Afterbursts

To ale

With all good wishes —
I hope you find it a
worthy read.

Copyright © 2025 Lucy Colback

All rights reserved. No part of this publication may be reproduced, stored in a retrieval system or transmitted in any form or by any means, electronic, mechanical, photocopying, recording or otherwise without prior permission of the copyright owner.

Most photographs come from the author's own original collection. Where images have been reproduced, the subject has permitted reproduction of their collection.

Cover concept Paul Friday
Section Three chapter ornament by Tracey Proulx

Published by Borderless Publishing, Hong Kong.

Paperback ISBN 978 988 76370 8 0
ebook eISBN 978 988 76370 2 8

Afterbursts

Reliving World War Two

Lucy Colback

Afterbursts (n.)

1. **Modern definition:** The reverberations of past wars that persist in today's conflicts. Echoes of ideological divisions and territorial disputes that continue to influence alliances and global tensions. The past resurfacing in new forms, never fully extinguished.

2. **Emotional definition:** The lingering effects of an event, such as memory, trauma, or consequence, that persist long after it has ended.

3. **Military definition:** The residual bursts of machine gun fire that continue after an initial volley, whether from mechanical recoil, delayed ignition, or the remnants of sustained combat.

To those in all theatres of war who gave their lives
for their compatriots. And to their surviving
comrades who could never forget.

Table of Contents

Foreword — ix

Author's note — xi

Section One—Fighting the war

Chapter One—You Can Breed Hate (*Indoctrination*) — 3

Chapter Two—The Desire to Go to the Front (*Idealism*) — 17

Chapter Three—It's a Duty (*Reluctance*) — 33

Chapter Four—Twenty-eight Stoppages (*In training*) — 45

Chapter Five—I Hope my Mum Got home (*Under bombardment*) — 65

Chapter Six—Tea and Chelsea Buns (*Serving in the rear*) — 79

Chapter Seven—My Best Friend Shot Me! (*Europe and North Africa*) — 91

Chapter Eight—Fire Machine Guns! (*The Eastern Front*) — 107

Chapter Nine—Thank Christ You Got Here (*The turning point in Europe*) — 121

Chapter Ten—They Ran Out of Petrol (*The importance of supplies*) — 141

Chapter Eleven—Verboten fur Deutsche (*Victory in Europe*) — 163

Afterbursts

Chapter Twelve—All in a Night's Work (*The Far East*) — 183

Chapter Thirteen—To Survive Was a Disgrace
(*The Far East II*) — 199

Chapter Fourteen—A Bomb Dropped on my House
(*Nuclear resolution*) — 217

Section Two—Children in War

Chapter Fifteen—Our Greatest Treasure (*Bearing arms*) — 237

Chapter Sixteen—Why Weren't You in the Resistance?
(*Under occupation*) — 253

Chapter Seventeen—Je Suis Mort! (*In the crossfire*) — 267

Chapter Eighteen—You Learn to Catch Very Quickly
(*Incarceration*) — 283

Section Three—Remembering the War

Chapter Nineteen—You Want to Say "Stop Crying"
(*The enemy*) — 307

Chapter Twenty—I Had to Bury Him (*Aftermath*) — 323

Chapter Twenty-One—When I See the Graveyards…
(*Remembrance*) — 337

Chapter Twenty-Two—A Huge Manipulation of Knowledge
(*Alternative truths*) — 347

Epilogue — 367

Acknowledgements — 377

About the Author — 379

Foreword

Inspired by a war-era photograph of an American GI and an old Chinese man lighting their cigarettes tip to tip, Lucy Colback left her job with the Financial Times in order to capture the memories of survivors of the last global conflict before they were lost forever. Over four years she travelled the globe interviewing those who endured WW II and documenting their experiences of close combat, as well as the thoughts and behaviour of people fighting for their lives. Proficient in Chinese and given extraordinary access to Chinese, Japanese and Russian veterans, Lucy's file covers the major land campaigns—terrible in their time but leading to a prolonged period of relative peace and prosperity that only now shows signs of unravelling.

The memories are recorded verbatim, but with notes that provide context and comparison whilst recognising that passage of time may have intensified or diffused the reality of the events into those lasting images deemed too vital to forget. The collection provides an invaluable resource for those trying to understand what motivates and sustains men—and it is mostly men—as they seek to kill each other in war and then what crystallises in their minds over the rest of their lives. For very few it seems that hatred for the enemy is eternal, but for others in the moments after the fight they are sharing family photographs and discussing the action, sometimes going on to form lifelong friendships.

Many stories in this compendium describe rapid emotional changes from fear into elation, calm into chaos, brutality into

Afterbursts

compassion. The shock of these violent transitions can unhinge the mind, but leaders must be reminded that what remains uppermost in soldiers' minds up to the point of dying is rarely the great cause for which the war is being fought, but the ever-enduring values of honour, home and duty.

Brigadier (retd) John Lucken
Military Assistant to the Chief of Defence Staff
during the Falklands campaign
Chief of Staff of the Army Doctrine and Training Command

Author's Note

This book is based on the 70-year-old memories of people who survived World War Two. While it covers true events as told by those who experienced them, given the time elapsed, these accounts may not always be historically accurate. They aim more to provide a small window onto the scars of war carried by the millions who were involved than to recount the specifics of who went where and when. The cast is only a hundred or so people—just a very small slice of the many millions whose lives were irrevocably changed by the conflict—but that hundred, no matter what their allegiance, all suffered wounds, either mental or physical, from what they had been through.

Of course, some combatants enjoy war for the camaraderie and purpose that it brings, while a very few embrace the brutality. I only spoke to one such and he wasn't a sadist; he just seemed to like a good scrap—with his comrades, mostly, since he never saw frontline combat.

The vast majority of people, however, endure lifelong trauma from war. This book brings together their stories, irrespective of their allegiance.

A brief explanation of the structure and its logic feels appropriate since, for anyone who understands the war in terms of engagements, the collection might seem somewhat haphazard. Although assembled in roughly chronological order, it is not focused on one event, nor does it cover every battle—it is simply a compilation of the memories of the individuals I met. Their accounts vary in length and some appear more than once. Several of the veterans talked to me for hours over several days, so it was not possible to include all of their experiences. I have selected stories that were for me most striking, be it for their emotional impact, unexpected humour, or coverage of unusual events.

The presence of so many "…" may also seem overdone. The testimonies are compiled from hours of interviews, often filled with emotion, which were seldom fluently delivered. The device is used when the speakers' hesitation was so pronounced as to be impossible to skim over, or to indicate a break when the stories jump to another part of our conversation. Mostly, they spoke in their own language, with just a few of the Japanese survivors conversing in broken English and therefore coming across perhaps a bit less fluently. The German, Russian, Japanese, Chinese and French interviews have all been translated from the original language. I chose to audio record rather than to video the interviews to minimise the intrusion on our conversations.

Memories can fade after so many years but, where possible, I have checked facts to ensure that at least the broader context is accurate. Locations may be confused; details may be embellished (such as with Roy and the "German ambassador's" son) and some perspectives altered by received knowledge long after the events. Especially for those who were children during the war, many of whom were preoccupied with it and spent much time reading about it in later life, they might present their wartime selves as more knowledgeable and prescient than they actually were. This backfilling of history may be a means for them to make sense of events that often were too inhuman to be sensible.

The sample of participants, being largely self-selecting, is not exhaustive—nor can it claim to be fully representative of all the nations and people who experienced the war. But collectively these men and women reveal the aspects of conflict that are, in the end,

Author's Note

universal: fear, bravery, loss, regret, sadness—and, occasionally, adventure and fun. I hope that these very personal accounts shed light on the human costs involved and give us pause for thought when our leaders speak glibly of war.

SECTION ONE

Fighting the War

Chapter 1

You Can Breed Hate

Indoctrination

For those of us in Western Europe whose formal historical education is limited to the very basics, we might know at least that World War Two commenced in 1939. I recall expending considerable effort as a child drilling myself to memorise the dates: "First World War, '14-'18. Second World War, '39-45." Details of how or why it began were only acquired later but were still confined to facts and dates—for instance that it all began with Germany's invasion of Poland.

For years, this remained about the extent of my extremely rudimentary knowledge. Somewhere between my youthful diligence and 2014 I had learned and subsequently forgotten about China's wartime history (from my degree in Chinese at university) and gleaned often inaccurate snatches of America's involvement from hours of Hollywood shows.

From a global perspective, of course, the history is not so neatly packed into that Western European timeframe. One gets an inkling of the complexity and the competing narratives of the war when you discover that not only does the start date vary according to continent, but the conflict is referred to by different names in different countries.

Afterbursts

The US did not become formally involved until 7 December 1941, when Pearl Harbor was bombed and the Pacific War commenced. The Soviets' Great Patriotic War began on 22 June of the same year, while China's War of Resistance Against Japan had been in full swing since mid 1937, with the northeast of the country occupied as early as 1931.

If all these regional clashes ultimately fold into the one we know as World War Two, it started, then, in China. At the time, this growing Asian conflict was initially considered more a local affair and Western nations, while concerned of a wider threat from Japan and broadly censorious of its unwelcome advances on its neighbour, did not wish to become overly involved.

The US offered some unofficial support in 1940, with Roosevelt secretly permitting a group of pilots to resign their regular commissions in the US forces and serve under the Chinese flag. America and Britain also imposed sanctions on Japan from July 1941 in response to the latter's occupation of airfields in Indochina and in agreement with the Vichy French government. The resulting oil and gasoline export embargo squeezed the Japanese government and threatened to hamper its regional ambitions.

One theory I first heard from a Chinese American school friend posits that the attack on Pearl Harbor was not only predictable, it was in fact deliberately provoked in order to give the US leadership justification for entering the war against Japan—and possibly, by extension, its ally Germany. I thought she was barmy. How could *America* of all countries, which balks at leaving even its bodies behind, be willing to sacrifice any of its youth to such a cynical end?

When a couple of US veterans I spoke with put it forward almost as a given, however, it seemed less outlandish. The way Issy Wolfe, who served making precision instruments at the US Navy Observatory, put it, it sounded like a plan gone badly awry due to American complacency:

You Can Breed Hate

I have to state a little history: that December the 7th of 1941, the Japanese attacked Pearl Harbor. And they had reason to. Because they knew that we were gearing up to take over the Pacific, as much as we could, from Pearl Harbor as our base. And I see a picture of the pre-Pearl Harbor Navy talking where they don't have all the things they wanted and they took many things from the East Coast, from Norfolk, sent it to San Diego and from there to Pearl Harbor.

And so at Pearl Harbor, not only were a lot of ships destroyed, airplanes, people and infrastructure, but, most importantly, almost every bit of naval navigation instruments that they had stocked up…They brought them over because they knew they were gonna fight. So they were stocking up on binoculars, telescopes, ship's compasses, alidades, theodolites…

I say, from my point of view, that yes: we [the US] knew we were going to fight Japan…We knew that the Japanese Navy had left port. We knew, we knew, we knew—and yet we didn't tell the people…Why? Because if you do some damage to me then I have a reason to load up on you and beat the heck out of you… But what happened is that your initial punch hit me in the gut, and I didn't realise that you were smart enough to do that. But, it got us into World War Two. Europe would have been decimated and Germany would have taken over. England was ready to fall apart, France certainly had. Russia was self-destructing…

Yoshio Nakamura, a second generation Japanese American, or *Nisei*, met with me the day after President Trump, in his first term, had assassinated a high-ranking member of the Iranian military. Yoshio was concerned about the justification for this act as a means to stop a war and he drew parallels as he mulled over the provocations on both sides that had led to Pearl Harbor.

[W]hen Pearl Harbor was bombed…I thought at that time the United States was a big country with tremendous resources and

Japan a little country that didn't have a lot of resources, and it seemed rather foolish for the attack.

But there were reasons why they would attack. I think that when you have an embargo, you cut off something that is very vital to the survival of a country…It's not like striking someone, but it's pretty close. And I think that's one of the problems that Japan had: the embargo of oil, which was very essential.

But the fact that they were into China and Manchuria, elsewhere…they were aggressors…You have to confront that and there were consequences of that, they should have realised. Who are you, taking over a country and not thinking that something else is going to happen? So I think that there's some miscalculation on both the US side and Japan side.

Pearl Harbor was just one of Japan's incursions in December 1941. Over the ensuing days it invaded various Western colonies and protectorates across Asia, including the Malayan Peninsula, the Philippines and Hong Kong. Thailand was also occupied. The second week of that month saw declarations of war between more than a dozen nations.

The genesis of Germany's war in Europe could also be traced to well before 1939—the Allies had in fact laid the groundwork with the Treaty of Versailles in the wake of World War One. Against the backdrop of a humiliating defeat and the crippling reparations imposed on them, the German people were open to manipulation by Hitler's passionate defence of their nation and susceptible to the corrosive racism he espoused.

Peter Gafgen, who had been a young boy at the time, believed that Hitler's appeal was quite simple.

When he was elected—because it was still democracy in '33—the women's vote went to him because he promised work for the guys. And they were hanging around home, or on the streets, not able to bring food to nourish their families. And he promised work…and he held his promise because unemployment was abolished. Immediately, there was zero percent unemployment, because it was not tolerated…You work, or you go to a camp.

If one of Hitler's goals was to provide his people more territory into which to expand, *lebensraum*, Japan's goal was also expansionism. Here, however, it was more about "modernising" than finding room into which the nation could spread out. The country needed resources such as the commodities it found in northwestern China in order to make industrial progress. It had looked towards the West and in the mid nineteenth century its elites had brought back science from their education overseas—as well as some observations of the contribution of the colonies.

Japanese veteran Nobuo Okimatsu studied history with the specific goal of understanding how Japan had gone to war, and how it had lost.

I learned that the Japanese government and the Japanese people made a huge mistake with respect to the Meiji era[1] [when] Japan incorporated western culture…While Japan incorporated industrial civilisation, it did not incorporate spiritual civilisation, since the government assumed that Japan was spiritually superior. Japan should have incorporated and studied rationalism, democracy and scientific thinking…

I was in the Japanese military, so I strongly felt the military's lack of rationalism and its unscientific thinking. They often referred to *seishinshugi* [having a strong spirit], *shichohei keishi* [a lack of military respect for logistics] or *bushiwa kuwanedo takayoji* [how a samurai pretends he has eaten when he has no food].

---

[1] The Meiji era began in 1868 and was the beginning of Japan's opening to the world

Afterbursts

This almost superstitious approach to inspiring its army meant that practical aspects—such as ensuring adequate supply lines—were ignored, as more than one Japanese soldier told me. When it came to rations, perhaps as a deliberate ploy to ensure that its soldiers would have to subdue local populations, several noted that the Japanese Army did not even provide more than a few days' worth of food to its troops when they sent them abroad. Indoctrination and unquestioning obedience were such a big part of Japanese education that none felt able directly to challenge the hierarchy and its more questionable edicts. While this empowered the militarists to march their people into war, it was also a major contributor to the country's defeat.

Those who were attacked, such as America, China and Russia, perhaps had the most easily defensible justification for fighting—self-defence. Allies such as Britain were bound by treaty to become involved. Even so, messaging played a part in persuading people to take up arms. Patriotism and propaganda were used equally by both sides—but each saw itself as justified while the other was at best naive and, at worst, evil.

After the event, many combatants came to understand that propaganda and indoctrination had been behind much of the hatred which had stimulated their appetite for the war and their ability to kill another human being.

Fergus Anckorn, a veteran gunner who achieved some renown in his latter years for being mentor to the magician winner of Britain's Got Talent in 2016, believed strongly that propaganda and popular entertainment helped to perpetuate the idea that the war was glorious.

> I'm sure it does. I mean, in the First World War, look at the volunteers. And in the Second World War: let's get there before it ends! And come back with a medal or something…I've seen propaganda films in the Second World War—derring dos and things like that—and they're film actors! I know them!…And

you see them "in the RAF" plotting all these things…So the propaganda is terrific, even here. For instance, when the Germans came over at night and all our anti-aircraft guns were firing at them, they wouldn't hit a thing. But the civilians heard our boys "fighting the Germans"…

No they weren't! They were just popping off shells at a thousand pounds a time. No one was ever hit. Our bombers that went to Germany…never, ever got within five miles of the target. They were hitting something else. How can you leave this country in the dark, in a blackout, get over to Germany and you're finding such and such a square—in the dark? And yet…it's "Bombs away!" It hits a school somewhere.

So all of that propaganda, "Our boys were bombing Kiel yesterday" and all the rest of it…They weren't. They were just dropping their bombs and trying to get home safely. Propaganda is a terrible thing.

Liliane Willens *was born to Russian Jewish parents in Shanghai, where she was relatively insulated from the war as a non-enemy foreigner and far from the Jewish persecution in Europe. From her unusual vantage point[2], she could see how both Germany and Japan had been mesmerised to fulfil their leaders' ambitions.*

Who would have thought of Germany, the most sophisticated country in Europe—with the most wonderful literature, the inventions, the music—that they would behave that way?…The doctors here [in the US]—future doctors—they studied in Germany, because it was the best school…How did Hitler…It was fear, that if you didn't obey the Nazis you'd be bayonetted? How did he manage to do that? It's true after World War One they lost so much, but he managed to mesmerise them to cruelty.

It's indoctrination…starting from age five and continue, continue, continue. You can breed hate…negative passion, hatred…No:

---

[2] Liliane's unique experience is covered in detail in her memoir *Stateless in Shanghai*.

Liliane Willens at home in 2017

the human being is not a good person. We need our laws to hold us down…

They [the Japanese] were brutal towards the Chinese…and I associate the Japanese mentality to the German mentality. From age five, the Japanese in their schools, as in Germany, they were told—and this is true, Japanese wrote about it—they were told that the Chinese is an inferior race. They were like rats…And when you're trained that way from age five to age 20, it's a part of your life. You don't look at the Chinese or the Jew as a human being but a rat whom you could step on…It's brainwashing…That's what happened in Germany and in Japan.

As Liliane observed, indoctrination in the Axis countries began from a very young age. In Germany, ten-year-olds were taken into the Hitler Youth to be groomed for the military.

You Can Breed Hate

***Peter Gafgen**, born in 1932 as Hitler was coming to power, noted that the autocrat had merged a minority pre-disposed to violence with this indoctrinated youth to create a willing group of enforcers. A robust raconteur, Peter did not mince his words as he expounded on the war over the course of a few days spent hosting me in France.*

Those bastards were five percent of the whole population—and those five percent born criminals you have in every nation in the world, and if they come to power, then you've had it. It is that few people. And you have to recognise it very much ahead of time, which the Germans did not—because why? It was their first democracy… and the Weimar democracy was for them a learning chapter. And this learning chapter, they failed. In other words, in a school, you get a bad mark, but there, the bad mark was the Nazis…

The SS was indoctrinated 100% by the Nazi—the Hitler—regime: the Slavic race is an inferior race. It can only be used for slavery… Of course, they had this famous five percent, which would do these things for whoever would govern them—it's their inclination—and those five percent were also a part of the SS. But [some of] the other young SS people were formed in these special schools, and outside of the reach of their parents. Indoctrinated by the system. And those Orden schools of the Nazis were fantastic schools in old castles. They were very well taken care of—they could do the sports, everything—but they were indoctrinated from morning to night…It's one of the first things Hitler did, I mean, psychologically he knew how to work on people…

The girls, which are the BDM—Bund Deutscher Madel—they could also go into these other schools which were for girls, and they were also completely indoctrinated. And if you see these parades when these young people go like this [*Peter gives a Hitler salute*]—the girls dressed in the uniform, the youngsters dressed in his uniform going like this—these are indoctrinated kids. And the white trash people, that could not support their kids anymore or had difficulty, they send them into these schools and said, "This is a way to get ahead."

Afterbursts

Ron Johnson, like many Allied soldiers, knew well the difference between the Nazis and other Germans—and was equally clear about why Britain had to go to war. His own motivation to fight he ascribed to an Oxford Union debate which had occurred in the early 1930s: "This house will under no circumstances fight for King and Country." Although the motion had won, when World War Two broke out the debate inspired Ron to the opposite course of action. He joined the Territorial Army in 1939, aged just 17, and was enlisted in the infantry. He described his battle engagements in largely unsentimental terms, becoming most impassioned when it came to commemoration and educating young people about the war.

What you have to remember is the aggressors were the Nazis… They were the ones that started the war. I mean, they went into Czechoslovakia, then they went into Poland…and when war started, they attacked France, if you remember. So, there's no question about it. They were the aggressors.

Now, not all German soldiers were out and out Nazis, but there were enough of them [who] were to make it really rather unpleasant.

Ron Johnson in 2019 holding a picture of his younger self

You Can Breed Hate

If the soldiers you were fighting were the general German soldiers you were a lot better off than if you were fighting the Waffen-SS, let's put it like that. Because they were ruthless. They were the out and out Nazis…We mainly met normal German soldiers at Arnhem—but there were, among them, some SS. And if you came up against them, it was not very pleasant.

Since any nation often assumes its own moral superiority, I was curious to know if he thought British people would be capable of something similar.

Oh, we've got people who'd be just as capable of acting like that. Oh, yes. There are thugs in this country—just as there are thugs in pretty well any country…

Not all German soldiers were Nazis, but the distinction between these zealots and the more general Wehrmacht soldier is often lost. **Jeff Hawards'** *varied encounters over the course of the war illustrated some of the differences and highlighted the extreme prejudice that drove the SS.*

'Course we'd fought the Afrika Korps…They obeyed all the rules—and that's what we thought the Germans were like. And when we came back to Europe, we were to learn a terrible lesson. Because… the Wehrmacht, they were all decent—and most other troops—but when you came up to the SS, they were totally different. They were mostly young and had almost been born and grown up all their lives under Hitler. And the first clash we had was with the 12th SS Hitlerjugend…You couldn't mess about with them, you know. You had to kill them—you know what I mean? They wouldn't give up.

I remember one time in the breakout, and we came across this German—one of the Hitlerjugend—and he was badly wounded in his stomach. And it was obvious [he was going to die]…Unless he received something immediately—it might save him.

And my stretcher bearer was Jewish. And we called him Nobby… and I said— because they had blood—"You going to give him a blood transfusion, Nobby?"

So Nobby said, "Yeah."

So he got this syringe out and he was about to stick it in this German. And this German looked up, obviously recognised he was a Jew, he said, "Nich Juden! Nich Juden!"

Didn't want a Jew to save his life….

So…[we] just left him. I'm sure he died…But that's what they were like. They were—well…translated into English, it was: "My blood is my honour." Because they all had their blood type tattooed under their arms.

Ernest Hilton's *family was among those who suffered most from the rampant racism that Hitler had stoked. Born in Germany in 1932 to a Jewish family, even as a small child Ernest could sense the mounting fear as the German leader's broadcasts became more rabid.*

The threat of Hitler…First of all, we moved to Holland in 1933…[My parents] had a radio, and they listened to Hitler's speeches. And while I didn't get the content, I got the emotion—of my parents and of the Hitler voice. I would say from four years old on I was aware that this man was a threat…

Ernest Hilton in 2019

14

You Can Breed Hate

My father insisted that we were safe in Holland because Holland was neutral in the First World War. He would have been right if we had been in Sweden.

We moved out of Aerdenhout [Holland] after the Germans invaded and took over Holland. And…maybe within 30 to 60 days there was a decree that Jews cannot live near the sea. So we moved to Hilversum for probably less than a year and then we were one of the first to be called up to move to Westerbork[3]…

I can only imagine that my grandparents were very upset that we were caught there, because they had the means to move us out, but my father was determined to keep his business in Holland…It must have been absolutely gruesome.

And in 1939 I was seven. Whatever I sensed, I didn't sense enough.

---

[3] Originally set up as a refugee camp by the Dutch government, Westerbork became a staging post for deportation of Jews to concentration camps

Chapter 2

The Desire to Go to the Front!

Idealism

Regardless of their nation's justification for the war, participants' personal motivations to fight were often quite similar. Axis and Allied soldiers alike could be fired up by patriotism—stoked by governments all manipulating their people into embracing the conflict.

Liu, *born in 1923, was in Nanjing when war broke out between China and Japan. Fleeing heavy bombardments, his family left the city before the Japanese arrived in December 1937. They were lucky to get away: Shanghai had recently fallen but had resisted the invaders so doggedly that by Nanjing the Japanese were eager for revenge. For several weeks after Nanjing was taken, Japanese troops marauded through the city, raping and massacring civilians in what is known as the Rape of Nanking, an event returned to modern consciousness in the late 1990s by a book of the same name.*

Despite their escape, Liu's family was not completely spared and his flight left him determined to fight. He was just 16 when he applied for military school—his lie that he was 17 readily accepted as the country was so short of men.

Afterbursts

In 2018 we met in the concrete-block apartment he shared with his wife in Nanjing, our conversation in Mandarin guided by the man who introduced us. The couple had returned to his hometown after the war, walking from the far west of the country with a young daughter in a cart and an infant son on his shoulders. Liu had fought for the Chinese Nationalists, China's leading political party and American ally during the war years, but he sported the navy blue padded Mao jacket that had been ubiquitous in early communist China. His black-clad son, by now 70-something and a Communist Party member, sat beside him nodding sagely at the story and occasionally adding context.

After the War of Resistance broke out, I fled with my family—from Nanjing first we went to Anhui...Because at the time, planes were bombing indiscriminately...the idea was to get away from the planes...

We were eight family members...I was the littlest...just a child in my teens...At the time we were completely reliant on my older brother because my father had died relatively early. My older sister was ill, too...She had tuberculosis. So she died during the journey...Aside from that, my nephew also got frostbite and died...

In the beginning, we thought it would be just a short while and then we could come back. We never imagined that the war would change so much and we would never be able to come back...that the Japanese bombing would get worse and worse. At the time we were only teenagers. I wasn't able to study...

Once we got to Guilin, I applied to enter military school, Huangpu Military Academy fifteenth cohort. But the obstacles to my application for the Huangpu Military School were considerable. One thing was my family's status—none of my family had been in the military, they were all scholars, teachers...and my mother, she was old.

In China in the past there was a saying—what was it? "A good man does not become a soldier and good iron is not turned into nails." It's an old way of thinking. These days it's just the opposite: good men should become soldiers. Haha.

The Desire to Go to the Front!

I was motivated to apply to military school by righteous indignation—it was the duty of a lifetime…and we young people had to fulfil the responsibility of our era. What's more, during the course of my flight, the things I saw and heard, the things I witnessed, made me incredibly angry. I absolutely had to become a soldier, I had to beat the Japanese devils.

Liu's family was still in flight when he left to enrol in military school, and when he visited his relatives towards the end of the war, they told him the rest of their ordeal.

By this time there were a few more in my family who had died, my sister-in-law had died…my brother's wife…Because of the war—what's more, she died tragically. At that time, the Japanese launched an attack on Guangxi and Guizhou. There was no choice, they had to flee. As it happened at the time she was ill, so my brother carried her on his back all the way. They hitchhiked…caught some means of transport, and finally at Jincheng River in Guangxi she died on my brother's back.

My brother didn't know until another refugee said, "This person's dead." Only then did he put her down. She was done…Done—what could he do? So he took a reed mat and rolled her up in it and buried her right there.

So my two nephews didn't know their mother. At the time they were both still very little. They also don't know where she was laid to rest—and now they can't find it. On a business trip they were passing by this Guangxi. They got out of the car, got down to have a look, pay their respects…So unbelievably tragic…

So, when it comes to the whole War of Resistance against Japan, families were scattered and their members died. Mine had a niece who also died in Guangxi—a nephew, a niece, an older sister, a sister-in-law…Four who died because of the war.

As Liu's family fled the bombs, Europe was teetering on the brink of war, with Germany annexing the Sudetenland borderlands in the summer of 1938.

Brother and sister **Ted** *and* **Em Hunt** *recalled how, just months later, Chamberlain returned from his "appeasement" trip to see Hitler*

Ted and Em Hunt at home in 2019

in Germany. They were not fooled that conflict would be avoided. The pair recalled stories they had heard about the Germans from their father, who had ferried the wounded away from the French lines in World War One, and how the segue into World War Two had been quite unsurprising.

As war loomed, the family lived in the East End of London, Emily, born with her twin Florence in 1915, was working for London Transport. Ted, born in 1920, was an apprentice lighterman on the Thames, like his father and grandfather before him.

When I met the siblings at Ted's home on the south coast of England, Em had recently moved in and as the younger brother tucked into a pint of beer and his story with equal gusto, his birdlike sister, nearly 104 years old, chimed in more tentatively, searching for words to convey the atmosphere when war broke out.

The Desire to Go to the Front!

Em: You said, "What was it like?" Well, we were aware that Germany was a threat…

Ted: Oh, yes!

So, 1938…Chamberlain came back. "I have a piece of paper in my hand…" And people have all sorts of ideas, "He let us down." But he delayed the start for 12 months.

Now, I used to catch a train from Eltham Well Hall station, and we would pass Kidbrooke, where there was a government military store…And what happened in those 12 months: they had barrage balloons and guns and all kinds of things…Industry went mad producing, preparing for the war, which came a year later.

So I see it that way: that the giving way over Czechoslovakia in 1938 meant we said, "Right, now…we know what's coming. We're going to prepare…"

Em: The parade ground and Woolwich Barracks were near us and we used to see the soldiers about…it was building up, we knew. And you thought, "The Germans. The Germans are coming."

And of course Dad had stories of the First World War, and so did my mum…I can't say that we were frightened…My mum knew what to be frightened of, but we didn't…

I remember when the announcement came out. I was with Ted.

Ted: I'd been working all Saturday night and Sunday morning, the third of September, the streets were crowded with people.

And when we got home, they said, "There will be an announcement at 11 o'clock…" And then, eventually, "I have to tell you now that this country is at war with Germany." And within an hour, the air raid warnings…

That Sunday morning we were all together as a family—

Em: But you and I went out in the street, just the two of us, and you said, "The Germans will come" and I thought *Oh, they'll come and rape the girls.*

That was a thing I worried about—because they were quite notorious for that, the Germans, you know. That's what they did. They captured these villages and raped the women…

Ted: Well you heard stories of Germans bayoneting babies—but that's universal, in war.

Ted was so keen to serve that, like his father before him, he lied about his age in order to enlist. He came to regret this in his first engagement in Norway, as he would later explain.

Ted: I told a lie to join up…and in Norway I was so frightened I'd have told any number of lies to have got out of it—I was terrified in Norway. But that's how I came to join up.

They'd said, "Well you can go home and get prepared. You're in the Army from Friday the 13th of October."

So I remember going home, saying, "Well, I've joined up, and I begin on Friday."

She [my mum] said, "Oh, Teddy! Friday the 13th!"

How often since…If I had joined up on Thursday the 12th, my life would have been completely different. I might have gone to 2-2-8 [Field Company, Royal Engineers] instead of 2-2-9, and they were slaughtered on the way to Dunkirk.

Franklin Medhurst *was born in Bristol in 1920 and was enjoying a carefree youth in the Somerset countryside as tensions in Europe escalated.*

What made me angry was the way that Hitler and Mussolini were just taking over large resources, without any opposition. Austria, Hungary—just walking into them. And Mussolini got into Abyssinia. And this was wrong. We knew this was wrong, but we could do nothing about it…

I applied to join the Fleet Air Arm. That was in the spring of 1939…Then war was declared on September the third and ten days later I received a letter from the Admiralty to say that there was no longer any enlistment into the Royal Navy, would I please reapply for the Voluntary Reserve. And I was so frustrated I went straight down to Exeter the next day and enlisted in the RAF…

At that stage I wasn't really asking questions, I was only determined…Because I had seen what was happening in Europe, and I decided that must not happen in Britain. And it was the attitude of

The Desire to Go to the Front!

Franklin Medhurst in 2017

youth at the time I suppose. You just think *Sod them, let's get on with this*.

And I remember where I was when war was declared: in a high street. And I saw the sign on a newsagent's placard, WAR DECLARED, and I thought, *Thank God*. You know, I just welcomed that, which of course was completely the wrong attitude, but at the time that was the atmosphere…

Most of the Air Force[4] was flying over Germany and bombing it—and I didn't want that, I wanted to fight the German Navy. We'd heard from the bombing students that they had no real means of bombing accurately and they had to drop their bombs on towns. And a friend and I discussed this in the NAAFI canteen over a tea and bun…We both felt inclined that we wanted to fight armed men, not

---

[4] In fact, Bomber Command was targeting only German industry in 1940, but accuracy on these night-time runs was indeed questionable

civilians, so we volunteered for Coastal Command…

But everyone else…the main aim was to get into Bomber Command—which, in retrospect, I think was a mistake. Because Bomber Command just bombed towns and cities—cultures and people—and it was the American Army Airforce that [later] decided they would not do that. They would bomb the ammunitions supplies, the oil fields. They would bomb the resources of Germany and not the people. And they did it in daylight and they suffered great losses—but that's what ended the war.

*The fighting spirit swept up even those less in a position to serve. Sixteen-year-old **Pat Mygind** could not wait to volunteer as soon as the war broke out. Her father, a butcher left deaf by World War One, would find the following war increasingly trying as he struggled to supply old friends and neighbours who clamoured for favours.*

On the day it started, I was working. I couldn't help volunteering for anything. They needed someone on the local telephone exchange—plugs in and out. Of course, I volunteered. Worst person possible. And as I was [working]…they announced the war.

Ran home. My mother made me get on my bicycle, go down to church, tell my father. And then of course the sirens went. It was all very exciting. And then we started the next day filling sandbags. And everybody couldn't wait to do things…Couldn't wait. I mean we'd no idea what war meant, really. It all sounded exciting…[I] couldn't wait to volunteer…

I had to wait some time before I was called up. I wasn't old enough, of course. So…we started off filling sandbags and then another person and myself joined the Red Cross Cadets—I thought I'd be a wonderful nurse—and passed the exams, so we went off to the hospital…And we went up on the ward in our uniforms feeling very important. And the friend I was with, she was taken over that side to hold someone's foot whilst they had an injection. I was on this side, holding somebody else's foot. [My friend] fainted when they put the needle in and I dropped this gouty foot. We weren't very good nurses!

The Desire to Go to the Front!

So they put us outside sorting out dirty laundry—and in the blackout, you never knew what you were going to pick up. But we kept at it...for as long as they could stand us...

We were optimistic, really, because another teenager and myself, plus a married woman, once every two weeks we would go to the local school and sit up all night in case an incendiary bomb dropped. And we had a bucket of water and a stirrup pump. Now, if an incendiary bomb had dropped, we would have run a mile. How were we going to put it out? But that's how optimistic we all were.

__Edwin Ledr__, born in Germany in 1919, was twenty when his country invaded Poland. One hundred years old by the time we met, he sported a sparse fuzz of grey hair on his mottled head, and with his mouth full of false teeth and sunken eyes he looked old and frail as he croaked out his story in halting German.

Edwin's home of Jagendorf (now Krnov) was in a historical region of Central Europe called Schleisen, or Silesia, that is mostly part of modern Poland. Edwin was an illegitimate child, but his mother had married a man he called "father" and who was a butcher.

I went to Heligoland because I wanted to earn money—because at my father's shop I didn't earn money. I went to the job centre and they told me there was a job in Heligoland. And there, I was examined and sent to Bergedorf as a soldier, artillery...

In the war, I did what I had to do...At first, I was not [proud to fight for Germany], but later on I had to be. When I became a soldier, I had to do what they wanted...I didn't know what war meant before joining the military, I was too young. In the war they punched out my teeth and I lost my hearing due to the artillery...

Canadian __Rolfe Monteith__, about to turn 16 when the war broke, also did not let his youth put him off attempting to enlist. Despite a landlocked upbringing he had long wanted to be in the Navy and the conflict allowed him to realise this dream. Canada declared war on Germany just a few days after Britain.

Well...from the age of eight living in Ontario, Canada—relatively speaking, the middle of Canada—I had a view of joining the Navy...

So, in 1940, the war had started. I was aged 16. My mum said, "We are going to Prince Edward Island for the summer…"

Down we went by train, and in the middle of Charlottetown, Prince Edward Island, was a recruiting office for the Armed Forces. So without saying anything to my mum, I walked in.

And—this is Fate—it was a Navy man in charge of it, a Chief Petty Officer. And I approached and I said, "Excuse me, I'm aged 16, I would like to join the Navy."

And he was like a father, looking across this desk at me and he said—I'll always remember this—he said, "Son, you're aged 16, you tell me. You can prove that?…Well", he said, "I could sign you up as a boy seaman. Now. But I'm going to tell you to leave this office. Go back to where you live…get senior matriculation…Reapply."

So, I spoke to my father who did the obvious thing: he wrote to the National Defence and said, "My son is interested in the Navy."

And back came this little booklet, which I've still got, *How to join the Royal Canadian Navy*. And I had to write exams and had to pass an interview and then pass a medical…

I did those three things, and my father received a letter which said, "Your son has been accepted and will be proceeding to Britain." That was the first idea that I would be going to Britain, straight away.

It took longer for the Soviet Union to join the Allies. In June 1941, just a few months before Japan's attack on Pearl Harbor, the country was invaded by Germany—something of a shock given the treaty between the two nations. Still, the Soviet Union was not entirely unprepared for combat.

Nikolai Kozlov *was born in Tambov, nearly 500 kilometres southeast of Moscow, moving to a tiny village "deep in Siberia" where he and his friends rode plough horses working the fields. His father had served with the cavalry on the German front in World War One and had primed Nikolai for war. In November 1940, aged 17, he was called to attend flight school. Old black and white photos show him turning from a fresh-faced young boy into a man in pilot leathers in just a year.*

The Desire to Go to the Front!

Nikolai Koslov in 2019

Nikolai in his youth

Afterbursts

Decked out in a dress uniform armour-plated with decorations, when we met in 2019 Nikolai's patriotism and pride in his service were evident. First a pilot and then a horseback artillery commander, he fought the full duration of his country's war in engagements that ranged from Russia through Ukraine, Belarus, Poland and Germany. He was almost always on the battlefield—but the most vivid images he described were of horses at war.

As we talked for eight hours, his middle-aged son took charge of refreshments—attempting to kick us off with vodka at 10am.

In '40, in November, I was called to a military drafting office and I was told: "You either enrol in an aviation school now or we will draft you regardless in spring."

I agreed and in November I departed to Kansk School, in Krasnoyarsk Krai…I learned [about fascism] when I started the school. I learned some history of Germany, the wars we used to have…We got enlightened. We discussed among ourselves what the teachers told us…

Most of our instructors in the school—pilots and navigators and combined arms military officers—were veterans of the [Finnish] war and they told us about the war. And in contrast to what was published in newspapers, they told us straightforwardly that war with the Germans would happen and we needed to be prepared, learn the aircraft…They had combat experience, and they shared that combat experience with us. And they nurtured in us not just a love for the country, but also for military service. I must also note that there was no panic or pessimism after the war was announced, there was pure patriotism.

I learned about the war for the first time on the 22nd of June [1941], at 12:30. At the time we were at the shooting range, at the Kam River…We were raised by an alarm and [had to do] 20 kilometres cross country, running back to the school…

The first reaction was to ask to be sent to the frontline…There was no panic: we believed we would win. Our army would not fight on our territory…

Everyone wanted one thing: learn the aircraft and go to the front to fight.

The Desire to Go to the Front!

Victor Harchev was just 13 years old when Germany invaded the Soviet Union. A softly spoken 91-year-old when we met, with his gentle manner and baby-smooth skin he did not strike me as an obvious military candidate, but as a young boy he had been keen to be a soldier. Based on his recollections, too, war was inevitable.

From as early as I can remember, I was desperate to be in the military…I was looking at the Red Army servants—commanders, of course…

Before the war, in Moscow parks there were children's military battalions where we would come after school and learn from real, active military staff. The idea was that in future, when you joined the army, you would have the knowledge…Weapons: rifle, machine gun, grenade…

The point is, we were getting ready to serve in the Soviet Army. Naturally, we were growing up with the idea that service is necessary. Why? It wasn't imposed on us, but there is a notion that in *Rus*[5] a man is first of all a warrior. A protector of the motherland, that was also in us…

On June 22, '41 our childhood was over. My father was summoned immediately, on the 22nd. He showed up and that was it—he left, drafted.

I was studying in that children's battalion…The desire to go to the front!…Because I thought I had some knowledge, for instance rifle operation, machine guns, grenades…but obviously, I was told: "Shush. Grow up. You will have enough time to fight."

Six months after Germany invaded the Soviet Union, the Japanese bombed Pearl Harbour. California at the time was home to a large number of Japanese immigrants and formerly integrated communities were divided by fears that Japanese Americans were spying or signalling to enemy submarines in the Pacific. Americans of Japanese heritage were rounded up and incarcerated in internment camps as anti-Japanese sentiment erupted.

---

[5] Old name for Russia

Afterbursts

Not everyone bought into the fear mongering, but attitudes were muddied by domestic propaganda. Despite accounts of squalid and inhospitable conditions in the camps, many believed government claims that the Japanese Americans had been interned as a form of protective custody.

Yoshio Nakamura *was born in America in 1925 to immigrant Japanese parents and was among the first to be incarcerated in Tulare. To him, the notion that his family had been locked up for their protection was laughable. His wry delivery underscored a heavy scepticism of the official line—both during the war and in the modern day.*

Imprisoned as a teenager, he could have been forgiven for not feeling patriotic, but he was committed to serving his country. When he reached majority age in 1943, he was given a "loyalty questionnaire" which asked if he would be willing to fight for the US. It was worded in such a way as to presume treason among the Nisei, but Yoshio swallowed his objections.

Number 1: 'Would you no longer swear allegiance to the emperor of Japan?'…If you answered yes, you *had been* [loyal to the emperor] and if you said no, it meant you continued to [be]…

And then the other one was: 'Are you willing to join the armed forces of the United States and go wherever ordered?' And I figured that's the same as volunteering and…you're in this jail situation and they're asking you, "Will you go and fight for us? We jailed you but we want you to fight for us."

Well, anyway, I said "yes"…

Our 442nd and the 100th Battalion were, very, very good in battle. They'd proven themselves very much, but their casualties were very, very heavy—the 100th Battalion was called The Purple Heart Battalion, that was the 1st Battalion of the 442nd—and so there was a need for replacements. So they had to find enough Japanese Americans to train them together.

So when I got my call for active duty, I went to Camp Blanding and there were people from Hawaii, and…oh! There's a guy from

The Desire to Go to the Front!

Oklahoma there and from Wyoming and several from Pocatello and Blackfoot, Idaho, and Nevada. And people from California and Washington, Utah…

Over in Japan, there was a strongly held belief in the honour of being a soldier. The country had been highly militarised since the 1930s and its education was designed to instil a strong sense of loyalty to the Emperor. Whole villages would turn out to wave the soldiers off to war and with so much honour accorded to the soldiers, youths such as **Ken Yamada**, *who described a fairy-tale childhood, were eager to serve.*

I was born in Fukuoka Prefecture, Asakura region. My father was a railroad worker. We were four siblings; my older sister who died, me, my sister, and my younger brother.

I lived in a house with a thatched roof and there was a watermill next to it which transported water into the house. We would put rice bowls in a big basket and wash them with the water…There was a small pond outside in the front and at the back of our house. We cultivated carp in it.

There were about 200 households in this village. During the summertime, we kept the house completely open and fireflies would come in from the porch. We had mosquito nets and the fireflies would rest on it. We would go to sleep while watching them.

Looking back at it now, it was like a dream. We were poor, but very content. In the olden days, houses used to have name plates hung up near the entrance…There would be the characters for Yamada, and then two characters on top of that. Once I was older, I realised it said *shizoku*, [samurai family]…We were poor, but we had pride.

In my era the Emperor—the royal family—came first. The Emperor's photo was even hung up in elementary school. Back then we used to say "*arahi togami*" (they are a God in human form).

Right from my school education, I just wanted to know how I could serve…When I was in 5th to 6th grade—the war was already taking place then. I thought it would be cool to become a military soldier…

Afterbursts

Yoshio Hara, *born in Japan in 1927, recalled becoming conscious of the fact that the country was at war from the age of about 10, when his country invaded the heartland of China.*

That is because the remains of people who died in the war against China were returned to Japan...People who died in war were called "*eirei*" (spirits of dead soldiers). School children also participated in these memorial services for people who fought for the country. That's how I found out that people who died in the war for the country became gods.

Since I was educated under imperialism, since I'm a male, [I felt] I would eventually go to fight for the country. I was a militaristic young boy—everyone was. Women became nurses to be useful during the war...

When the war broke out, the Second World War, the population—which was nearly 100 million—all people, including young children and the elderly, became one in spirit to fight the war. The phrase 一億一心 (100 million, one mind), this is the kind of era that began...

I didn't think about it; it was a matter of course. But looking back now, it was a sad era that had begun.

Chapter 3

It's a Duty

Reluctance

Not everyone was eager to serve in the war, but dissent was far more challenging than going with the flow. This was particularly, if not solely, true in the aggressor nations—despite the general national mood, some of Japan's citizens were anti-war, particularly in more recently acquired colonies such as Taiwan and Korea. Among the Allies, although patriotism and shock at being invaded often fired the young to take up arms, enthusiasm was not always a given.

Okinawa and the independent Ryukyu kingdom of which it was part had been rolled into the Japanese empire only in 1879, shortly after the renaissance of the Meiji Period. With absorption still so new, the government was unsure of the loyalty of the island inhabitants. Ryukyu schoolchildren like **Yoshiko Shimabukuro** *were subjected to stricter indoctrination than the rest of their compatriots and punished if they used the local dialect.*

I was born January 16, 1928…My father fought in the [first] war against China. He was a peace-loving person and told us he was against the war—although it wasn't an easy thing to say at the time… He used to tell his children that war was terrible, but back then people who said this would be branded a liberal or socialist and taken away immediately. So, while on the outside he said he'd fight and do what is best for the country, he used to tell us it would be best if there was no war...

We lived in a two-storey house in the countryside. He would hide strangers in our house, and I would ask why a man was hiding there, and he would tell me they were very good people so I should never tell anyone at school...

I didn't understand why my father was hiding these strangers, but now I think he did an admirable thing...I mean, he was able to hide people who were against the war, in times like those...

Kenpei military and *tokko* policemen were tracking down traitors and came to our house, but my father was the village security leader, so even though they thought they might be here, the military and policemen didn't directly ask my father if anyone was hiding in our place...

[He hid] about two to three people. They stayed about five to six days, and then they would go somewhere else. Then another person who was being tracked would come...One of the people we hid, Kaneshi Saichi, later became the mayor of Naha City, so I later thought my father had had good judgement...

When I entered elementary school, the war against China had already started so I was educated throughout an era of war...At the time, it wasn't so much fighting for the country, it was fighting for the Emperor, giving your life to the Emperor...At school, we would bow to the Emperor first, in front of the Emperor's photo, and then bow to the guardian god of the village—but it was the Emperor first...That's how we were indoctrinated.

It was an era without radio or the internet—there was only one radio, at school. Even if we were losing the war, we were always told that we were winning. If Japan bombed one of the enemy's warships, we were told Japan bombed many. If we shot down one aircraft, we were told we shot down dozens. The news was all lies, and we had no way of investigating by ourselves...So we all believed Japan would surely win...

It's a Duty

I thought the Chinese were our enemy and when the war against the US started, I believed Americans were not human...*Kichiku beiei*[6] means not human...they were the enemy. Back then, as a part of the *kichiku beiei* education, we made straw dolls and practiced piercing them with bamboo spears. But the teachers taught us that we shouldn't immediately take out the spear—they said we should twist it before drawing the spear back. It's dreadful...the teachers would make us practice this repeatedly.

When war began in China in 1937 **Xu** *was eager to fight, but at 16 he was too young—even if his father had been willing to let him go.*

He was nonetheless required to undertake war work. By late 1937 Japan had occupied most of China's major ports and the besieged Chinese government knew that it would not survive without supplies. It ordered that a road be built from Burma, then a British colony, into China's south-western province of Yunnan so that materiel could keep flowing via the port of Yangon. Later this road, too, would be cut off and Americans would keep China's war effort alive with airlifts over the Himalayas.

Xu helped to lay a section of the Burma Road in Yunnan. With fighting-aged men already conscripted to the army, the labourers were mostly the elderly, women and children. They had no explosives, no medicine, and no mechanised equipment.

China's remote regions were so undeveloped that one of his fellow workers, observing a plane for the first time, asked Xu whether it was edible.

In 1937...there was the Luguo Qiao [Marco Polo Bridge] incident, and the Japanese began to invade China. Everyone resisted... the whole population...Later, because Yunnan was in the rear, it became the front line for defence. So after Long Yun[7] came back from a meeting in Chongqing[8] he rushed to build the road...

---

[6] A wartime slogan meaning "American and British demons"
[7] Governor of Yunnan
[8] This is more likely to be Nanjing. China's capital moved to Chongqing only after Nanjing was sacked in December 1937.

Afterbursts

Xu

Xu as a young man

It's a Duty

In my family there were three brothers, I'm the oldest. Even though I was 16, I had to fulfil the government's labour order…If you had money, you could hire a substitute to go and build the road, but because my family was poor, they sent me…

At the time we didn't have excavators, bulldozers…We carried hoes…We also had a cart as a bulldozer. In the middle was a wooden plank to push the earth. It was pretty useful, less effort than one person by himself…

All along the road there were tens of thousands of people…Very old, very young, grandfathers, grandmothers, those with bound feet, people carrying babies on their backs…There was one woman of thirty or more, who didn't wear any clothes…the skin on both these sides [of her shoulders] was rubbed raw. It left a deep impression on me.

It was incredibly hard…Even though it wasn't a battlefield, it was the same as a battlefield: the sounds of crying, whispering, explosions, people dying…As soon as there was dynamiting, stones would fall down and kill people. And cave-ins…When you went to dig, so much earth would come down it killed people…

Once the road had been laid, you had to press it down. There were no road rollers; we just used a big, honed stone. If you were on a flat road it wasn't too nerve-wracking, but when it was on a downward slope, people were crushed to death…After the construction was completed there were so many people on both sides [of the road] who had been killed.

Zhang's introduction to service for his country was possibly even worse. Born in 1927 in Sichuan, he was press-ganged as a teenager[9] and taken from his family. When we met in late 2016, the octogenarian was living with his daughter in a village courtyard house, a mountain of corn cobs piled in the centre to dry for the winter. After the war he had settled not far from Tengchong in Yunnan, the region where he fought most of his battles, never returning to his parents and siblings.

---

[9] Zhang says he was 16, however this is likely to be Chinese counting which starts at one from birth, so in Western years he would have been 15.

Ten years prior, his efforts to find what remained of his Sichuan relatives had drawn a blank. Nationalist soldiers such as he had not yet been embraced by the China Communist Party. By 2016, though, times had changed and he had recently been back to his hometown, where, with government sponsorship, he had been welcomed as a conquering hero. His siblings had all died, but his nieces and nephews and their families turned out to greet him.

I went to become a boat apprentice when I was just 14 years old…I went for more than two years.

When I was 16 we were transporting army rice from Chengdu to Yibing…Once we had offloaded the rice, the soldiers came—to press-gang us. They grabbed seven from my boat. The ones that were paid a wage, the boss wasn't too bothered about…The ones he didn't pay for, those people he cared about. Afterwards, the boss came to try and keep me, but they wouldn't let me go, there was no way…

We went from Sichuan to Dali in Yunnan, we walked for more than three months. More than three hundred men. Two hundred were held under gunpoint, like prisoners…We weren't tied, they just directed us with guns and the newer soldiers walked in the middle. There were a lot of mountain passes, and a lot of rain.

*Although not press-ganged, Briton **Fergus Anckorn** also did not feel he had much choice about becoming a soldier. Like compatriot Franklin, he was enjoying his youth exploring the countryside when his call-up put an end to his carefree days.*

We met not far from where he had grown up and as we chatted over a pub lunch, he entertained us with the sleight of hand tricks he had learned as a youth: he had been the youngest member of the Magic Circle and was by now the oldest.

The war came, I was the first man in Kent called up—my number was SGB1…and I didn't want to be in the war. I lived a glorious, happy life and I was going to go with these soldiers. They told me they swear all day long—I'd never heard swearing—and these nasty sergeant majors who'd get you out of bed at five in the morning. I thought I would die.

It's a Duty

And so that was it, they'd take you away from your home. The next thing there's a train and they'd shove you into it. Then the train would stop and there's a big boat. And, "Everybody out..!" And you're going up the gangplank like sheep. You don't know where you're going... "Get up there!" And off goes the ship and you're all seasick, of course.

But where are you going? No one ever tells you where you go. And eventually you're in the war...

Hans Walter's enlistment was equally unavoidable. Born 17 May 1923 within the boundaries of modern-day Hamburg he was drafted to serve in the military along with his peers.

I started school in the Weimar Republic 1929. In 1933 Adolf Hitler came to power—and I must say, I come from a family which had a Social Democratic orientation. My father was no Nazi. I never became one.

My father once said, there is a German saying, "My dear son, have a close look at everything. Not everything that shines is gold. Make up your own opinion and act based on that." That's what my father taught me...

My age group was drafted to serve in the military. I was taken in due to my age, in February 1943, to the Air Force.

Hans was trained in communications in Denmark and transferred to the west of Germany onto the Wurzburg radar, directing night fighters to incoming enemy planes. He was then reassigned to the Soviet Union, but after reaching Ukraine and failing to locate his unit he received orders to move to Poland, where he witnessed the prejudice pervading the German system.

Posen was a city which was mixed, Polish and German citizens lived there—there were about a quarter to a third German citizens, but the majority was Polish—and the first thing I realised was that the damn tram is going along and the front car was empty and the one following was completely full.

I asked why this was so and the response was, "Ja! The Polish citizens sit in the back." They were only allowed to use the trailer, and the Germans got the front wagon.

Afterbursts

Hans Walter in 2019

I said, "You must be joking." I shook my head that something so stupid could be taken seriously.

But the theory of the Nazis was that these were not equal citizens, the Polish. They were thought to be far beneath us Germans—all said with arrogance. I never understood…

I got to know a woman, a girl, and I wanted to go out with her. And there were cafés only for Germans, and the Polish had other cafés. She said—she spoke good German—"I am very sorry, but I am Polish. If we are seen together then I have to go to a prison camp and you are going to get punished. I am truly sorry, but it is not possible, it cannot work."

When you were out at night with a girl by your side you were questioned at least three or four times, either by the Wehrmacht or by the police. You were controlled all the time…It was terrible…

At any point in the war did you think about not obeying orders?

I never disobeyed orders, because it would have endangered my life. It would have meant that I'd have to defend myself

It's a Duty

at a court-martial, and the verdicts in these situations were harsh. Either you would be sentenced to death or years of penitentiary, or prison. At this time there was something called a criminal battalion. Everybody who was previously convicted was sent to the front line of battle to let them die the death of a hero. They had to fulfil impossible missions and that is something I aimed to stay away from if possible.

So yes: I always obeyed my orders…But I did it in a way I felt comfortable…I followed them depending on the circumstances, because I…I always had a certain rule in my life. That "what" I had to do, but the "where" and "how" were my decisions to make…I was not a rebel, I only tried to survive the war—because it was not my war.

Although he could in later life understand how the Germans had been beguiled by Hitler, **Peter Gafgen**'s *family was clearly against the war. As in other countries, there were veterans who had already waged war against their neighbours and did not want a repeat. Peter's father, Heinrich, had served in the horse-drawn artillery in France in World War One, during which time he fell in love with the country. He survived only by sticking close to a man who had already fought for two years. At the end of the war, he had his lieutenant's stripes torn from him by a mob at a German train station, leading him to question why he had fought for them.*

He was an officer in reserve—because all these guys that became officers during World War One became officers in reserve, not professional officers…and then he was called to arms again in '38… From that moment on, I saw my father either in Army camps or on short leave at home…

As a five-to-six-year-old, you have of course the opinion of your mother who says, "This is a foolish thing, and we are suffering because your father and my husband, he is gone. Whenever we see him, he is in uniform. And why all this for the stupid guy there in Berlin?"

And my father always said, "It's a duty…It's the best way out in order to avoid becoming a Party member…"

We had a cult of friends of my father from World War One. I knew that my parents were against the system because they had parties and let the shutters down and danced to the Lambeth Walk…Turning around, *Hi!*, and so on—and that was forbidden. But that was, for the young guys…it was the thing to do and it was against the regime…

You see, the blocks in which we lived, in Mannheim, were being walked around by a guy called the block warden, and he was an extreme Nazi. And he could report what kind of music—you were not allowed to listen to BBC, to *Dong dong dong DONG*. And…I think: why did BBC continue through the war to have that sign, *bee boom boom boom*? Because from the outside…if somebody heard *boom boom boom*, he knew you were listening to BBC…

Of course, at home we listened to BBC…We got all the information from outside of Germany and we could be critical. And it confirmed what father and mother thought about, and they had to get prepared, to survive the dictatorship. Well…he went back into the Army…Difficult choice…

I remember when the war began. I had a problem with it…I don't know why, as a kid, I foresaw the problems…I was running around on what they call a ruderrenner, a vehicle which you could use like a rowing boat…the more you pulled the faster it went and with your feet you could steer. And I remember when the announcement of the beginning of the war on the radio happened. And then I went to play…and I said, "Shit. This is probably the end of your youth…"

I was only six years old…I still remember that, sitting on that ruderrenner and saying, "Shit."

…My dad was in manoeuvres, being prepared. And one time he came back from the manoeuvre in Montebaur, where they trained the artillery, and he of course was on horseback, organising his regiment. And he said Hitler was there on a high stand. "And doing my duty, I approached that high stand by about 50 metres."

And he said, "Peter, I could have shot him." He had a pistol all the time, because he was an officer, and he said, "I was so close, I could have shot him."

Well, of course [he wished he had], but he didn't dare! He had a family, and a kid and so on.

It's a Duty

*While **Rodney Armstrong** was not reluctant to serve, he elected to cure rather than kill. Born in Atlanta, Georgia, in 1923, his family had some early awareness of the war as some cousins had been evacuated from Shanghai on "one of the last boats to get out…and they watched their house burn up in Shanghai."*

I met Rodney at his home in Boston overlooking the ferry piers, surrounded by antiques he had gathered in Europe on a trip he had taken just after the war to get over his experiences. He spoke with a gentle southern drawl and wry understatement particularly marked when he recounted his most difficult memories.

There I was at boarding school and, on a Sunday, sitting around in the common room of my dormitory and talking to my fellow students at the school, came the announcement of Pearl Harbor.

And at that point I remembered only too clearly my conversations with the fathers of classmates and friends who had served in France and who had been in trench warfare. So I was a smartass and decided that the last thing I wanted to be was in some trench some place. And so I applied to go to an officers' training affair at the Merchant Marine Academy on Long Island.

Well, in order to enter I had to get permission from the draft board. So I went to my local draft board in Atlanta…and they were exactly what you would have expected to be on a draft board. Men and women—all whites of course, no blacks possible—men and women of a social class who would have never crossed the front door into my family house. But earnest. Wanted to do right. Determined to fill their quota from their draft board.

And I should expand that of course I lived in a section of Atlanta which was populated by rich white people…people well beyond 50 years old, and rich! Bank presidents, head of stock brokerage firms, doctors, that sort of thing. So there I was, one of my draft board's few shots at filling the quota. Well, they told me they weren't going to give up on me for any merchant marine academy appointment, thank you very much…

I had a childhood medical record which was lousy and I thought it was very unlikely that they were going to take me…But they did.

And so I went out to our local fort one day to be inducted into the armed forces…The doctor examined me and looked at me and looked at my papers and said, "For God's sakes what are you doing here? You should have never gotten this far in the process. There's very little I can do to help out now. What I can do is I can stamp on all your service *Duty inside the continental United States only.*"

So, the next step was, I discovered I was in the Navy…and we set off to a Great Lakes training camp outside of Chicago, where I went for six weeks and where I learned such handy things such as how to salute an admiral from a rowboat with ten other men, flipping the oar out of the water as you go past the admiral, or running hazard courses in the dark…

After six weeks of this nonsense, they looked at all of us and said, "Well fellas what do you want to do?" And they looked at me and they said, "Well you've passed all your examinations so very well, we can offer you any of the training courses we have, and the most exclusive one deals with radar."

And I looked at them and I said, "Listen I can hardly add up…I'd be a disaster…Besides that, I come from a family where the enthusiasm for killing other people is minimal"—a lot of my family were Quakers—and I said, "I really don't want to kill anybody. How about the medical corps?"

Well, there was a sigh of relief because the medical corps was about four down on the preference list. I had six weeks' medical corps training, which mainly consisted of lectures. And of course, I listened very intently to every lecture on venereal disease that there was, but I didn't listen very much about what to do when somebody had their leg blown off…

Chapter 4

Twenty-Eight Stoppages

In training

Even for willing participants, entry into the forces could be a rude awakening. Young men on both sides of the conflict were equally likely to be underwhelmed by their training, or by the paucity of their equipment. In the Soviet Union, Pilot Nikolai Koslov discovered that there were not enough planes for him to continue flying after he was shot down early in the war. In Japan, Nobuo Okimatsu lamented the inadequacy of Japanese technology. In Britain's Coastal Command, Franklin Medhurst manned aircraft that now seem to belong to another era. At the start of the war, biplanes were still in use around the world. By the time Franklin was called out to the Far East to replenish the stock of Allied pilots, the two Swordfish he had flown in Gibraltar were no longer serviceable.

America was even less prepared. Hollywood films gloss over the fact that at the start of the war the US Army ranked just nineteenth in the world by size. When I first came across this statistic in *War and Nationalism in China*, I recall finding it hard to believe. Throughout my lifetime the US has been a major—and lately the only—military superpower. But as several of the US survivors reminded me, when war began they had barely emerged from the Great Depression of the 1930s which had meant soup kitchens for many and, for at least one of the families I spoke to, suicide. In switching its under-utilised economy to make war, America rapidly caught up. World War Two was the making of the country in the modern era. (Britain, meanwhile, would only finish paying off its World War Two debt to its former colony in 2006.)

At the outset of their involvement, a country's general mood tended to be one of optimism and confidence that the war would not go on for long. The reality was quite different. I met British veterans who had fought from 1939 until victory against Japan in August, 1945; Russians who had traversed Europe from Siberia to Berlin, fighting from June, 1941 until the May, 1945 surrender; and Chinese who had resisted the Japanese occupation for more than eight wearisome years. Evidently, few individuals anywhere had any idea what they were committing to when it began, and most had very little control over their circumstances. Rodney Armstrong's observation best summed it up: "You have to realise that the whole experience had a tinge of happenstance and pure fate and chance of all sorts…"

Jeff Haward had just turned 100 when we met, but he had a cheeky manner that belied his years and his insults against both friend and enemy were delivered with good humour. As he recalled his youth, his octogenarian girlfriend ("I'm a cradle-snatcher," he quipped) supplied us with tea and biscuits.

When he talked of bravery, like so many other veterans, it was of others' and not his own. His memories of the rapturous welcome his unit received on England's beaches after their flight from Dunkirk still moved him to tears.

I was born in Finchley, North London, in 1919, and I grew up there, and when I was 18 I joined the Territorial Army—not that I wanted to be a soldier, but because a lot of my friends were in it, and the cheap beer and the canteen. And the girls used to like someone with a uniform on. And also it was a mechanised unit, so…I knew I wouldn't have to walk too much!

When Hitler invaded Poland on the 1st September 1939—which was a Friday, I still remember—the news came over the wireless,

Twenty-Eight Stoppages

because there wasn't television then, to report to your various drill halls, and so off I went. And we stayed there for about three weeks and eventually went to an Edwardian barracks in Aldershot. Oh dear—quite a change from the comforts of home!

I was in a machine gun battalion…and we weren't at all trained. So in January 1940 they decided to take my battalion to France and finish our training there. Well, we just about knew which end of the machine gun the bullet came out of! 'Cos it's very technical: there were 28 stoppages[10]—reasons why it suddenly stopped—and you had to know all of them…

We were stationed at a place called Gondecourt, not far from Lille in northern France, and one of our regular battalions was stationed there, and so they were able to send their instructors to us every day and knock us into shape a bit—until the Germans started their onslaught and they invaded Belgium and the Netherlands.

Teenaged **Rolfe Monteith**, *eager to join the Navy in Canada, had been told to wait for a year. He was still just a boy when he was accepted as a cadet. We met at his home in Plymouth where he had settled long after the war.*

So…Joined the Navy, given a ticket to Halifax, put on a troopship, arrived in Britain—no uniform—war on in Britain…met by a Canadian Navy officer who said, "Right. You're going to the Naval College, no time for uniform!" So we appeared in the Naval College in whatever we had on.

And the Royal Navy people said, "You have a duty, because we have this slit trench overlooking this beach. And you'll take turns manning it …"

We were lined up behind this slit trench and Petty Officer Daekin—who was a Royal Navy petty officer, from World War One, and he called us "lads"— "Lads! Line up!"

So we all sort of got ourselves in the line.

"Now, lads, you're going to get a weapon."

---

[10] This tells us that he was instructed on the Vickers MMG.

And we had already been issued a gas mask…We had a brown overall, gas mask, steel helmet. And on came this motorised cart. And Petty Officer Daekin got the seamen that were running the cart to distribute what the cart contained…Dozens of long wooden poles and a pile of rifles. And the rifle was given in a very haphazard fashion: you just happened to get a rifle or didn't. And if you didn't get a rifle, you got a wooden pole.

So there we were, a hundred of us, lined up, looking rather unimpressive…and I was given a 303 rifle…

I thought to myself, *Hmm. I better tell somebody that I've never ever had a rifle before.* So I put my hand up and this Petty Officer Daekin…"Yes, lad?"

And I said, "Sir, please if I could say, I'm from Canada. I've never had a gun before in my life, and I have this. If you felt it appropriate, maybe if I had a couple of bullets, I would try, if it was important…"

And…I guess he was sort of waiting for it. "Now, lads, I want to tell you something. There is no ammunition. If the enemy arrive on the beach, and you're in this slit trench: do your best!"

…You know it's only on reflection in my later years that I look back on it and think…Mr. Churchill was up in London saying, "We will fight them on the beaches. Fight 'em in the lanes, in the fields."

I don't know—everybody else maybe had bullets, or ammunition. We didn't! And there we were, "ready" for the invasion.

Rolfe was ill-prepared for war not only because he had never fired a gun.

Back in my hometown—when I joined, I had to make a decision: which branch of the Navy?

I looked at these three headings and they didn't mean a hell of a lot to me—except the first two sounded like being like my father, who was a bank manager…The third option was Engineering.

And I thought *well that's very practical* and without thinking—you know, I was supposed to be fighting a bloody war…I ticked the box in my application form to do Navy, Engineering.

Twenty-Eight Stoppages

I got to Halifax and met my other 30 Cadets from all parts of Canada…and this particular chap, having breakfast with him, and he said, "What did you select?"

"Oh," I said, "I selected Engineering."

And this bloke said to me, "You selected Engineering with a war going on? You're going to be getting an engineering degree! The branch to do the fighting is Operational."

I said, "Really?? You must be joking…"

I made my way to the Royal Navy College, at Dartmouth. And we were all split up into what's called "divisions". Quarterdeck was mine and we were taught the fundamentals of weapons, marching, saluting. Each Saturday was the payday and you lined up and you had to salute your commanding officer…and if he wasn't happy with your salute, you didn't get your seven shillings…

We had a fantastic group. Europe had just fallen so we had Norwegians, we had Danes, we had Belgians, we had French, we had Indians, New Zealand, South Africa…a hundred of us.

Eventually so many others of my shipmates said, "You're going to miss the war!"

So you had to put things in writing. So I wrote this little note… [that] simply said "I wish to transfer from Engineering to Operational. Rolfe Monteith, Cadet."

A runner came and found me one afternoon at suppertime and said, "Monteith, you're wanted by your divisional officer, Lieutenant Commander Brooke, in his cabin." (Even though it wasn't a ship, still called a cabin.) "1700…"

So up I went, knocked on his door…

And I'll always remember this moment. Lieutenant Commander Brooke was standing in his uniform. He said, "Monteith, come in." And he had in his hand my note…

He said, "Monteith. I have this request to transfer from Engineering to Operation." He said, "I want you to pay careful attention…Just look at me. I'm Lieutenant Commander. I'm quite old. I was an Operational chap during World War One. I have nothing to offer the world. Fortunately, this war came up and the Navy said, 'Please come back in.'

"This war, Cadet Monteith, will finish, and I tell you…if you stay with Engineering, you will have a profession. Not a war profession. You can't live off a war profession—but engineering. You will have that for the rest of your life. Please would you let me tear up this bit of paper?"

Now that was a huge, huge moment in my life, and I was 17 years old.

I said, "Sir. I'm most grateful…Yes, please."

Tore it up. "Well done, Monteith. Dismissed."

Rodney Armstrong, *with his "lousy" medical record and something of a reluctance to kill, had elected to be a medic in the Navy. His training had begun unpromisingly, with what seemed to amount to messing about in boats, and the impression he gave was that, initially at least, the army had no more idea about what he should be doing than he did.*

We eventually ended up in San Francisco, and then I was assigned to go be a hospital corpsman at a Navy hospital which had been set up in the grounds and buildings of the Oakland California Country Club…to work with a doctor who specialised in burns, helping in the operating room and in treatment.

And as you may know the great wounds of the Second World War were burns, rather than bullets. And let me tell you…working with a surgeon who was very skilful and who was a fine man, a patient would come into the operating room to be treated…He'd come in screaming and he'd leave screaming…

And I did that for some time and then I was transferred to a hospital in San Francisco to work with a psychiatrist, and that was fine—except I developed pneumonia. And I was in bed when my orders came in for me to go with the marines to Guadalcanal…So my group went to Guadalcanal without me and not one survived…

Twenty-Eight Stoppages

Eventually my orders came up to report to a marine camp north of San Francisco, so I went in there and reported to the captain I was supposed to get my assignment from. He cheerfully admitted he'd never heard of me before, didn't know what to do with me, had no job to offer me and he said, "What I will do, is I will get six other men and put them under your charge and I would like you to make me a rock garden in front of my office here."

So, I duly started to work as a landscape gardener, which would have given my mother, if she had known it, a great laugh...

Rodney was kept on this detail until a race riot upended the military installation and he was sent back to San Francisco.

And I was assigned to go on a Dutch merchant marine ship as a passenger to an unknown destination...So, here I am along with maybe 1200 other men, bouncing along, and we went to a nasty little island in the South Pacific, and off I get. And of course you're carrying your whole worldly possessions with you. It was 110 at least in temperature and I had this heavy bag full of my winter uniforms and my pea jacket and all this stuff.

So I reported in at a shack to a bunch of smartass yeoman. They looked at me and I looked at them and I handed over my orders. And they took their time about looking at it...

So finally, one took a look at my orders and he calls out to another one behind the desk, "Hey, Joe, look at this—you won't believe it."

So they looked at my orders and they started to laugh. And they looked at me and they laughed harder. And they said, "Those fucks in Washington don't know that ship went down six months ago..."

*Over in Russia, young **Victor Harchev** was in the capital as it was besieged by the Germans in early 1942. Desperate to go to the front despite his youth, he and his friends joined a long queue to register as Naval cadets, just missing the cut-off. The following year, the 14-year-old finally made it onto the list.*

In July '43 I received the call-up letter: "On August 23 come, packed, to the Frunze district military drafting office."

Victor Harchev in 2019

On the 26th at six in the morning we [got on a train] and arrived at Arkhangelsk on the 28th.

We were given uniforms. The robes were like diving suits—wouldn't bend…It took two to three washes to get better…

There was the following order for the naval fleet: any ship going to the Solovetsky islands had to take a group of people…A minesweeper that was on duty in the White Sea stopped in Arkhangelsk to refuel…Its base was at the Solovki[11]. The first 50 ship's boys were put on that minesweeper and sent to the Solovki…

Our way there wasn't without adventures. There were 25 people in the minesweeper's crew, and we 50 cadets were squeezed everywhere where there was space…Fifteen of us were put [in a cabin of 2 by 3 metres]. We all slept on our sides. Like herrings. Like sprats in a can: if one turned, everyone had to turn.

---

[11] The Solovetsky islands

Twenty-Eight Stoppages

We were instructed not to leave our rooms while underway so that we wouldn't prevent the crew from fulfilling their military duties. When the first storm began… Oh!…Something felt different—not being accustomed to the sea waves and so on…But we lay down and at night a military warning was announced and an extremely dangerous situation arose at the entrance to the White Sea: there could be a breakthrough of the German submarines.

As there were not enough forces at the entrance to the White Sea, all the military ships were sent there urgently. So our minesweeper, halfway, turned right…It was given a square and it headed there to prevent the submarines from going through. And a whole day and night we were at sea with them guarding that area. That's why, instead of eight hours—the normal time that takes from Arkhangelsk to the Solovki—we spent almost two days getting there.

As that minesweeper was on duty, its food supplies almost ran out. And everything the crew had on board the minesweeper—some had biscuits, canned goods—everything was gathered together, and we would take a bite of bread, sugar, some soup…The entire crew was [eating that]. So, we powered through, survived.

Later, we arrived at the Solovki…[The previous year's cadets] came to bare land, to build. We had to finish the construction…We didn't have any servants—everything [was done] by our hands…all the housework—sawing firewood, splitting it…to cook food, to heat the dugouts, bagna [sauna]—of course…

The study process began in November. In December '43 we took the military oath. From that moment we started learning our specialisations…Clearly, everyone tried to study well. The incentive was that those who graded in the highest and the first ranks would be able to choose in which fleet to serve. Because I graduated in the first rank, I chose the Northern Fleet. Because this is where the war was—the war was everywhere, but especially there.

Unlike Victor, **Leonid Fyodorov** *had no such dreams of being a soldier. He enjoyed his studies and was aiming for university—but,* *aged just 17, a year younger than drafting age and still at school, he was sent off for training.*

Happily, he had fulfilled his childhood ambition by the time we met: after a career as a military prosecutor he had written several books about his war and, finally, become a law professor—comfortably into his 90s, he was still tutoring students.

He was a thoughtful and bookish man, recounting his battles in minute detail despite all the ground he had covered during his years of fighting. Our brief meeting therefore allowed him time to share only the most memorable experiences of a service that had taken him from Ukraine through Moldavia, Romania, Poland, Germany and Czechoslovakia. Most striking was when he talked of defending key heights in eastern Romania in battles which fielded inexperienced soldiers and where individual heroism redeemed an undignified retreat.

Like several of the Russian veterans I met, he had a habit of switching between past and present tenses as he got into his narrative. Many of them also had a tendency to describe the crops in the fields through which they fought.

When the war began, I had only finished nine years of school. Always with distinctions. It was New Year, '42. I decided to apply for Frunze Higher Naval School, in Leningrad…I submit an application and I fail the eyesight test—I was very short sighted…

And literally a week after that commission—I was only 17—I'm summoned to Kirov, the military drafting office. With my belongings. They gathered us—about 30 people from Ufa, 10th-graders, first-year university students…and we are transported…in cargo train cars. First to the west, to Kuibyshev, which was a hub station, and then the train goes to the east…

We spent a month on the train. The train was not rushing, of course, and 70 kilometres away from modern Orenburg—Chkalov back then—the train stopped at some small station and we were ordered to get out and line up. And we marched for two to three days towards the south, away from the railways.

Twenty-Eight Stoppages

We came to a huge Cossack village, Krasnokholm, on the Ural river. There was nothing military in that village. We were accommodated in schools—on the floor, on make-shift beds…No basics: no food, no uniform…But there were frosts, winds…And we were constantly in training, mainly outside. We were given warm food once a day—there was a small hut and the line of cadets was going through for the entire day. We survived…

So, we didn't have machine guns for a long time, no rifles. No weapons, no uniform…I won't even talk about the lice that were eating us alive. But the most interesting is the following: in June—when we had studied for no more than three months—they lined up the entire school and for all who were born in '23 or '22 or older there was an order to provide them immediately with uniforms, sew on sergeant shoulder straps, and send them to Stalingrad to be unit commanders—including our machine gunners—while we studied

Leonid Fyodorov in 2019

for one more month, till August. And in August, I was awarded lieutenant rank. I wasn't 18 yet and I was already a lieutenant. And right after graduation, I was sent to the 13th Guards Division…

After Stalingrad, where that division suffered big losses, it was moved to Saraktash village to replenish its resources and I was assigned as a commander of a machine gun platoon which was mostly staffed with convicts…thirty people, maybe…criminals. Grown men of 30 years old and so on. And I started teaching them the machine gun…And we all knew in a week we would go back to Stalingrad.

And, suddenly, an order for me to show up at the staff office of the Southern Ural Military District. Unclear why. There, I received deployment to a reserve regiment. They probably looked at me, at a boy… [*He laughs.*]

This is how I twice avoided Stalingrad. If I had gone there, probably you wouldn't be talking to me right now. [*Laughs.*] You understand? My fate worked out that way. When I came back to Ufa after the war, I couldn't find any one of those people I studied with. Not one.

Xu had been too young to fight in the early days of the war, if not too young to help with building the Burma Road. On his return from that labour, his father apprenticed him to a shopkeeper in nearby Baoshan to keep him out of the army. But by 1942, eager to serve, Xu would no longer obey his father's instruction to be a merchant. He gathered some friends and walked for several days to enrol in military school.

When we met in 2016, Xu lived in a courtyard village house in Yunnan, not far from his childhood home of Tengchong. He was a tall and handsome man and, like Liu in Nanjing, he wore a navy blue Mao jacket—his with a dove of peace pinned to the breast.

Xu had ended up serving with the US "Flying Tigers"—later the 14th Air Force—and in the manner of Errol Flynn he had a red scarf arranged rakishly around his neck.

All the instructors were military school graduates. Every day we had three meals and two naps, it was very intense. They said to you, "You don't know when you will have to fight the Japanese." We were all about 20 years old, none of us dared disobey.

Twenty-Eight Stoppages

Even when we were sleeping, we were nervous about having an emergency assembly—because the time for emergency assemblies wasn't stipulated. They could be at two o'clock in the afternoon, or three, or eleven. As soon as the whistle blew you leapt up, two people to a blanket that you had to fold like a piece of tofu. The tofu piece had to be folded properly, your puttees had to be tied, clothes on, bullet bag on, gun slung and neckline buttoned. There were quite a few things you had to do. There were a few classmates who were scared of having an emergency assembly at night and so they never undid their leggings…because tying up your puttees really took time.

In those days almost everything was done at a trot…Going out to the exercise field: trot. Emergency assembly at a trot. Going to class at a trot. Even going into the loo it was at a trot. Aiya, it was intense!

I remember one time when we were having a meal…they yelled out, "You lot! Come to the front!"…They ordered us to crawl forward, like it was a training exercise. They told us to lie on our stomachs and eat…

In the end at the graduation ceremony, there were a few army commanders, division commanders, regiment commanders and high officials and the like on the stage. "You must all go to the battle front line and obliterate the enemy, the Japanese dwarves. What are you afraid of! Go and beat the Japanese out of China…Serve the motherland." That kind of thing.

After graduation I was assigned to the 11th Regiment of the 6th Army…I reckoned I was going to become a soldier, take a gun and fight the Japanese. After I got there, the regiment assigned me to be a company instructor…

After a while…we were stationed in Nanjian, for military training. Nanjian County tended to flood easily, so our regiment went to help build a big ditch…We also put on theatrical performances… Sichuan opera. I'm from Tengchong and I can't speak Sichuanese but at the time I was 20 and my physique was fairly standard. Even though I couldn't speak Sichuanese I played an unmarried older Sichuanese girl…

Then we had to relocate to Yunnanyi airfield. When we left Nanjian I remember the common people came to see us off. They liked us—we had built a large ditch for them and they hadn't had to pay us!

Over in the US, **Richard Dayhoff** *had no family holding him back. He successfully lied about his age to enlist with the Marines aged just 16. He had been a bare-knuckle boxer and admitted to me that he had quite liked fighting.*

By the time we met at his care home near Gettysburg he was a gruff and weather-beaten 91-year-old and almost entirely blind, but he could still see the events of his youth, which he described with a sort of sad bewilderment.

I went through training in Parris Island. Camp Lejeune. And… they had me wearing a gas suit. Ahhh. That was the most miserable damn thing. Tied around your neck—for flames and stuff. It wound up; it was hot. We took a 14-mile hike with all our gear down along the railroad tracks…and we're having manoeuvres 14 miles out there and…I'll never forget, we had two-man pup tent and two guys in it. And they had a guard on the water tank—you couldn't get but a of quart of water in 24 hours, and you washed and brushed your teeth with it too. Now could you picture using a quart of water to do all this?

It wound up, we're out there and I went to chow. The other guy in my tent, I come back and he's still in there, sawing them off, and here's a snake crawled up on his chest. And I went and got the officer of the day, I say, "M-m-m-my buddy in my tent with me there got a snake coiled up on his chest."

Well he said, "Get a rifle…"

And he took his carbine and then he gets down there and he pulls that trigger and that damn guy got straight up—took the tent and all!—and he run into a damn tree when the major shot that snake—it wasn't funny but you had to laugh—cos he couldn't see where he was going…

And another thing that happened that I wasn't too proud of: we're going to go through the obstacle course where the two machine guns is shooting right across your head and…They should have went through that obstacle course first, before we went through it…to see there are no snakes. And, Jeezus, we had to go down in a pit, come up a ladder and then sneak out. And they're shooting these bullets 15 inches across your head—now, that ain't far! Live rounds, yes…

They didn't go through the obstacle course and this one kid, he was making a furrow with his helmet, pushing. And he stopped and looked up, and there was a snake in front of him and he jumped straight up. Practically got cut in two with 17 bullets…

It's uncalled for, this stuff, you know? He was a young kid. He gets cut in half with a machine gun. For training…

Many of the youngsters, of course, got a kick out of letting off guns. **Mel McMullen** *recounted with shades of adolescent glee his experience of target practice—a pastime which offset somewhat the fact that his pre-service lounging around on beaches had been rudely interrupted. He and his wife of 70 years (and a Rosie Riveter), Jennifer, bickered fondly as they recalled his training.*

I went to basic training in Buckley Field Colorado and the only thing available to me at that time was gunnery school, so I didn't become a pilot…So I didn't improve my attitude at all. I was not a very good soldier…I'd get an assignment and I wouldn't bother going.

Things settled down actually when I went to gunnery school, because I did realise we were in the Army…I got over the fact that I was not going to be a pilot…

My first job as a gunner was on the back of a pick-up truck, and there was a gun mounted on the back…and we'd ride around this circuitous route, and somebody would shoot a [clay]—like it was skeet shooting, and you had to track it…That was just several weeks…

But then, more sophisticated—and probably a forerunner to all these arcades—we went into a big barn area and the whole wall was a picture, a screen, and there were aeroplanes flying across it. And there was a mock-up of a turret and you had a gun, and you had to pick out which of those fighters were friendly, which were foes, and you'd pull the trigger and they could track how many you hit of the enemy and how many you hit of our own planes…

And in the meantime we learned about weather, about cumulous clouds, about circa cumulous clouds and all those things, so there was a great deal of training…[for] something like 12 to 15 weeks…

Then we had our first air flights in our training, and each of us tried different turrets…We were training in B17s which is a very sophisticated plane. And my first experience—since I was smaller—was in the ball turret. And it was quite a sensation to be sitting inside of an airplane and then, according to instructions, you'd turn it down, and all of a sudden you were hanging 10,000 feet above the ground looking down!

And then, our further training—where we actually used guns—and our pilots there were young ladies, and they were in airplanes that were towing [a target] flapping in the back of it, about 100 feet from that airplane, and you could shoot at the target. And because you were using incendiary bullets, you could see—what a waste of bullets!—how close you were coming to it…All the girls were safe…I never really heard of 'em being brought down.

*Fellow Californian **Yoshio Nakamura** was not enjoying his training quite as much, although he recounted the experience with twinkling humour. A second generation Japanese American, or 'nisei', he had been interned by and then asked to fight for America. At Camp Blanding, he and nisei from all over the US were thrown together to train.*

It was not fun!…You see, you have to train for battle, so you have to learn to run over obstacles and run and march and use a dagger and all these terrible things.

It was in Florida, so at about two o'clock in the afternoon there was always a shower. And we would be marching and you couldn't do anything until you got orders…So the at the very head of the march, the commander says, "Put on your raincoats…" and M company—we're way in the back—by the time the order came to us, the sun was shining again…

But we were trained pretty well and…These were Caucasian non-commissioned officers training us and they couldn't pronounce our names. Especially names like "Matsushita". They would pronounce each syllable and—ooh! It comes out pretty bad…We had one guy who kind of stuttered as well. So, gee, roll call was painful…

And so we trained there and we were ready to go overseas and an epidemic of measles had been spreading and someone in our replacement group developed measles. And then the second one got measles. And then a third. And before long our whole group was quarantined. I got the measles, too. And so in order for us to be sent overseas, the quarantine had to be lifted and we had to wait till everyone got measles and recovered…And I think that probably saved my life, because it took about three weeks for the measles to run its course…

By the time we were ready to go, we were sent to Nyack, New York. And when I saw the boats that we had to go into—they were called Liberty and Victory ships—well, they look like rowboats to me! And I get seasick easily. Well, I was sick before I got on the boat!… And it took us a longer time to get there, and we were told "If you get sick, just get up on board and feed the fish."

As a boy, **Ken Yamada** *had thought it would be "cool" to be a soldier, but he found the reality quite different. Despite his enthusiasm, he was rapidly demoralised and his disappointment was still palpable when we met in 2018 at his retirement home not far from Hiroshima. Long before any suggestion of the corona virus pandemic that was to come he wore a face mask, giving the impression that he was trying to hide something. As he recalled his training days he spoke steadily, if somewhat laconically—perhaps because the memories were so difficult and so much worse was yet to come.*

Later, when his tale progressed to his combat experience, his pain was evident. He did not wish, he said, to talk about it—and yet he kept returning to describe images from the jungle which he had not shared since the war. Saying the words out loud, he said, was cathartic. For his listeners, it was hard to hold back our tears.

Afterbursts

First there was a military soldier exam. You line up and take all of your clothes off except your underwear…

Because I passed with the top score, I entered the military troop, in Kurume…It was hell. I wanted to run away. They slapped me every day—every day, with a slipper—and it affected my jaw. I cried in the bathroom…Being slapped for no reason, it was miserable…Because it was so painful, I wanted to go to the battlefield as early as possible…

After those three months, your rank was determined. I don't know how it was decided, but it seems parents bribed the military to have their sons placed in good ranks…

After the ranks were determined, the recruits were sent to war.

[From Japan we went by] ship, about 20 days…The height of our room in the bottom of the ship was low, very low, and we had to kneel, about 1500 of us…It was dark and it was like hell…It was so miserable that some people just killed themselves. [We were allowed out] for food and the bathroom about 5-6 times a day…

There was not much information coming from the battlefield, so I was worried. We thought maybe things weren't going so well… [My commitment] was becoming weak. I felt uneasy…but when I imagined my mother those feelings disappeared…

When we got off at Singapore, we couldn't walk, our muscles became so weak…The people who were able to walk stayed there for two to three days and then we left by train. Those who couldn't walk recovered…

I went from Singapore to Bangkok by train. I saw the Southern Cross from Malacca for the first time. It was amazing…The roof was open. They used lumber for fuel and we would get burnt from the sparks…

When we got to the battlefield [in Burma], we were first sent to the headquarters and we were assigned to a unit there. I was assigned to the joint headquarters—soldiers with good grades were sent there. I later found out my mother sent money to the unit…The senior officer told me that I would be assigned to the accounting department and take the exam…I went [back] to school in Singapore [for about 2 months. What I remember most is there were many British residences. Since we couldn't study in such places, we studied in buildings made out of bamboo…There was just such a big difference between the British residences and ours.

Japan may have precipitated the war but it did not have the resources at home to match its ambition. Its situation became materially worse as the conflict progressed and, unlike the US, its production did not accelerate. With so many resource-rich occupied territories, I wondered whether Japan's inability to keep up may have been at least as much due to the workforce as it was to a lack of commodities. So many brutalised and starved prisoners of war undertaking slave labour for their Japanese captors in mines, production and engineering throughout Asia could not have been as able or motivated to work as men fighting for their freedom.

Nobuo Okimatsu, *assigned to train as a kamikaze pilot towards the end of the war, was concerned with how far behind the US he perceived Japanese equipment to be. The country's Zero fighter planes were well-regarded, but Nobuo felt that its bombers were unreliable and its technology could not keep up with the progress in America.*

I was born in 1925 in Kure City, Hiroshima Prefecture. There was a navy base in Kure City and I wanted to be a soldier from childhood—this was the general tendency for all children back then. Nowadays, when you ask children what they want to become, they say a soccer or baseball player, but in our day eight to nine children out of 10 said they wanted to become a soldier…

My mother's cousin, who was a soldier, built a military academy. When the war broke out, he was a high-ranking officer, a major general, so I also wanted to follow his footsteps and applied to the military academy.

I was 16… [I began in] the logistics unit which managed military equipment—food, ammunition. It was a very important unit. The military cannot function without an active logistics unit, but in Japan we were not taken seriously. I believe that was one of the reasons why the Japanese military failed. A typical example is the Imphal Operation: they sent the soldiers without equipment.

Back when I graduated the military academy, there weren't enough pilots...Since Japan had a shortage, I was transferred to become a pilot. I began training with a glider plane, then with bombers...After graduating from the military academy one can immediately become an officer, but in order to become a pilot you have to start your training from scratch, so I didn't like it very much...

I thought the Japanese airplanes were no good—and that's what I also felt while attending the military academy about automobiles, we used automobiles when I worked in the logistics unit. During school, and in the military, I remember there were one or two US automobiles, it was either a Ford or Chevrolet. The engines would start easily, but Japanese automobile engines wouldn't start, even in new cars. Japan was probably behind by about 20 to 30 years.

It was the same with airplanes. When comparing performance, Japan made unrealistic claims that our airplanes were fast, but when flying the plane, I always felt there were major differences in our technologies. For example, Japanese pilots controlled the airplane manually when flying over the ocean, but US airplanes were automatically controlled by machines...US airplanes also had radar systems. Japan only developed radar systems and automated control systems towards the end of the war. Japan was very behind in this field...This was clearly due to shortcomings in technologies and natural resources. So in Japan many capable, talented people died in the war because of this.

Chapter 5

I Hope My Mum Got Home

Under bombardment

Across Europe and Asia, bombing campaigns designed to demoralise civilian populations and undermine support for the war were conducted by both sides, making the rear no safer than the front. Bombing combat zones might assist ground troops—and in some instances in Russia prevent their own side from running away from engagements—but such devastation wrought so far behind the lines seemed far worse. More than one Allied soldier I met expressed regret at what they had encountered in the aftermath.

Roy Cadman recounted what he had witnessed as the Allied troops advanced through Germany after D-Day.

> God Almighty…Oh my God, they dropped tonnes and tonnes on a defenceless town. Women with babies, and heads blown off. I hated the RAF. I literally hated them. A woman had a child in her arms and she came up and spat at me. She had a baby in one arm and she was trying to hit me with the other one. All the old men and old ladies and smoke everywhere…There wasn't a

Afterbursts

German soldier within two miles of it. I've never seen anything like it…

Harry Rawlins, who served with the King's Royal Rifles, had been keen to be a soldier and was awarded a Croix du Guerre for his actions in battle. Despite his eagerness to fight, he felt a similar compassion for the beleaguered Germans.

> It was terrible for the Germans…I didn't think much of Churchill and all those people…They make him out to be a great war hero and all that, but he was just as bad as anyone else—I mean, the bombing of Dresden…I know the Germans started this bombing of civilian populations, but it was murder in Germany. You look over Hamburg…you just see chimney stacks, because that's the strongest part of the house…Terrible, what they went through, really. I think all the people like that—the Germans, the British, the French—suffered…I remember seeing a film of some people after a bombing raid or something in Japan and there was this little Japanese boy—he was only about so high [*he indicates about three feet tall*]—and he was trembling…I felt so sorry for him.

Ted Hunt, too, mused about his side's inability to judge harshly their own bombing tactics while condemning those of the enemy.

> You are likely to have met veterans who declare that they can never forgive the Japanese for what they did, or they can never forget the Germans for what they did. And I meet people who are pure racists and are quite ready to insult some German in the cemetery who's looking for his hero of an uncle. And that makes me very cross. Because…in war, and afterwards, if you're a true historian you put it down…warts and all, without bias or prejudice…

Most people don't want to hear what I have to say about this.

I say, "Why is it that you hate Japanese?"

"Look what they did to our prisoners of war!" etc etc, take yer pick of attack...

"Well...what did we [do] in return?"

"We didn't do that!"

I say, "Well, Tokyo was made of wood. We bombed it with firebombs. We burned to death thousands of Japanese children—and find an excuse for it. But you don't excuse them treating our prisoners of war as they did."

In Hamburg, we only killed hundreds of—burned—hundreds of children alive. It must be the most painful of deaths...

I've learned a thing or two in the last 70 years, and I know that the Chelsea crowd see the Arsenal foul and the Arsenal crowd see the Chelsea foul. And that sums it up.

In many countries, the war was heralded by bombardments, with Germany setting the tone from its September 1939 invasion of Poland. In Western Europe, the first attacks notionally targeted industrial facilities, but in later raids everything became fair game. In China, Japanese bombing campaigns were indiscriminate from the start, and when the western Allies with their superior firepower got involved, Tokyo was subjected to firebombing raids that razed whole neighbourhoods of wooden residential housing to the ground. Those who had been schoolchildren in Hiroshima before the A-bomb was dropped recalled that their school duties included demolishing houses to make firebreaks.

The first bombardments of the USSR were even more abrupt. Many Soviets had suspected that they could not avoid the conflict raging in Europe, despite the Molotov-Ribbentrop Pact between Germany and the USSR, but the ferocity of the attack shattered any pretence that peace would last.

Afterbursts

When Hitler moved on Western Europe, Rotterdam was among the first cities to be blitzed and under threat of further bombardment, The Netherlands surrendered the following day. **Max van der Schalk**'s *family lived not far from where the bombs fell on Rotterdam.*

I was just four years old—it was May 1940—and what I remember is that we had a broom cupboard indoors underneath the staircase…And my father had made that into sort of an escape place. He had put mattresses on the floor and blankets, and we all were put in there when the bombing of Rotterdam happened.

And I remember that we were all lying in there and that all the time you heard very loud explosions and the house always shook. But my father said, "You shouldn't be afraid because we're so safe. Even if a bomb hits the house the staircase is very firm and underneath there, it's the safest place."

In the evening—it was dark, in my memory, so it must have been 8 or 9 o'clock—we left the house, my father being the first, who had a white pillowcase filled with, I think, money, and maybe some jewels,

Max van der Schalk

and maybe whatever was in the house of value. And then my sister, my elder brother and me. My mother was behind, also carrying something, and we walked down the street. It was dark but there was clear light because there were fires all over the place and it made a lot of noise, the burning, and it was in smoke and it was quite close by.

And then we walked away from there and we went to the house of my grandparents…And some of my cousins were there also, the sisters of my father, and we stayed there and that was just a little bit further away from the fire. And then…the wind which was blowing from the west turned around…and then it was safe there. So we stayed overnight and waited for more bombing, and then the next day most of the fires were out and we went back to our house again. And that's what I first remember of the war.

Over in England, the Channel presented no barrier to airborne attack and the population there, too, learned fairly quickly what it would mean to be at war. After failing to overcome the Royal Air Force in the Battle of Britain, Hitler began a campaign aimed at bombing the United Kingdom into capitulation. **Em Hunt** *had volunteered to train with the St John Ambulance through her employer London Transport, but she was not ready for the fear of the first blitz, which came almost exactly a year after war had been declared.*

It was a Saturday afternoon, and I was up in town. We'd been to the theatre, enjoyed ourselves…and I was just waiting for a bus to take me down to Woolwich and the sirens went…

And you looked up and you could hear them—you could actually *see* the devils…This was the first blitz, you know. You couldn't believe what you were looking at.

Then of course the air raid warden came along. "Come on. In. In. Shoo. Come on…" They shut us up in a safe place until the blitz was over. And I think *How am I gonna get home?*

I went behind the Westminster station and there was a bus…So I came all along the Old Kent Road…

It was the smell to start with. It was the smoke and the smell. And the noise. And, 'course, there were fire engines, and ambulances and the police, and the gutters were full of hosepipes and we managed to crawl along. We knew the docks had been burned—we could see that, hear it…Smell it, really…I remember looking out and seeing all these hosepipes, flat on the ground, waiting to be used.

And then as we get across onto Blackheath we could see all the smoke over on the other side of the river. And, of course, the houses…Pathetic. A bedroom, with all its windows and wall gone and there was this bed…almost toppling out. So pathetic!

All you could think of was *I hope my sister got home. I hope my mum got home…I hope my dad got home…*What were you going to find? Were you even going to find a house?

Later on, when we got them more frequently—the Blitz—the siren would go down the river somewhere…And we had a dog and suddenly she'd get up out of her chair and go underneath it…She could hear it…

My dad built an air raid shelter…He was able to build it in the bottom of the garden—because it went on a hill, and he was able to build it inwards…We'd be in there, listening to the bangs…

"There's one. That's one. That one's a bit nearer. That one's nearer still. This next one didn't—it's over there. It missed us."

And dad taught us to play whist—in an air raid shelter! And, course, we used to start listening, "Where did that one go?", "Who's that…?"

"Pay attention to your cards!" That was my dad.

War in the Soviet Union was also heralded by bombardment. **Nina Danilkovich** *and her family lived in a village now part of Belarus. In just the first few decades of the twentieth century the region had been occupied by Germany, declared independence, been absorbed by the Soviet Union, ceded to Poland and then handed back to the USSR when Germany invaded Poland in September 1939.*

Nina's village was among the first to witness the German invasion. Not quite 12 at the time, Nina was deeply affected by the attacks and the subsequent occupation which inspired everyone in the area to resist.

I Hope My Mum Got Home

Nina Danilkovich in 2019

By the time I met Nina, she was nearly 90. After a long career as an academic she was running the Moscow State University Veterans' Association and had arranged for me to meet several of her fellow veterans who still taught at the university. Afterwards she led me to her office, a long skinny room where we crammed up to a conference table squeezed along a wall covered in books. On the single desk at the end stood stacks of papers and a Bakelite rotary phone.

On June 22nd, near morning, we heard shots…The railroad was being bombed…It was horrifying. Civilians were under attack from shelling. Many died…

In the forest, across from the railway, there were many of our soldiers…with no communications whatsoever…They didn't know what was going on at all. My parents told them that on the highway, which was on a different side from us, there was a steady stream of German cars with heavy military vehicles. It was the main highway: Brest-Minsk-Moscow. That's why they were going in a dense stream…

Afterbursts

They agreed how to get out of the encirclement…Sometimes there were gaps between the vehicles, but most of them were end to end. One could either find one of those gaps and pass through at night or, if not, then make an ambush attack and fight one's way through…

Once, there was combat because the Red Army soldiers were noticed. In our house we had a stove and mama hid us under the stove because it was bulletproof. The engagement went on for a long time. When it was over, one of the Red Army soldiers happened to be in our backyard. He was singing songs. It turned out he got really tired and buried himself in hay. The Germans were stabbing through the pile of hay, but all the stabs missed him.

As soon as the Germans left, he got out and started singing… Turned out he was sleeping and heard nothing and didn't realise what had happened.

Less than six months after the Germans rampaged into Russia, Japan attacked Pearl Harbor with similar ferocity, dragging America into a war that until that point it had largely been observing from the side-lines. Ask almost any American old enough to remember Pearl Harbor and they can tell you where they were when the bombing was announced, irrespective of whether or not they witnessed it—although many did not know at the time where the base was.

Paul DeNatale, *born 1922, Army Air Corps*: I was playing for Alcatraz, football. I was at City College and one of my buddy's fathers was the head-keeper at Alcatraz…Alcatraz against Angel Island. So, I took the boat, went to Alcatraz and then Angel Island, and I was ready to play football and then the big loudspeaker says, "All civilian people get off the island!", that Pearl Harbor was bombed. So I was there, December 7 1941.

Mel McMullen, *born 1925, Army Air Corps*: We were at home… and the phone rang and I went over and picked it up and it was [my brother] Jim, and he was all out of breath, and he said, "The Japanese have just bombed Pearl Harbor."

And I said, "Huh?" I knew what Japanese were, but I'm not sure I knew where Pearl Harbor was…And then all these young guys said,

"We gotta get in fast because this is gonna be over in 30 days. We're gonna wipe the—" even though we didn't have an army or anything at the time…

The Japanese had been bombarding China for some years by then. Over a three-year period from May 1938 the Chinese capital Chongqing endured more than 200 bombing raids using incendiary and fragmentation bombs. In 1943, **Xu** *also witnessed a raid, the catalyst for his decision to run away and fight.*

He had laboured on the Burma Road and then been sent by his father to Baoshan, 150 kilometres from his hometown of Tengchong, to train as a shop apprentice.

As soon as the Pacific War began [in 1941], the Japanese seized Yangon… China's overseas Chinese fled Burma to Baoshan, where they would be safe. At the time, the vehicles came from the Burma Road one after the other, it was pretty fraught…

In May 1942 a group of Japanese soldiers infiltrated a column of refugees fleeing the Japanese advance through Burma. The chance discovery of their presence at the Huitong Bridge, about 200 kilometres from the Burma border, thwarted their progress into China. Shortly afterwards, perhaps in frustration at this failure, the Japanese delivered airborne retribution to the Yunnan region.

On 4th May '42, Baoshan was bombed…Baoshan city did not have designated market days, so it was very crowded. Both sides of the street were filled with goods, because the overseas Chinese had brought a few things with them—you could buy ten yuan trinkets for seven or eight yuan…

There was an alarm, and suddenly 54 planes flew over. Fifty-four! Japanese planes, with machine guns, bombing indiscriminately… Just think how many people there were, refugees and people on the street, who died right then—more than ten thousand…There were ten city archways, all blown up.

We were in the shop and our boss hugged us all around our necks—so that if we were going to die, we would die in a pile…After the bombing was over, I went outside very quickly. Inside the shop it was all shattered. So after it stopped, I ran.

Everyone was scattering…We were all trying to save our own lives. Out of the south gate, just outside, there was a whole family, dead…There were piles of seven or eight…all dead…There was an old lady in the corner of the city who sold ground soybean soup. Her head was gone but she was still sitting there…

The bomb craters made by the bombs all over Baoshan city were all exploding with water…And there were germ bombs…

Afterwards, looking around as far as the eye could see across Baoshan, there were people weeping, yelling…collapsed houses… Everyone was panicked. The next night I fled. On the 6th or 7th May '42 I made it home…My father said, "I was looking for you, worried about you. It's good you're back."

*Born in 1934, **Feng**'s earliest memories are of fleeing the invading Japanese as a child.* From when I was able to form memories…those are definitely of war. At that time, we had begun to flee from the war… Japanese soldiers came…and we got out of the way. We went into the countryside…I was probably about five or six…At that time there was no pollution. Green hills and clear waters. It was very pretty…

Then the Japanese left our hometown and we came back…

In 1942 there was a huge famine. Henan suffered from crop failure. Three million people starved to death…We saw people who had starved to death. That's a very strong impression…I also have a very strong impression, and that's that our family home was in Tanghe county—Qiyi town, it was a small town. We, the family surnamed Feng, had lived in that area for several hundred years, so our relatives all lived in a big courtyard. Such a remote area. The army—the Japanese—came to bomb it…I don't know why they came, because there wasn't any army there, but they still came to bomb…

I had an older female cousin—probably about three or four years older than me, something like that—who was killed by a bomb in that bombardment…My brother, he was about the same age as that cousin. They were at primary school. The alarm went off and everyone ran outside…running, running, running…They were running together. My brother, he was a bit younger, probably. He wasn't paying attention and on the road was some cow dung, cow poo, and he fell over. Just because of those few seconds, he didn't die.

As many of the British veterans noted, the Allies were also not above bombing civilians. From Germany **Peter Gafgen**'s *father had gone with his regiment—newly converted from horse-drawn to motorised artillery—to serve under Rommel as a major in the Afrika Korps. Back at home, Peter and his mother tried to maintain a normal existence while dodging the bombs. Children's schooling included instruction on dealing with bombing raids and their aftermath.*

The only assistance I could give somebody during the war was phosphorus burning. He didn't even realise it was phosphorus on his body…

Well, you don't get water. Use some wood which is lying around and scratch the phosphor off…even to the point that it hurts the guy because you're scratching on the skin. And then when you have scratched the excess phosphor onto the ground, there is still the rest of the phosphor on his skin—and a part of it maybe has already penetrated the skin. The next thing you do, you gotta keep oxygen from the phosphor…[so] it cannot continue to burn and make a hole… So…you take some of his garments, wet them with some water…if you don't find: pee on it…and then very tightly close the area where the phosphor was with this wet garment, because it prevents oxygen going through the wet for some time until it dries. And this gives you time to transport the guy into some hospital…

It was a residue of Mr. Harris's[12] bombs—because [on their way home] they poured the phosphorus[13] out of the planes and it fell on

---

[12] Arthur Harris, also known as "Bomber" Harris, led RAF Bomber Command from 1942 to 1946. His uncompromising approach to bombing German civilians made him a controversial figure even as the war drew to a close. https://www.english-heritage.org.uk/visit/london-statues-and-monuments/arthur-harris/

[13] Not specifically designed to do harm, phosphorus was used in flares dropped by Pathfinders to mark bombing targets.

Peter Gafgen in 2019

the ground someplace. And this guy knelt down in his field near the river, doing some work there with the vegetables…cauliflower or something like that, and smeared that phosphor on his skin. And he didn't know…

I said, "What do you think it is?"

He said, "Glue from a snail." But I knew that the phosphor was all over this area, because Mr. Harris, the night before, had bombed…

Bomber Harris had invented how to bomb cities. And Schuth's house…he was one of the dancers there on the Lambeth Walk…was one of these fantastic confirmations of Harris's "theory".

First you send a bomb down in the house, you get the roof exposed and then you send the ignition bomb—and then the whole thing goes up like a bonfire, no? And that happened to Schuth's house and there was not enough water around to extinguish, it was burning too much.

So he had time to remove some furniture from the ground floor, damaged furniture, a safe distance from the burning house. He could

I Hope My Mum Got Home

still have access to the cellar...and when the dawn came, Schuth was sitting in the *fauteuille* in his garden having two or three bottles of champagne, looking at his house on fire.

And this was—we thought—great...This guy...Incredible!

The fire brigades—it was hopeless, they couldn't extinguish the fires. So then a heat developed from the fire, went up in the air and pulled fresh air in so fast that it was a storm...with very high speed... full of sparkles, still burning material, and you had to cover your face if you went out saving part of your household...

If your house was not hit, you stayed put but you sat around with a wet towel around your face...And they [the firestorms] were very dangerous because, also, of the gases. Even if your house wasn't hit, all of a sudden in your cellar where you were sitting, some smoke and gases came in, carried by the wind.

I remember the first one that hit Mannheim and then came a second one. And in the meantime, [my aunt] suggested to my mother, "Listen, sooner or later you two are not going to survive a firestorm. You have already survived two. So why don't you come to Wiesbaden...because Wiesbaden will not be bombarded during the war."

The Allies had thrown communications down from the planes in good German to tell the people: "Listen, the war is lost. Why do you continue? It's much better when you are occupied by us than what is happening now..."

They flew around and you were being punished when you collected them and showed them around. So on the way to school after an attack—we had to go to school every day and when our school was bombed, we were assigned a new school—we looked around [to see] if we could find some of that stuff. Some were funny...The one for Wiesbaden rhymed. It said:

Wiesbaden wir werden Dich schonen

Denn Spåter wollen wir in Dir wohnen.

"Wiesbaden we will not destroy, because later on we want to live in Wiesbaden."

Mannheim…the house of mother and father was hit by an explosive bomb—not a big one. By that time, we were already in Wiesbaden…[My mother] went, after she heard that her house was bombed, with a woman whom she knew from her student days to look—what could they save?…And when they were in Mannheim we heard in the news that there was an attack on Mannheim again. And the woman that took care of me while my mother was gone and I, we heard nothing from my mother. We didn't know whether she was hit during this air strike or not.

And Wiesbaden main station was not too far away from the school I had to go to. So…before school I stood there in the station, on the track where the trains from the south came in, looking at the people. And after school, I went back and stood at the track, looking…Because that was the train that should have taken my mother back. And we had no news. No news. And I did this for five days. And then we got the news that they are unhurt and that they would be coming.

Chapter 6

Tea and Chelsea Buns

Serving in the rear

The war affected the lives of almost everyone in the participating nations, whether or not they were under bombardment. The home front was the hub of defence and support—and in some cases it was the only option for service. Among Western Allies women were ordinarily not sent into combat, those at the front mainly fulfilled medical roles. Back home, many took on jobs traditionally considered the preserve of men, in factories producing materiel from aeroplanes to ammunition and across business.

For military-aged men, service behind the lines came with different emotional burdens than those carried at the front. Liu told me how he had for decades felt ashamed of his relatively safe job training soldiers in north-western China.

> Mostly I was training mid and lower tier officers—because at the time we didn't know how long the war would go on and there had been a huge sacrifice of junior officers…Later on I felt quite inferior because I did not directly go to the front line and take part in the hard work, face to face and gun to gun

with the Japanese devils…But afterwards, Xi Jinping said in a speech at the 70th commemoration of the victory of the War of Resistance, where a commemorative medal was awarded: "No matter whether you fought on the frontlines or behind enemy lines, no matter whether you directly took part in the war or supported in the rear, all those who took part in the War of Resistance are war heroes, they are all the People's Heroes." This made me very happy…It was a huge consolation.

For British soldiers, service at home was perhaps more common early in the war when the UK was priming itself for invasion. My secondary school headmistress related to me how, as a child bicycling in the lanes in the south of England, she had had to take care not to be knocked off by the tanks out on manoeuvres. When the wind was blowing the right way, she could hear the bombardments in France.

Although the Germans never did make it across the Channel in any great number, the odd man did slip through. **Fergus Anckorn** *served with the 118th Field Regiment, Royal Artillery, but was fortunate to be skilled as a magician—a skill which would save his life in a Japanese prison camp. At the beginning of his service his talents kept him in the UK, entertaining the troops and defending the coast.*

I caught a spy. Down at Eastbourne…Our guns moved up and down the country, to Scotland and Wales. Every time there was a thought of an invasion coming, we were moved to that part of the coast. And I was down here at Eastbourne on a roadblock at a place up the road called Hand Cross—lovely Sunday morning—and walking down the hill towards us was an RAF officer. And he stopped to talk to us. He was a very nice chap.

And I said, "Where's your cap?"

"Oh", he said, "I didn't bother with it today."

So I said, "Get hold of him."

And there was a garage next to the house and we asked them if we could use the garage and we held him in there…And that afternoon MI6 [sic] turned up and took him off.

He was a spy. He spoke perfect English, but he crashed because he didn't know you don't take your hat off. And most of the spies make a silly mistake.

There was one when we were in Norfolk. He came, I think, by submarine and walked into the nearest village—I think it was Swaffham—and there was a pub there. And he went in, dressed like an Englishman, and asked for a glass of champagne. Outside there was a board all about champagne, which was long forgotten by then, and he'd gone in—"Glass of Champagne, please." And they caught him with that silly mistake.

And most of the spies had dropped something like that. What they used to do here, "Who won the '39…football match?", or something. They don't know that.

And our spies…All their buttons, they sewed them on the English way. In France they sewed them a different way. Every bit of their clothing, the seams would go one way—ours—and they would get that wrong, of course, they wouldn't know….They had a cuff here, that we wouldn't normally have…So all our spies' clothes were taken apart and made the German way, or the French way or whatever, and it was the way the thing was sewn that no one would know about it but the people that had to. What a job!

And all the German spies that came here—when I was in this company—*all* of them were caught within 24 hours of arriving. Not one German spy got anywhere in this country, and they were all caught with some silly little mistake.

***Roy Cadman**, born in March 1923, went to enlist on his 17th birthday. Although exempted because he was an apprentice in an aircraft company, he signed up for the infantry so that he could be released:* I said, "I want infantry." Stupid, innit? I think I said something like, "I wanna kill Germans." I must have been a nasty little boy at 17, mustn't I? *He was posted to defend the coast with the East Kents during the Battle of Britain.*

Some 79 years later, smartly turned out in the beret and green blazer of the commandos, he painted a vivid picture of his early days

Afterbursts

Roy Cadman in Normandy in 2019

in combat, embellished with sound effects and plenty of energy—but the uncharacteristically long pause after he described his first kill spoke volumes.

I wanted to be right down in Dover, where they used to shell it every now and again. And the fighters used to come over and shoot up Manston Aerodrome. And that's where I finished up: ground defence on Manston Aerodrome. And that was in between Ramsgate and Dover and it was 3/4 of a mile from the beach.

And they used to come over there first light in the morning. Four—a flight, four—yellow-nosed Messerschmitts. And the alarm used to go because we could pick 'em up on this big, huge electronic thing with a hut underneath, and there was WAAF girls in there, with earphones on…and we could pick them up as they were starting their engine about six or seven miles behind Calais[14].

---

[14] This appears to be a conflation of radar detection with the acoustic mirror, a system not operational by WW2.

Tea and Chelsea Buns

Roy had been in the air cadets and the Home Guard from the age of 16, so he knew how to handle guns. One day in August 1940, an air raid alarm went.

I thought, Right! *This is it!* And I was down a pit and I had twin Lewis guns…when I shot down this Messerschmitt…And all the smoke came out the back and the engine was going *chop chop chop chop*, and I had an officer down the pit with me and he said, "Corporal, you've got 'im!"

And the nose went down and he was doing 400 mile an hour! *SCHUUUNK!* But I had me guns up—I pressed the trigger when they were about three or 400 yards out and he went right through it *p-p-p-p-p*. And after it was all over, he went down and we jumped in a truck, with the officer.

We had to try and find out where it came down and we saw smoke going up…round the other end of the airport. It was about two, three mile away, and we got there and it had landed flat.

The pilot was dead—cos he was all stitched all across his chest. Blood all over the place. And the RAF blokes had just got him out of the cockpit, laid him on the floor…Stone dead. He was only a young bloke. About 22, 23…

The Bofors gun, the other end of the airport, they fired five rounds. It's a 20mm shell [sic] and we heard it as the thing went over the top…and it went *ponk ponk ponk ponk* and we just thought, "Well, that won't do it, we've already done it!"

So we got there and it was a major out of the Artillery chucking his weight around…"Here you are, this is what we did."

The only thing that was broke was the propellers and there was a hole…right in the middle of the wing…One of the shells had gone *boomp* all the way.

One of those 109s—it would have flown back to Germany or France with half a wing, I don't know about anything else. They were very strong aircraft, used to take a lot to shoot 'em down…

Anyway, he's lying on the floor and this Artillery major was saying, "Oh, look. Look what we've done."

And my young officer—'e only had one pip, 'e was about 22, 23, 'e was a lovely bloke…'e said, "Ah come on, fer Chrissake!"—'e didn't call him "Sir" or "Major" or anything—'e said, "That? That wouldn't bring anything down!" 'E said, "This is what brought 'em down!"

And right at the front where the yellow middle of the spinner was, right from just above that, there was a whole line of my bullets all the way through the cockpit, chest high—that's where all the blood came from, out my bullets—and it went through the back of the cockpit and out the side. And there was all this row of all these bullet holes. And we tried to tell 'em, "For Chrissake that's what brought it down."

And my officer, 'e put in for [credit for] it. The artillery major, he put in for it. So they decided to put it in for a court of enquiry…We thought, *Oh, 'ere we go…'e's a major…*

And…I stood up and I told my story. My officer stood up to back me up—cos 'e was down the pit, as well—and then the Artillery… There's not a lot they could say—they fired five rounds and that was all. The three officers went away for about half an hour and they come back and the senior one said, "We're going to give you half a Messerschmitt each."

And my officer, he said, "Whaaaaaa'?!" he said, "It's a bloody…!" He went berserk. Yeah…

Angered by the outcome, Roy volunteered for the Commandos. After training months spent running up and down hills in Scotland, he was sent overseas with a number of his fellow East Kent "Buffs" comrades. On the shelf in his room at the Royal Hospital Chelsea, a renowned London veterans' home, he had a photo of his unit: twelve fit young men, grouped casually with their guns. Roy was the only one to make it home.

Some home postings offered more respite than others. After a terrifying first operation in Norway, **Ted Hunt** *returned to build defences.*

When we got back to Scotland, we built an anti-tank ditch right across Fife, from Kirkcaldy to Newport…And you think, *Well, this is rubbish—a bit like the Maginot Line…all they're going to have to do is come around the end!*

But it was lovely, because the Scots thought the world of us. And the girls…Oh, lovely!

So, life was good, the Germans haven't come yet…We built pits on either end of the bridges over the River Bure, in Suffolk, to blow up the bridge with depth charges and make this fantastic gap…Building machine gun posts in crossroads in Essex…

And, boy, what a difference! The summer of 1940. You go out in a 30-ton truck—and because I was a corporal I'd be up the front, no windscreen…and it'd be a lovely fresh morning. Essex! And you're going to build a machine gun post at that crossroads…And you do that and then the maid comes from the local mansion: "Lady so-and-so would like to know how many jugs of tea and Chelsea buns." And—Oh! We felt so happy. We were going to *meet* these Germans when they came. What a difference to my feeling in Norway…

But, having arrived back, we were given 72 hours' leave…I came home, with my Norwegian furry hat, with the white fur with ear flaps and the lot. And I remember coming to Shooters Hill—knocking on the door and stepping back. And Flo, my sister, looked through the window, and I can see her face, "It's TEEEEEEED!!!" Ooooh!

Of course we had to go home with our rifles, because—who knows—they might be coming tomorrow. But, oh! to climb up stairs with carpet on it. Little things…I'd been walking up bare stairs, with hobnail boots, *bang bang bang*, and I could walk up the stairs at Shooters Hill…The feeling…

And how my mum must have felt—because she didn't know…She must know I'm in Norway, though I'm not allowed to tell her I'm in Norway—I can't even say it's cold…because the letters were censored. And then suddenly I arrive, dressed in Norwegian gear. Ooooh, what a day!

And then of course, back up to Scotland…I reckon if the Germans had landed in Scotland, they could have come right down through and won the war. Yeah. Because no one was prepared. If they'd landed in Fife, come down the Great North Road, nothing would have stopped them. We'd have lost the war.

Over in the US, the threat of a land invasion was more remote—although there was the odd scare, such as when a weather balloon was mistaken for a Japanese air raid and Los Angeles went into full defence mode. A few bombs were also floated by the Japanese into the US interior late in the war.

In the main, though, the country was safe to focus its efforts on regearing industry towards the war. While women filled in for men working in factories—and occasionally flying planes—there were also young men who were considered more valuable at home.

Issy Wolfe's *parents had immigrated from Eastern Europe. He was a student working several jobs to help support the family before America was thrust into the war. Taking an exam on a whim, he found himself winning a job at the US Naval Observatory, part of the Navy Yard in Washington DC.*

My brother Harry, who was three years older than I, in 1941 was a clerk in Washington DC…and right after Pearl Harbor, I came to visit him…and had nothing to do on that Monday. And so I took an examination…Apprentice, mechanical trades…mainly physics, mathematics and general knowledge. And so, of the thousand kids that took the examination, I was number nine, having a 96.25. So I was appointed as an apprentice instrument maker and I came to work in Washington…

And most importantly—in the situation—a good many of these instruments that were very precise measuring instruments had been bought from Germany before the war! And this country at that time had very little equipment or infrastructure for that…Universal Camera—most of the optics that they got came from Germany.

And so they sent out posters all over the country: "The Navy needs binoculars. If you have a binocular go to your fire station. There's a carton there. Put your binocular in…"

Tea and Chelsea Buns

Issy Wolfe in 2017

Now, you have that situation and you have also the fact that at this time, early on, you had German submarines sitting what we call "on station" off of our east coast—off of Florida, in the Caribbean area—torpedoing merchant ships as they left the United States to go to Europe to supply England and France and all the Allies. And on one of those ships, as a radio operator, was my Uncle Joe Davis, who my aunt Lily lost—her love of her life—and she went bonkers...So we had a personal desire to do something.

My brother didn't get any draft notice. He called his draft board and said, "What's going on?" and they said, "We lost your file."

And he said, "That doesn't stack...Let me tell you something, gentlemen...Twenty feet from my desk is the office of General Hershey, who's the head of the Selective Service...I'll give you two weeks to find my file. If you don't, I'm going to tell your name to General Hershey."

So they found his file. He was drafted. He became a medic in the Battle of the Bulge. And he got a bronze star...

[I was making] binoculars, telescopes, ships' compasses...Working on experimental sextants [for] airplanes...The binoculars that people were sending in, 90% of them were World War One signal corps binoculars, which were made of brass. We decided that we would use the new medium of plastics.

The shift from brass housings to plastic presented a considerable challenge to the mounting of the prisms, and as the team experimented Issy made a contribution to the design which finally enabled them to produce a workable solution.

Nobody knows it, but the binocular that you have today, and you buy for $49.95 from Indonesia, is exactly the binocular we did...

But we have also...these German submarines...They had periscopes that their objective lens, the one that faced outward, had a coating on it, it was non-reflective. The American submarine came up and if there was a star, sun—any ambient light—[it] reflected off of that periscope, so German submarines knew that there were American submarines in the area. And what did they do? They sunk them...And so the German submarines were able to stand, as I said, on station...They were invulnerable.

But the people that I worked with devised a little way of coating lenses with a non-reflective surface that was hydrofluoric, which etched the glass itself. They built a dome, had an electric [wire] to a crucible, put some flakes in there, they had a shelf with holes in it that they can put lenses. They evacuated [the dome], gave it a charge... and they [the flakes] embedded themselves in the glass: non-reflective glasses.

So what happened? The tide changed. You will read books where they say our anti-submarine forces took over. Yes: because they now had the same capability as the German submarines...So now, we had convoys going across—hundreds of convoys. To Russia, to England... And I was part of that group of people in that establishment that was able to turn the war around without being in uniform at that time.

Despite deserved pride in his war work, Isidore noted that the contributions of able-bodied young men who served at home were not always appreciated by society at large. He pushed to serve overseas. As the war was coming to an end he was sent with the Navy to repatriate soldiers—and provide cargos of beer for R&R breaks at Kwajalein.

After her ill-conceived attempts at being a nurse, **Pat Mygind** *had joined the Women's Royal Naval Service (Wrens) aged 17 and a half in late 1940. While her job was far from danger, she worked on the fringes of loss. She was assigned as a continuity girl making films for the Navy, which included filming planes as they landed on aircraft carriers, as well as the post-crash therapy for pilots as they eased themselves back into the seat of a Spitfire.*

A lot of [pilots] were so brave…I mean, you knew when you went up there, I'm sure, that you might never come back again—a lot didn't, did they? But they couldn't wait to get up…They thought it was so wonderful to be flying…

Pat Mygind in 2019

I lived in this village and one family, they had this only son. Fair-haired boy, really nice. But of course, he got shot down. And…that hit the village somehow…I always felt sorry for that family. They'd waited so long for this boy.

People…they wanted to be pilots, didn't they? Anything to be a pilot. One of the ones that we met in Scotland that had been shot down…I don't think he ever went back [to flying]…There was a lot of waste wasn't there really?

As the Americans massed for the D-Day landings, Pat was on the south coast and she saw them off as they left for Normandy.

Even today I…I just want to cry…We were on a camp, between Winchester and Southampton…And they had a camp further up the road. And they used to come down and chat and we sort of had at the back of our minds, *why are they here?* because we didn't know anything.

But they were very nice. Really nice young men. So innocent and young and not wanting to be there, really…But they'd come and take us out in their jeeps. And one particular one…There was never any romance, really, it's just they wanted to talk. We were sort of like their mothers in a way. And…this one had a wife and children.

I wish I knew…I never knew his name, except…his Christian name…Such a long time ago. And I remember every night, "See you tomorrow."

Then one night they came and said, "We won't. We won't see you…"

You feel…so sad. Awful…And I thought, *what can I do? He's giving his life for me.*

I knew he'd never come back. The officers…They were all so young and the first lot to go over…And…All I had was my signet ring. I gave him that. It went on his little finger. And I always say to [my son], "I wonder what happened? Is it in the sand, or did his wife say, 'Who did that belong to?'"

Often wonder…That was it, you know. They'd gone.

Chapter 7

My Best Friend Shot Me!

Europe and North Africa

In the West it took some months for total war to commence. In fact, after the initial declaration in September 1939, such was the inaction that the period up to April 1940 is often referred to as the "Phoney War". Hitler had not yet moved aggressively against Western Europe and the Allies were reluctant to engage. Even during that lull, however, there were strategic considerations at play, and one of the less well-known early operations was a British plan to occupy neutral Norway and deprive Germany of iron ore.

Ted Hunt was among those sent to the Nordic country in the spring of 1940, and although he had been keen to enlist, he realised that he was not at all prepared—he was also, more than 70 years later, quite clearly unimpressed by the perfidy of this attempted invasion.

We were going to invade Norway[15], did you know that?…Well, that's a story on its own, really worth telling because it's not denied, but it's not put on the placards…

I was in a Royal Engineer field company. And we got on a train, and we went to Glasgow from Ripon, in Yorkshire…We arrived

---

[15] Most accounts say that the Allies were going to lay mines and be ready to respond to German aggression rather than invade

in Glasgow docks, and we're in the warehouse there, and there's a ship alongside, the Polish ship *Batory*, a passenger ship…And it was the 4th of April, and we went aboard the ship and were issued with Arctic clothing—wonderful Arctic clothing…Double sleeping bags, one nesting inside the other…Leather boots, rubber boots two sizes too big and three pairs of submariners' gloves. Perfect! If the Germans had had this gear, they wouldn't have suffered frostbite like they did.

The 4th of April…And I'm told that as a ports man, knowing about cranes and ships and berths, I'm going to be on the advance party as we're going to invade Norway—peaceful, neutral Norway—because we wanted the ice-free port of Narvik.

Narvik was warmed by the Gulf Stream. Now, the Swedes produced all the iron ore but the Baltic would be frozen up in the winter, so all their trains went to Narvik through the mountains…And this is why we were going to invade Norway and kill Norwegians…so that we would have the advantage of the Swedish iron ore supplies.

Now secrecy was so bad then that the Germans knew that we were going…And on the 9th of April we woke up to the news that the Germans had got there first and were marching down Oslo High Street with a military band. And we were in our hammocks, on the *Batory*, on our way. So overnight, instead of invading Norway, we became potential liberators…

So we landed in Norway with the Scots Guards and Irish Guards, to liberate, about 20 miles from Narvik, and we built an airstrip. And when that was completed, the hurricanes landed on Sunday the 26th of May, and we captured Narvik on Tuesday the 28th. And having captured it, we were told, "Do as much damage as you can."

Can you *imagine* how we felt?

So, as sappers…blowing things up, that was our business. So we did damage in the railway tunnels, and cut the railway lines, and my advice was asked, "What do you think, Hunt, you're the waterman?"

I said, "Well if we blow this jetty and the crane falls in, we get rid of the crane and the jetty and it ruins the berth." We did all that.

In early June, Ted and his unit were packed back onto a ship at Harstad, where they had first arrived in Norway.

And we said to the crew, "Where you taking us?" thinking that they were going to take us up to Tromsø, even closer to the North Pole, to carry on the fight.

"Oh, no", they said, "things are going so badly in France, they want you back home."

"You're taking us back home?"

Oh!!!! One of the happiest days of my life, when they said, "We're taking you back to Scotland."

I was *terrified* in Norway…We were in a little tiny hamlet and we were building an airstrip and the planes would come over and drop bombs on us…I was so frightened, I felt ill. That's not an exaggeration. I thought, "These other blokes can't feel as bad as I do. Why did I do this? Will I be alive—when they queue up for breakfast, will I be queuing up there or will I be dead?"

Terrible! Untrained. Immature. That's no exaggeration at all.

When we stood in that warehouse on April 4, the long and the short and the tall, a group of men—soldiers—came in and they were solid khaki. And as they got nearer—they're all the same size! Scots Guards. They were regulars who had served their time, were on reserve and were all called up…Boy, were they soldiers! And we realised we were rubbish…

While the British defeat in Norway might be ascribed to a lack of lead time, the Dunkirk evacuation that took place in June 1940 was the culmination of a rout that occurred despite months of preparation. The disaster offered the first major indication that the war might not be an easy win for the Allies—and yet, in the end, it has become emblematic of success against all the odds.

*The escape of **Jeff Haward**, who had been mobilised to France to complete his training, epitomised this unlikely victory. He described his unit's retreat after Germany made its move.*

We immediately moved across the borders to a place called Louvain, on a river…which was exactly what they wanted us to do[16], so that they could surround us. As soon as we got there…on one side were the French and one side were the Belgians, and they weren't performing very well and every time we took up position, one side or the other fell back, and we had to fall back to correspond.

By the 25th of May, Jeff was at Wervik on the river Lys, which at that point was the border between Belgium and France. Following some intelligence which Jeff's unit had gleaned, the divisional commander Montgomery shifted it sideways through two others to the Comines Canal—just in time to blow up a bridge and halt the advance of the Germans.

We were there for five days while evacuation from Dunkirk took place, and on the last night we decided these French troops would relieve us, not get involved in too much—they were quite good at that—and just give us sufficient time to get out, and then they would surrender.

But they made a lot of jabbering, like these French do, coming in. The Germans, we assume, heard them and sent a fighting patrol across to see what was going on. And in the darkness and confusion they got amongst us, in a big old farmhouse. And it was these Froggies and these Germans and us, and we didn't have time to say, "Excuse me. Are you with us?" and my best friend shot me! Shot me in the shoulder…His name was Johnny Hunt. It was only a flesh wound, but that put me out of action.

Anyway…we managed to hold on and move back to where our transport was, behind the lines. Got in our transport, moved close to La Panne, about 20 miles up the coast from Dunkirk…And we left all our transport in a field, took our guns out and ran the trucks over them to destroy it, and then walked on foot into La Panne.

And when we got to the outskirts, I remember there were two officers standing there and they said, "Just carry on to the beach and

---

[16] The Germans wanted the British to advance into Belgium in order to be able to cut them off from the rear, having taken out the French defensive line.

when you get there someone'll tell you what to do." And of course, this La Panne was all on fire, and the walls were dropping down…

Well, we got to the beach and there was no one there. And five companies in our battalion walked into the water in a column, and it must have been about four o'clock in the morning when it starts to get light at that time [of year]. And I said to my friend who was walking behind me, "As soon as it gets light the old Luftwaffe will be over."

And I was up to about my waist and when the waves came in, they went over my shoulders. Of course, the Luftwaffe never let us down. As soon as it got light a whole line of Messerschmitts came machine gunning the beach…we were like sitting ducks.

So they took us all out of the water and decided that instead of making too big a target, each machine gun crew of about four or five would make their way individually under their own NCO into Dunkirk and see what they could do.

So I was walking with my best friend up the beach and we saw this coaster…It was lying on its side, because the tide went out a long way there, on the sand. It appeared to be on fire—all smoke coming up from it—but when we got close we saw some squaddies getting on it. What it was…the sailors got a big oil drum and they were burning oily rags to make out the ship was on fire…

So, we got on it and we had to go down into the hold…And some of the last ones on were four Belgian soldiers. So we were all lying on the floor in the hold and these Belgians were standing on the ladder that went up, they were going to be the first up…So…we all decided everyone would have a fair chance, and we told them to get off the ladder, but they wouldn't…There was quite an argument.

So this sailor looked over the side of the hatch, down at us and he said, "What's going on?"

So we said, "These bloody Belgians won't get off the ladder!"

He said, "Well don't argue with them…Just get hold of them and throw them over the bloody side!" Well, they got the message….

I was so tired, I fell asleep on the floor. I remember waking up during the night, and I could feel the boat going up and down on the waves…The next thing I knew was someone shaking me by the shoulder saying, "Wake up, we're coming in to Folkestone."

It was eight o'clock the next morning. And of course, waiting on the beach were all these lovely ladies, with their cups of tea and their slices of bread and jam. I mean, we'd just lost a war and they were treating us as heroes…

In the early days of the war **Ray Whitwell**, *too, was moved to France with the Royal Army Service Corps, assigned to deliver petrol. His company was caught off guard as the French defence crumbled.*

And I was left near a place called Lille and we was ordered to Dunkirk, and when I got to Dunkirk it was hopeless…All the British who had been sent to Dunkirk left their vehicles on the approach a mile back from Dunkirk and then we were sent—I was on the rear party—to stop the German army getting to Dunkirk…And eventually the British ships came and took all the English soldiers off—and we were still held back, being the rear party. And by the time that was done I couldn't get off.

Ray Whitwell in 2019

My Best Friend Shot Me!

So…I "borrowed" a vehicle…and I called at my lorry, which was parked in a wood and it had been bombed overnight, and I got four of those [petrol cans] out and put them in the little Austin that I'd borrowed and set off…

And then I was 16 days on the run and if the French people wouldn't let me in a garage or out of sight anywhere, I had to find a woods and hide in the woods all night…

I got to Lille station and I met another Englishman and he could speak French, he was an officer. And we found the stationmaster and with his pidgin English, we asked for permission to go to Le Havre… And there was a discussion for about half an hour.

In the meantime, I went around the station and I found 18 English nurses. They were all aristocrats and they'd got lost and didn't know what to do. So I took them back to where my colleague was talking to the station master, [who] after a lot of deliberation decided we *could* go on a railway train—when he saw the nurses. So he put us all on the railway train to go to Le Havre, which is about 250 miles…and we were told to keep out of sight.

And in the meantime, I had got two boxes of bully beef and two boxes of biscuits and I brought those, so we had plenty to eat. And when we got to Le Havre after about 10 hours—it was a slow train… it was in the evening, about eight o'clock at night—but when it was light nights—and we walked down to the harbour, and in the harbour was this Dutch fishing boat.

The man spoke English, and I told him what we were doing.

"Well", he said, "I'm going to Southampton in the morning. You can come along if you like."

So, back to Southampton we went…Good luck!

After the retreat from Dunkirk, Britain regrouped. Two and a half years later it achieved the first major Allied win of the war in North Africa against German and Italian troops. **Jeff Haward** *was there.*

I was attached to the Gordon Highlanders for the first attack at Alamein and they mostly came from Glasgow…And these Glaswegians had had to walk all across everything that the Germans could throw at them: shells, bullets—kitchen sink if they could get it—and they were very upset by the time they got up to [the frontline]…

So…we could hear all these Italian voices jabbering away in the dark. So we mounted our machine guns and each fired 500 rounds rapid fire in the direction of where these voices were. And then the jocks went in with the bayonets, and all the shouting stopped…

We were supposed to get through this minefield. It was unmarked. And…people were getting their legs blown off everywhere on these personnel mines…

Oh—for the attack, they'd given me a pickaxe—why I wanted a pickaxe to dig a hole in the sand I don't know!… I had it stuck down the back of my small pack and every time I fell over when the shells came over, it came up, [and] hit me in the back of the neck. So I got someone to pull it out and throw it away…

When it got light, the plan was that our 2nd Armoured Division was to go through the minefield—which the engineers with us had cleared and made a gap—straight into the Germans.

Well, the gap wasn't made, so in due course, when it got light, behind us appeared the 2nd Armoured Division. They started banging away at the Germans and Italians in front. In next to no time on the ridge in front of us appeared the Panzers of the 15th Panzer Division. Started banging back.

Now, these tank shells don't go over like artillery, they go straight, 'cos they're high velocity. So there was us in these little holes in the sand and all these armour-piercing shells just passing a few feet over the top. Not very nice… We were stuck there for five days before we could move and it was pretty nasty. We were cut off and no one knew where we were and eventually some of our own shells started dropping around us. Our wireless set had been knocked out, so we had what was known as a runner, and he was old enough to be our father, he was reservist. His name was Sam Sleeth…

Anyway, he volunteered to go back to where the artillery was, to tell them where we were. And—this is true—on the way back he got wounded four times—only with small pieces of shrapnel—but he was able to get back and tell them where we were in these holes in the sand. And he assisted to fetch a relief force back—'cos, you know, difficult to find a hole in the sand—and he got wounded another four times, fortunately only slight wounds, and fetched them back to us. And for that he was awarded the Distinguished Conduct Medal—which for a ranker is second only to Victoria Cross. Old Sam, he was a…good old boy…

Rommel had been in Germany being treated for a tropical disease, but on his return, realising that his position was untenable due to overextended supply lines, he ordered a retreat. Hitler countermanded the order, leaving the Germans, who had by now left their positions, exposed in the desert to the Desert Air Force as the British ground troops pursued them.

The first real fight we had was a place called Homs, which was about 20 mile from Tripoli…It was night-time, and it was the only place where there was some hills, along the coast road. And we were going through these hills and the Germans were up in the hills, firing down at us. Well, we couldn't elevate our machine guns enough to fire back.

So I remember, our officer decided we would fall back a bit and try and find a way around these German positions. And we hadn't gone long and up came this Jeep. And in it was our divisional commander, Major General Wimberley…Fiery sort of a person, he was. And he jumped out and he shouted out. "Who are you? Who are you? And where you going?"

Well, this officer, Humphrey Wigan, he conveniently disappeared.

He [Wimberley] said, "Who's in charge?"

So I said, "Well I suppose I am at the moment."

He said, "Well, what are you doing?"

"Well, we just got ambushed," I said. "We can't fire back at them. If we stay there, we'll all just get wiped out."

He said, "Where do you live sergeant?"

I said, "Finchley, London."

He said, "Would you like to go back to Finchley, London?"

I said, "Yes, General."

He said, "Well bloody well turn round, go through those hills, go to Tripoli, and when you're finished, get to Berlin. Then you can go home to Finchley!"

And he disappeared in a cloud of fume!

So now, our officer'd miraculously reappeared. So we went back a little way and we saw a track going off to the right. So we went up this track…And at first, we could hear the firing going there [*pointing*], then it was there…

So I said to our officer, "I think it's about time we had a look. See exactly where we are and where the Germans are." It was just starting to get light. So the two of us ploughed up the top of this big hill and then we could look down in this ravine.

And it was mostly I-ties—with some Germans, to see that the I-ties didn't run away. And when we looked, they had these two field kitchens and we saw smoke coming out the chimneys…So by now we got two of our machine guns up. And when the grub was ready, all these I-ties lined up for their breakfast…

War's not very nice, you know…

And so we waited 'til they were all lined up. Perfect target. And we opened fire. And, of course, slaughtered them. And they all got very confused. And to the left side of us was the only way out of this ravine and we'd got a machine gun lined up on it.

The Italians had these 10-tonne [sic] "Lancias", they were called. Of course, we were ready, when the first one came round, for the I-ties trying to get away. We were able to open fire and hit it. I remember it turned over on its side, that stopped all the I-ties getting out. That was the only way out…

Course…didn't take much to persuade them to surrender. And the worst part of it was, most of these lorries were full of tins of spaghetti and I hated it…For months afterwards all we got was bloody spaghetti!

Having also survived Dunkirk, **Ray Whitwell**, *too, was redeployed to North Africa and then to Sicily, an invasion that ultimately had little* *strategic significance but provided memorable encounters for more than one soldier I met.*

I was put in a company called 250 Company, RASC, and we supplied ammunition and food to the front line and we were sent out to North Africa with the First Army. And I was in Tunisia for—oh, several months…And then from there we invaded Sicily.

The British didn't have enough aeroplanes or gliders, so I was put on with the Americans, in an American glider called a Waco. And we set off towed by an American airboat—and they were green. They hadn't been in before, and they were casting off too early and a lot went in the sea…We landed on a cliff top in Sicily, not far away from an Italian anti-aircraft battery.

So our officer said, "Come on we'll have to take them."

And at that moment two of them came out, marching, carrying a white flag…And they took us in and—we had about 18 of us in this glider—and…we had coffee and cakes and waited for the sea party to come. As simple as that. Luck.

I supposed their hearts weren't in it.

No. Which is sensible when you think about it. Who wants to die? Nobody. I don't. I didn't, either…

Ray might have found the Italians guarding Sicily a pushover, but his later experience in Italy's mainland was of a different order.

We were there for about 3 or 4 months, fighting up the coast side past Bari—we talk about it in a few minutes, but really it was days and days…

The Italians didn't want to fight. The Germans did…I call them "nasty people", especially the SS. And of course, being RASC, and taking supplies up to the front line, I was always in mixed up with the fighting in the front line…

But I was lucky all the time. Missed me! I was frightened, but I always had the belief that I was coming home…It's horrible though. You don't know who you're shooting…but it's somebody's father, somebody's son. But you haven't got to think about that really. You just think, "Good, he's gone."

Afterbursts

Roy Cadman's *encounter with the Germans in Sicily was equally tense.*

I wouldn't know [how many Germans I killed] cos I used to have a German Spandau and I've knocked a lot off. I think the nearest I ever got to one was a young lad in Sicily, a German para, and we were 40 miles behind their lines…

I was the leading scout for One Troop and we came across open ground and there was a bushy-topped tree on the right and there was a German Spandau parachutist sitting behind the gun and he got it lined up on me. And the corporal, he's what you call an *obergefreiter*, and 'e's got binoculars on me, cos 'e didn't know—'e thought I was one o' them, cos we were dressed the same: short sleeved KD [khaki drill] shirts, KD long trousers, gaiters.

We were exactly the same, everything, except they wore a round metal tin hat—camouflaged—and we had a green beret. And I didn't have the green beret on. Otherwise, I'd have been dead. I had it in my battle dress front pocket…And he didn't know what I was.

I'm walking across the front of this thing, it was about 20 yards away from me. At that stage I had a Tommy gun and I had loads of pouches—I had a special belt made with four pouches with four magazines on each pouch and one on the gun. And I thought, *Well, I'm gonna get myself killed here.* And I thought *Bluff! Bluff 'em!*

So I got a packet of cigarettes out, and I lit up—and he's still got these binoculars on me—lit up [*Roy sucks on an imaginary cigarette and waves*] and I waved at 'im and 'e waved back and 'e sat down alongside the gun and 'e got cigarettes out and 'e puffed at 'em.

And I walked on to the edge of this wadi—an open dry riverbed, 20 foot down—and I looked down and I thought *Oh my Gawd!*

There was thirty or forty German paras all lying down on the floor. Some of 'em were reading, some of 'em were writing and they were a reserve company, and we walked right—Well, we were forty mile behind their lines, you see…

My Best Friend Shot Me!

So I got to the edge of this ravine and my section came up—there were nine of us left at that stage—and they all lined up at the edge, laid down. And there was a path went down to the bottom and coming up the path was a young German para with a rifle on his shoulder. 'E'd been sent, thinking…They thought that we were them! And this young lad had come up to take me down to the officer in charge of that lot down the bottom.

And I thought, *Oh I'm gonna 'ave you, mate,* and I cocked me gun—you can have it on single shot, or automatic, and I put it on single shot—and I thought, *You take that rifle off and point it at me and you're dead.*

He came up and I said, "Hande hock! Du bis mein gefange!"

That's "Hands up! You are my prisoner" and 'e looked at me like I was a nutter.

"Nein!" he said. And he got his rifle off his shoulder…I went *bang! Bang!* Two single 45 shots…'e did a double back somersault—*doink*—and as soon as that went, they were up on their feet, they went, "Where are they?"

I got it on automatic and I'm spraying it around and all the lads had opened fire with their rifles and whatever weapon they'd got and then suddenly there was a *burp! burp! burp!—whack!* Right in the middle of my back.

And I thought *Oh, Gawd.*

That bloody Spandau that we'd walked in front of, they've realised they've dropped a right clanger by letting us get where we were and they've picked it up and turned it round and let us all have a whole belt of two hundred rounds. He sprayed the whole lot of us. Out of my nine section there were five outright dead—they got huge holes in their backs—and the other four were very badly wounded. Our officer…dunno where he went, but he'd gone…

And—*whack!*—something hit me in the back and I thought, *Oh, bloody hell, I'm dead.* And the blood pouring out of me mouth…and I flopped onto the ground and there was a big cheer and about

50 or 60 of them came charging across, rifles and bayonets, and I thought they were gonna stick the bayonets in me but the corporal in charge of the nearest three, he gave 'em a right choking off—cos one of 'em, he pulled it back to thrust…and 'e made 'im stand to attention in front of me, and 'e were more or less saying, "You don't kill a wounded man—look at the state of him," and he made those two pick me up and take me down the bottom of the ravine…

Well, I got a bullet went in under me shoulder blade, into the lung, through the lung, and it came out right next to the ear. If it had been an inch that way it woulda gone in the middle of my throat, right up through the middle of my head and out through the top 'ere and I'da been stone dead.

Roy was interrogated by the German officer commanding the group in the wadi. As Roy recalled it, the officer's father had been the German ambassador to the UK and the son had been educated at Eton and Oxford. When war broke out, the ambassador was put under house arrest in London while his son joined the German army. The officer was home on leave when his father appeared at the front door as the family was having dinner.

In fact, the last pre-war German ambassador to the UK left shortly before war was declared, but the general gist—that the officer's father was an official well-treated by the UK—was probably accurate.

The ambassador [sic] had been nine months under house arrest and an officer came in and said, "You're being set free."

And they put 'im in a plane, a Swiss plane to Switzerland, transferred 'im over to a German plane, landed 'im in Berlin, and he knocked on the front door and…they're all looking at him and they said, "What you doin' 'ere?"

And he said, "They let me go!"

He was sent home! That's why I was treated as I was treated…

[The German officer] gave me the chance of getting away…didn't help me, but left me on my own and I was able in the middle of the night to get out, all the German soldiers were all sleeping…

I just had to get out, up the side of this hill—I'd lost loads of blood and it was about 150 feet up and I stayed there, overnight, and the next day I could see 'em all scurrying about up and down. But nobody came up after me. He left it to me to make my own way back.

I think it was purely the fact that I was ultra fit, being a commando…That got me through, really. I kept pushing—I wanted to jack it in, I just wanted to sit down and let the world go by—and I kept saying to myself, *You're not bloody doing that. You're gonna get back to the lads. Go on! Get up! Get up!*

Chapter 8

Fire Machine Guns!

The Eastern Front

Germany invaded the Soviet Union almost two years after war was declared in Western Europe, but this was no phoney start—the country went straight into combat. Over the following four years, the Soviets sacrificed over 20 million lives to the war, many of them civilians. Civilians were engaged not only in support work: there was also an active resistance of partisan fighters who agitated to drive the Germans out of occupation. Meanwhile, Red Army soldiers marched across miles of Soviet and neighbouring territory on their progress towards Berlin.

A few months after the British retreat from Dunkirk, **Nikolai Koslov** *was beginning his pilot training in the Soviet Union. The country would not be invaded by Germany for another half year but the lead time was not sufficient for it to build up its equipment production and most of the airmen were placed in reserve.*

After months of inaction Nikolai was "elated" when he was chosen for an elite reconnaissance squadron bound for Stalingrad.

One of the unit commanders, Ostraverzhenko Georgiy, picked me as navigator of an excellent aircraft—dive bomber—at the time, a PE-2. Everything that depended on the navigator—i.e. route and bombing calculations, photographing—that was my responsibility...

Our task was reconnaissance, meaning searching for enemy formations and photographing...Everyone had only one [thought]: what would be the best way to accomplish the mission they had?...

December 9th '42 was tragic for us. We left in the morning...A mission to look for tank units...Found them, took pictures—but we were unlucky, because when we were taking pictures, we were attacked...there was strong anti-aircraft fire, the photos turned out blurry. We returned to our base around 10 o'clock.

When it turned out that the photos were blurry, we went for a second flight around 16:00. We found the concentration of tanks around Debaltsevo. Again, there was anti-aircraft fire—and when you are taking photos you can't change speed or altitude. That's why at that moment an aircraft was a very good target...

We left the anti-aircraft fire zone unharmed but were attacked by four aircraft...They were afraid to attack from the front as we had five machine guns and we were shelling the front area, so they were attacking from behind...The gunner-radio operator had two machine guns: one at the top that can be moved and another one at the bottom which is foot-operated and immovable. That's why the rear while the shooter was alive and resisted was okay, but once he was killed—a bullet hit him as he had hardly any protection there—then they started basically to bully us, from the right, from the left.

The right engine was set on fire. The pilot, Georgiy, he was an excellent pilot...He made that aircraft perform its best, even though it was a new, metal aircraft that pilots didn't know very well...So, with the right engine ablaze, we managed to fly to a bank of the Volga and stuck it in the sand.

We got out and even managed to take the radio operator out, even though they kept shooting at us...Senior Sergeant Buzaev, I still remember him and will never forget...The airdrome crew came and took him, while we [left] with another car.

Fire Machine Guns!

Nikolai and his crew were fortunate to land in an area where they could be picked up. But with no more planes to fly, they were again put in reserve as they waited for equipment to be built.

The Germans had already reached the Volga, Stalingrad was already cut off...Around that time, a general from the army and an air force general arrived. The army general said bluntly: "You're sitting here devouring pilot rations. Can you see what's happening in Stalingrad? This where the fate of the motherland is being decided... Those who are in favour of defending Stalingrad with a rifle in hand, right now, take three steps forward!"

The majority stepped forward, including me. Two companies were formed...I got into the second company, second platoon. We were provided with supplies...green flasks, green backpacks, a rifle that was one and a half times longer than me. Some press cake—I had never eaten anything like that in my entire life...They loaded us in a truck and took us to the Volga. There was a command to dig trenches. We were preparing to cross...

What I remember especially vividly is when infantry was being transported [to the other bank] and they were shelled with mortars... not everyone would make it. Some people would die in the Volga waters...The first platoon of the first company started crossing and the Germans, of course, with six-barrelled mortar...In short, there were casualties...

We were in trenches, waiting to be transported across the river, but somebody remembered that pilots are scarce and we left, at night...There was a railroad along the frontline—right on the sand. Our second company was loaded into two train cars, 25 people in each. Bunk beds, hay...And we took off.

We were on the way, on the way...After three days, we stopped to receive hot food. I get off—Sverdlovsk. We protested. "We asked to be sent to the front, not this!"

No. The poor commandant was running around and [later] he came out and told us that we're being taken to Chita for retraining.

Eventually, the veterans were persuaded to knuckle under by generals who convinced them of the need for artillerists and promised that they would return to flying once there were enough planes.

Nikolai graduated from artillery school in March 1943, two days after his twentieth birthday, and was assigned to be a control platoon commander with the 7th Guards Cavalry Corps based at the Don River, bordering Ukraine.

The cavalry corps were fulfilling the role of a mechanised army. Vehicles, tanks...Not enough. The cavalry could go through any landscape: marshlands, forests, fields...This is why, especially in Belarus cavalry corps were used along the Prypiat River. Six people could easily move a cannon—for short distances, a couple of horses could also move the cannon, while six people could gallop 40-50 kilometres a day. That was normal...

The [battery] control platoon had 20 people in it. Out of them, 12 were combatants, and the rest are horse guides—for each two combatants, one horse guide. The horse guide's task was to take horses to the rear in combat conditions, take care of them, and when needed bring them back into the battle...[The horses] were trained and stayed calm. If the rider is killed or wounded and fell down, the horse would stop and wouldn't leave him—if the rider trained it well. On the battlefield they understand each other very well...

The morale at the front was high. My artillerists were writing "For the motherland, for Stalin" on the shells, with chalk or coal. Nobody forced them—the shell was going to be fired. No one would see it...

I was very lucky at the front. I don't know who was guiding me, but to have such a military path—always at the frontline and survive—that's rare...

One of the examples is from Belarus. I was with the orderly. It was in marshland. We needed to pick a spot from which to fire. After searching for some time, I found a small glade with a fence—Byelorussians were growing something there. I told the orderly to wait while I walked around to see how best to bring the cannon.

Fire Machine Guns!

I stepped away maybe 50 metres and—mortar!—the Germans attacked. I turned around and saw that the horses were on the ground and there was no orderly...I went back...The horse guide was all covered in blood, his heart wasn't beating. If I hadn't stepped away, that would have been my fate...His [horse] was dead. My Burat was looking at me...I knew that it was his end. His stomach was open, it was very hard to look.

I took out a pistol and put a bullet in his temple, finished him... He was going to die regardless, but in pain.

Leonid Fyodorov *had twice avoided fighting in Stalingrad due to his youth and was instead assigned to train recruits. In February '44 he was finally sent to the frontlines to serve in the 50th Rifle Division, part of the Second Ukrainian Front under Konev.*

I was told, "You, Fyodorov, take a group of recruits and take them to the 2nd regiment."

I met the group recruited by the field drafting office...None of them had uniforms or weapons...They ask me, "Comrade Lieutenant, we don't know a rifle. Are we really going to the frontline?"

I'm walking with that group, and we saw lightly wounded soldiers walking in the opposite direction, from the frontline...And I assured them, "You will study in the rear...you will receive new uniforms, weapons. And only then you will go to the frontline."

But of course, I couldn't imagine myself what would happen next. Those wounded—some an arm, some walking with a stick—were walking to the rear...and one of them said, "And you, lieutenant, will go straight up to the 'horseshoe.'" I didn't know what it was...

I arrived at the regiment headquarters. The officer didn't even look out of the headquarters and sent us all to the 3rd Battalion. I found its commander in the rear. He looked out of the dugout. "Everyone on the horseshoe!"

It was getting late. And this is when I saw the 'horseshoe'...the key heights. From there, Iasi was clearly visible—we hadn't taken Iasi yet—and that horseshoe was encircled by Germans. Their trenches and our trenches were 200 meters apart.

So, I warned the soldiers that we would be going up to the horseshoe from the rear, but if anyone saw a rocket—and their rockets burned for a while—everyone should lie down, otherwise they would get hit by bursts.

So, we were going up. The Germans were close, I couldn't scream, "Lie down! Down! Down!" [The recruits] are running back and forth…I left them close to the top and told them to stay low there and wait for a command. I kept going up.

I found a company commander on a breastwork and told him that I brought 30 people. He didn't say a word and suddenly grabbed me by the collar and pulled me down…the machine gun was firing and the ground was pouring on our heads. So, I reported, and from that pit we commanded [the green recruits] to go up. We counted them—everyone came…

Our troops tried to hold that horseshoe so as not to fight for it again. It was high. There was a famous monastery to the left, to the right, a valley. The most reliable machine gun, as I thought, was in the centre. There, there were newly equipped soldiers who had been in hospital, young. In the right and left wings the soldiers weren't even re-uniformed…Same situation in the company: half were newly equipped, and the other half—not really…

I'll tell you…I learned more about our machine gunners in battle.

The first impression is about the central machine guns, where I thought there were very reliable gunners, together with a shooting platoon commander…

"Germans! Germans!"

I used the connecting passage to get to a machine gun. I see two big guys lifting a machine gun…I see their arms trembling. They just need to lift it to a platform, ten centimetres, and it will roll by itself. And I see that the wheels are stuck and they can't lift it, while the Germans are here, shooting. So, I grabbed it by the trunk and pulled it up. They quickly gave me the bullets and crawled back…

[During another attack], the number one position commander, he was shooting. I thought everything was ok—he wouldn't let the

Fire Machine Guns!

Germans near. I'm to the right of him and, all of a sudden, he abandons the machine gun and goes away. The machine gun stops, the Germans are getting closer.

I give the command to prepare grenades. The soldiers are also shooting—from rifles, from guns...One of the hand machine gunners turned his back to the Germans, covered his head and starts yelling, "Fire machine guns! Fire machine guns!"

I'm thinking, "You have a machine gun!" But his machine gun is silent.

Maybe the machine gun has stopped working? I go behind it. It works just fine. I resisted the attack. I give a sideways glance, thinking the machine gunner has been hiding. No, he is shooting from a carabine. After everything was quieter, I asked him what happened.

"Comrade Lieutenant, I only know how to load...I don't know how to use the machine gun."

I had two such cases. This one and another one in winter, on German territory, when somebody drank machine gun coolant: it had alcohol, glycerine, water...We literally stumbled upon German machine guns and happened to be unarmed. The sergeant pulled out the machine gun for me and it wouldn't start, just managed one shot. That was scarier...When I learned that people didn't know how to use a machine gun, I started teaching them how to load it, unload, etc.

That was when the hardest defence battles began...Konev's orders were to take over Iasi by May 1st...Our horseshoe was the closest but we couldn't take it. Many people died. The dead bodies weren't taken away. It stank...

I think there were ten divisions concentrated on a narrow part of the frontline, four of them tank divisions, and our division was at the junction of two armies—the 52nd and another one—and it took the most important hit. Terrifying battles...Tanks, constant bombing... We saw our forces retreating on the right and the left...

At night...we received a command to quietly, unnoticeably for the Germans, pack up and leave those trenches on the horseshoe.

Afterbursts

We were told that we would be replaced by a different unit—and we saw our replacement. It was a reinforced platoon of the first battalion.

They took over...

And what happened in the morning? We observed at dawn how the Germans moved around that horseshoe from the rear, which I had predicted...And we saw with our own eyes how they all surrendered. Horrifying. I understood that we might have ended up in the same way.

After maybe half an hour, we saw about 30 tanks moving along that hollow straight towards us. I thought, *That's it*—especially because the third company, with the company commander in the lead, tore off their shoulder straps [and ran away]. We managed to keep our soldiers [from running]...

After that company's flight, all of a sudden, the tanks turned around...started moving back to their rear. It was hard to understand: the company had run away, there was no one...After about an hour we received a call. I picked up the receiver...

And this is when I heard for the first time that Private Semeschuk hit back at them and resisted the attack...Saved not only our battalion but the whole regiment...with grenades and bottles[17]. [He was from] the third company, the one that ran. He received a "hero" [medal] literally within eight days.

He explained, "The boys ran away, but my legs were weak, I knew I couldn't ..." In total, he crashed six tanks...

On the 5 [June], early in the morning shelling had already started... mortars, artillery...And I was commanded to leave my trench and move to the one in front to the right. I told my soldiers to run with machine guns towards the blasts as the dust would mask them—and of course a shell wouldn't fall for the second time [on the same spot]. It was surprising to me that we crossed those 400 metres without anyone even getting wounded.

---

[17] Molotov cocktails

Fire Machine Guns!

The trench was occupied…There were machine guns—without anyone operating them for some reason—and shooters, an officer, senior lieutenant—evidently a company commander…

My soldiers settled in the trench and there was another tank attack. That time there were about 10 of them moving towards our position…They stopped 150 metres away from us…I thought, *Probably, Semeschuk taught them a good lesson.*

They stopped and fired towards our trench. Then I saw, behind those tanks, a crowd! I thought *Germans!* Turned out those were our troops, with sergeants or officers running in the front…

I took a position at the entrance of the trench and one of the soldiers lifted himself like a gymnast and jumped out of the trench—and everyone did the same thing and left for the rear, including my soldiers…

I saw how the senior lieutenant got into some sort of hole in the trench and came out of there with a wounded arm—he shot himself!—and then he legitimately left the trench and the rest started running behind him. I realised that if I ran behind my soldiers I would get shot: there was an edict not to leave your position without a direct order. I decided to stay. I was the only one…And I stayed there an hour longer…I knew that even if I left 200 metres behind [our men], any officer could shoot me following that same order: 227[18]. That's why I stayed there as long as possible.

Eventually, I started thinking that I needed to go back to join our unit. Otherwise, if they came back—and they could come back, as the tanks stayed put while the trench was still ours—they would think that I was waiting for the Germans…

I, calmly, in a coat with lieutenant shoulder straps, started walking…It was about 800 metres that I needed to cross, through an open field. I decided not to run but just walk. The tank crews could see that clearly and started shooting at me—one quite close, another fairly close, the third one, really close. Hit me in a temple and on my side.

---

[18] An order, whose strapline was "not a step back", designed to disincentivise Soviet soldiers from deserting the front lines.

I thought I was killed. I lay down and started to feel [my head]—no blood, just earth. I stood up and kept walking. There was a small hill. I thought if I could manage to reach those bushes the Germans wouldn't kill me, but our soldiers would meet me with a pistol.

Indeed, when I reached those bushes and could look around myself, I saw our artillery positions about 400 metres away. The officers there could see me very well, through binoculars and so on. I kept walking at the same pace. When I reached the battery, there were heavy cannons. It was evidently our artillery regiment, 202.

A captain, tall, dark, with a pistol. "Lieutenant, where are your soldiers?"

I responded calmly, "You probably met them a while ago."

[*He laughs.*]

"Take a battery defence position…!"

We held the defence at that place until the attack on August 20 [the second, and successful, Iasi-Chisinau offensive]…

There were many interesting moments. I refused to follow my division commander Ruban's order to fire machine guns at our soldiers who were making friends with Romanian soldiers.

I told him, "I won't give such a command. If you want machine gun fire, give that command to my gunners yourself."

And he knew that they wouldn't follow his order. They were supposed to only follow my orders. Thank God it worked out.

Ruban later admitted that he gave the command, "When soldiers were running away, I ordered the artillery to shoot at our own infantry."

As Leonid's troops made a weary advance pulling their own machine guns and Nikolai Koslov's cavalry thundered across Poland with the First Belorussian Front in pursuit of soldiers such as **Hans Walter***, that German soldier was retreating across the country with Germany's First Ski Division.*

Unexpectedly, the Russians broke through the line of defence… From there on they marched all the way to the Upper Silesian industrial area and occupied the cities Beuthen [Bytom] and Gliwice

Fire Machine Guns!

[Gleiwitz] without much resistance…until they reached the German army along the Ratibor-Rybnik line. Then the forward German positions were pulled back by train to Rybnik. There we exited the trains and had to build up the cannons straight away, because the Russians had already moved so quickly that they were at the city limits of Rybnik.

We were equipped with everything you could think of when it comes to weapons. Germany, in 1944, produced more weapons than in the whole time of the war before that put together. No matter the bombing of the Allies, we had everything. There were cannons, tanks, everything…

But the greatest handicap of the German army was, from '44, there was no fuel: the troops could not take their vehicles with them because they weren't getting any fuel. Then the so called "wood gasifers" were introduced, which never worked, and there was not enough experience with these vehicles. The motor was heated by burning wood—it was a new German patent—but whenever there was a small hill, the cars which pulled the cannons had to pull up the wood burners because they did not have enough power…

We took firing positions straight away, and then it started. Rybnik was freed from the Russians and the battle lines were drawn. The line was back under German control, and the last coal mines Germany mined until the end—in the neighbouring town the Russians were already in control, but they still transported coal toward Germany.

On the top of the conveyor tower we had an artillery observation station. It was a front, but the Russians did not attack with reinforced troops. They just held the line and did not move…

The civilians were still there in the towns. They were never told that they had to evacuate, or…at the point they were warned it was often too late and the tanks were already rolling into the town. It was terrible to see.

Edwin Ledr, too, was fighting on Eastern Front. He could not recall exactly where he had served, only noting that he had ultimately been captured "somewhere in Russia".

Afterbursts

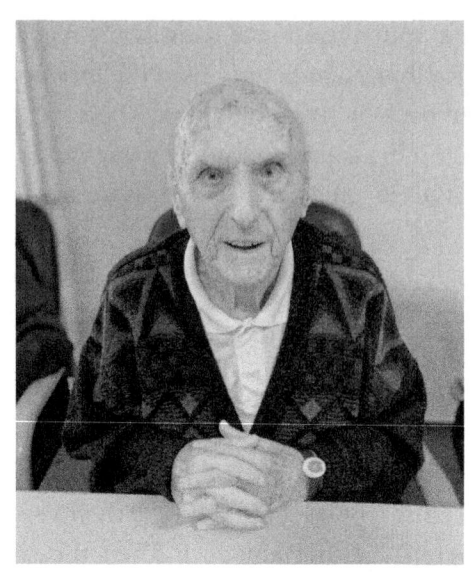

Edwin Ledr in 2019

I was trained to be a radio operator. So I marched with the batteries—we had three…I always communicated with all three. If we were in position, I was informed via radio. I was an observer. I told the artillery the distances and how they needed to adjust in the battery, and then I said, "Fire!" and then they [the shells] came…As soon as I could see them [the enemy], I said, "Fire!"

One time I nearly shot myself. I told them to shoot one kilometre too close…And so I added another hundred metres afterwards, and then—*boooom!* And then I saw them, how they flew out of the bunker, the Russians…They flew out when we hit it…Ah! I don't like to…I don't want to see it…to say it…

There were at least 10 men in the bunker and they came out… Flew out…Like butterflies…

Must have all been dead, that's all I can say. But other than that, directly, I did not shoot anybody—I shot a lot, but if I hit anyone, I don't know…

I always observed carefully, and I had a radio station up in a tree, and each time, for two or three days I was in the tree non-stop as an

Fire Machine Guns!

observer. And afterwards I had two to three days' free time about three kilometres behind the line of battle…

I got the Iron Cross because we always pushed forward as observers, we put the enemy troops under fire. I saw them: there they were, about two to three hundred men marching forwards. None of them had guns—they had sticks, like a walking cane. I don't know what they wanted to do with them…

We all waited for the war to end…to be finally over. Always freezing cold, we hoped the Russians would march further and we could retreat. We hoped it would be over soon—but capitulation? That was never spoken of.

Chapter 9

Thank Christ You Got Here

The turning point in Europe

In June 1944, almost exactly four years after their retreat from Dunkirk, the British forces finally returned to continental Europe. While the Soviets pressed the Germans from the east, the Allies squeezed from the west with their return to France and from the south with their advance up Italy.

__Roy Cadman__, still with Three Commando, had escaped from captivity in Sicily and made it back to British lines. By spring 1944, he had recovered from his wounds and was again fit enough to be on the UK's south coast training for a significant deployment.

We knew [we were training for D-Day] but we didn't know when it was or where it was. It was a dead secret...We were in this big camp run by the Americans—all barbed wire all round it. We weren't allowed out except with an officer on exercises, speed marching round up in the coast...

They had big marquees with sand tables—made by people out of the intelligence corps, from the aerial photographs—and they'd made a beach just like it was: barbed wire, bunkers, slit trenches... And it took up about a two-mile stretch of Sword beach...[So] we knew what the beach was like but we didn't know where it was—'cos the Germans thought we were gonna land at Calais and it was a big shock to them when we landed where we did…

We got on the landing craft in Southampton…LSIs—landing ship, infantry…They take a front hold and a rear hold…and you get 30 in the front hold and 30 in the back. You go downstairs. And down there there's just enough to sit round a table and nowhere to sleep except sitting on the form. We were loading up the Bren gun magazines and everything and priming the grenades…

I think there was seven boats for us, one for each troop [of 60] and one for headquarters troop. Nobody knew [where we were going]…Christ…the people didn't even know it at home until we were halfway across the Channel, it was kept such a secret…

It was a very, very rough trip. I mean these boats are quite big. And to get off 'em, on the deck on the port side and the starboard side, you had a long plank…and it was on six wheels: two at the front, two in the middle and two at the end. And for the landing there was one matelot in charge of that one, and a matelot in charge of that one. And their task was to run it along the deck and if you did it quick, it would go down properly. And then, as soon as it was down—we were all up the top, all lined up, ready to gallop down once it had been in position.

But the weather was so strong…and the waves were three foot high on the beach! And the boat went in sideways cos a wave caught it, swung the back round and I was halfway down the plank when it all went *rrrrr* and I went *zhooof*, right over the side, Bren gun and all…

I thought, *Oh I'm done now. Glub glub glub glub glub*. And my feet reached the bottom and I pushed, and me head broke through the water. I was in that deep of water [up to my chest]. If it been six foot I'd have been drowned. I bloody would! And all the lads were all saying, "Oh. Oh Christ!"

Six Troop were the unlucky troop. They got a direct hit on the rear hold where half of Six Troop were. The whole 30 of them were

Thank Christ You Got Here

killed and blown to bits. The Navy immediately turned it round, hooked it on one of the boats that were going back and they took the whole lot back…They had to sort the mangled remains and work out who they were and what they were. All full of bits—legs and arms all over…So we had no Six Troop in the landing…Good start…

We got the German end [of the beaches]… Because our job was to get up with the 6th Airborne [who had landed by glider the night before] and hold this bridge over the Caen canal and the River Orne—the two rivers with a stretch of land right the way up to Caen…

Well…the Germans were there, about 400 yards up, with Spandaus and mortars and they were plastering the bridge, all around that area, when we got there. And we were told that once we got there we were "three minutes late"—that's after the performance on the beach and all the bloody nightmare getting up there…

As we came up to the bridge there was a couple of para lads down a trench with a Bren gun, all camouflaged up. As soon as they saw us coming, they all jumped up, "Waaheeeyyy!"

We did a little dance together—cuddling each other all giving a dance—because…the lad on the Bren gun, he said, "We've been worrying ourselves sick here because if you blokes didn't get here there was going to be another bloody Dunkirk and we were gonna be it!… Thank Christ you got here."

So we carried on…up to the bridge where the cafe was, right by the bridge. And up in the top there, there was a little girl waving a French flag and as I went by I waved at her. And that was Arlette Gondree, who runs the cafe now [in her 80s]…

Roy inched his way into France over the following weeks, fighting to regain territory from the Germans. Every year from his retirement to the 75th anniversary of D-Day he would go to Normandy to lay wreaths and remember his fallen comrades—including his best friend Jimmy, cut in half by a German machine gun as he raced across a French field.

Ted Hunt's *father had served as a canal barge master in World War One, transporting wounded men away from the front. Ted had* *wanted to serve in a similar capacity and, at Normandy, he finally did. In charge of a fleet of ferries at Gold Beach, Ted was hugely instrumental both in ensuring the successful landing of equipment and the swift repatriation of wounded men from the bloody engagement—just as his father had been.*

When the time came for us to consider going back [to liberate the continent]—where should we go back?

Now, the Germans knew we had a thousand LSTs [Landing Ship, Tank]…about 360 foot long, nine foot deep at the back and three foot deep at the front. They had doors and a ramp. The tank deck below was full of vehicles and so was the deck…

So the Germans said, "When they come they will arrive on beaches which have a lovely slope of about 1 in 30 so they come in—bang! Doors open: *Don't get your feet wet, lads. Up the way and kill some Germans.*"

So all those places were defended so heavily it would have been suicide to attempt going there…Hitler was convinced that we might land in Norway, so he had about quarter of a million troops in Norway—all true!—doing nothing…So, all the way down to Spain or Portugal, has got to be defended.

Now, the "bad" beaches that were impossible for landing ships to land on were the ones that had a slope of 1 in 300…Normandy had an approach slope of 1:300—and then this short beach of 1:40. The LST's keel has a slope of 1:50…So the Germans knew that if LSTs arrived in Normandy at any other time than high water springs…they would come in, run aground, and sit there, sitting targets, before they could get rid of their load…

So they said, "They won't come here." So it was comparatively lightly defended. Guns and pillboxes, yes. But compared with the "good" slopes…

Rommel was sent to be in charge in 1943 and when he arrived he said, "Why are these beaches not properly defended?"

And they said, "Well, they won't come here because the only time the LST's could get rid of their load is three or four or five days at a specific time, [only] for two hours in every twelve could they come in and get rid of their loads."

And he said, "They will come where we least expect it, and we least expect it here…We will put stakes in the beach just where the approach starts…If they're going to come at high water springs… that's where we'll catch em."

So 70,000 pit props, as we call them, wooden stakes about 12 foot high—driven in they were about eight foot high altogether—and on the top of each was a teller mine or a booby-trapped shell. The locals called them "Rommel's asparagus".

And [the Germans] said, "Right, *now* when they arrive where we least expect it, high water springs some time, we're gonna blow their heads off."

So it was decided here that we would go to Normandy and the last mile would be done by shallow craft and these would be called the ferry fleet.

My invasion barges[19] were floating platforms…180 foot long, 42 foot wide, made up of 180 separate boxes. Each steel box was five foot by five foot by seven, joined together. When my "Rhinos" sat on a mine, we'd lose ten or a dozen boxes. We would have a hole in the middle and we would carry on working—and we did. I had 15 of them and three of them sat on mines—I was on one when it sat on a mine…

So these LSTs…loaded up with vehicles on top and in the tank deck, they towed us from the Solent and we left the Needles at 11 o'clock at night. It was still a little bit of light because in those days we had double British summer time, two hours…

So we spent all night towing across the Channel and when we were a mile or two offshore we stopped. The ship dropped its anchor, put the Rhino crew aboard…let go the Rhino from the towing wire, brought it round to the front [of the LST] and then the ship opened

---

[19] These were called "Rhinos" due to the conical posts at one end to which the loading ramp was attached.

its doors and we backed up and we married up [to load up the vehicles]…

We put all these vehicles ashore in two foot six of water. So most of the men…having slept aboard a landing ship, been put aboard a Rhino…they went into France with their feet dry…

Brave sappers had gone ahead[20] in front of us, opening up a hundred-foot gap—and we were 42 foot wide. We drove straight in and as you got straight in, you found you drifted sideways and then you'd run up on the beach. And then ashore they'd go…Goodbye.

And you'd say, "Go! Go go go go…!" And because it was four hours before high water…Rommel's asparagus didn't do anything. You see men running across the flat with flags and ahead of them all these posts, high and dry…

One in four…LSTs went over loaded with tanks and vehicles and whatever we needed, but added to the crew was a team of RAMC [Royal Army Medical Corps] surgeons and male nurses…These ships were fitted with pipe cots all along the tank deck…and they carried flag "M" for medic.

First man to be wounded was Sgt Shepperd—9 o'clock, D-Day morning. He had shrapnel wounds…As Shepperd went in [to the beach], the big guns over beyond Arromanches caught him and a shell burst killed a lot of soldiers, but it wounded him—lots of shell splinters in his back. He was taken to casualty reception station, where someone decided that he could be moved, that he wouldn't have to stay. A label was put on him, he was put on a stretcher.

Six stretchers were put on a "duck" [DUKW]…a lorry which can go on land and in water…and they waited for orders. The Rhino would go to the medic ship, take all the tank deck and go ashore… and then go back to the medic ship to load the remaining cargo… When we [on the Rhino] were half loaded, we would see a whole convoy of "ducks", 16 "ducks" usually, [steaming] round in a great big circle…

---

[20] Sappers had been sent to remove underwater mines and other booby traps which were laid out on the flat approaches of low tide.

Thank Christ You Got Here

Eventually, the last vehicle comes aboard us and the ship is empty. The ship would raise its ramp—"Go!"—and we'd storm into the shore [on the Rhino]—and when we looked back, we'd see how the ship had lowered its ramp in the water and the ducks'd drive straight up into the tank deck and unload inside the ship—fill up the pipe cots [with wounded] and then fill up the deck…I think it's forty thousand wounded men came back to the UK on the tank deck of a landing ship.

So Shepperd had passed the Needles at 11 o'clock at night, arrived over there 9 o'clock in the morning…got wounded, taken to casualty reception, labelled, stretcher, duck, landing ship and the ship left for UK and he was in Netley Hospital, which is on the Solent in the Southampton water, at one o'clock next morning…It took my dad's patients a week to go from the front line to the coast. My man had done the return trip in 30 hours. He didn't survive. He died in Netley[21]…

Now when my men—it brings tears to my eyes to think about it, honestly—when my men looked back and saw 16 ducks running up out of the water into an empty ship, thinking *They'll be in England tonight. If I get wounded I'll be going home this afternoon*, they said, "We don't know what's happening ashore, sir, but by Christ someone's looking after them."

And…morale boost? Boy did we need it any more. On D-Day! To get a morale boost on D-Day! We're gonna win the war!

After the war, Ted Hunt followed the family tradition to become a waterman on the Thames, serving as Queen Elizabeth II's bargemaster between 1978 and 1990.

Mervyn Kersh's *family originally came from Poland, several generations before the war. His neighbourhood was bombed in the Blitz, leaving craters "the size of several buses" and killing his swimming teacher.*

In June 1943, when he was 18, he was called up during a heat wave and sent for training in Scotland, where there was deep snow. I met

---

[21] Regrettably I could find no records of Sgt Shepperd

Mervyn Kersh in 2019

him at his home in northwest London and as he plied me with tea and biscuits he described his arrival at Normandy.

We were [the] first ordnance depot to go [to Normandy]. And on our order of battle, it shows we were supposed to go, I think it was D plus 5…but before that Colonel Gore, our chief commanding officer, took nine men with him and as soon as they left us in Billingshurst, Sussex…we knew that it was going to begin.

So we started out the next morning. We went down to Gosport, which was a very moving journey through villages and towns with waving civilians lining streets. And as soon as we arrived, Colonel Gore appeared—and we were very surprised, because we thought he was in France.

He told us that the ship they were on had been blown apart and he was on deck talking to the skipper and was thrown in the sea. The others were down below sleeping and just got blown to pieces. He said he was picked up and brought back and wanted replacements…volunteers, to replace them. And I think it was 10 volunteers

Thank Christ You Got Here

he wanted. I stepped forward...That's how I went earlier than D5 as planned...

It was just like going on holiday [going to Normandy]. I had only done that once before, I think, to the Isle of Wight, on the ferry. I didn't think much about it—I was just concerned with all the junk I had hanging round me—but I did make a point of sleeping on the deck, whereas all the others I was with all went below.

I was the only one who stayed on deck. I found a nice coil of thick rope and lay on that—with my rifle. We'd been told to go to sleep, because we didn't know when we'd get to sleep again...

We woke up at five o'clock in the morning. The seamen woke us up. You could just see the outline, in the dawn light, of France. It was then that I began to realise we're not playing games anymore...You could hear shells going overhead, both ways, from the big ships...I've never seen so many boats... mostly small craft, but they were packed. Like being in a park somewhere, on a pond—"Come in number 11!"—or something. Really close together...Then it struck home what we were going to.

As it happened, luck—or whatever you like to say—was on my side, because the Germans had been so hit by the first landing, and disorganised, there was no opposition to us. The opposition didn't materialise for another day or two. So we landed quite quietly apart from this big *voooooooooom!* going overhead. But nobody bothered to fire at me, thought I wasn't worth it. I was pleased with that...

It was very emotional [when I later went back to visit Normandy]. You see so many graves...particularly in Bayeaux, or the American ones...Partly because they were obstinate, they didn't use the wire cutters, tanks. That was one reason...

You've heard of Hogarth's Funnies? He was a British officer and engineer, who before D-Day—years before—invented different ways that tanks could be adapted to make them more useful. One was to have a flail—big drum in front with chains going round and round—hitting the ground ahead, blowing up any mines before the tank got there. Another was one that laid what looked like branches of trees, to cover muddy patches, streams…ditches and things like that…There was another one where a big pair of what looked like scissors—wire cutters—came out ahead of the tank and cut barbed wire.

The Americans said that's not needed. So when they landed on their beach, Omaha Beach, there was lots of barbed wire at the bottom of the cliff…They had to get out of the tank and cut it manually, with hand wire cutters. And of course they were just shot each time. That's one reason why they had so many casualties…

But the Americans [in general] relied a lot on their equipment rather than on themselves…Bit of bravado—which the British troops didn't have, you know, they were more serious. The others thought we were in the Wild West somewhere, playing Cowboys and Indians. That was my impression at the time.

Although D-Day marked a decisive turning point for the Allies, not all the operations that followed were a success, with Operation Market Garden at Arnhem in Holland being one of the more disastrous. Thousands of troops were committed to capturing several strategic bridges, but the manoeuvre failed to press the advantage from the Normandy landings, giving the Germans too much time to regroup and counterattack.

The attempt was also hampered by tactical errors: many of the soldiers were landed too far from their objectives and their supplies failed to reach them. **Ray Whitwell**, *who had returned to England from Italy, was delivered by glider. He and five comrades were among those surrounded by German troops, who shelled them like clockwork at 9am and 5pm.*

There were five of us, and we dug a trench, and then behind that we dug out a square, got some boards from a hut that had been bombed nearby put them over the top and put all the soil on top. So only a direct hit could get us.

With it being flat in the Netherlands, we were lucky, we were on the top of a slight grade and we could see for 500 yards. And we'd know where the Germans were, and as soon as they were coming out—we were all camouflaged in, we'd broken trees down—we could put some shots and they never got very near. And they didn't know where we were. They sent a tank out to find us but he didn't know where to look and he couldn't come into the trees because the tanks couldn't get there. The trees were only that far apart [*he indicates his arm span*]…

There was no food…They sent resupplies by airplane but they were dropped in the wrong place, they dropped where the Germans were and we never got anything to eat for ten days. You couldn't do anything.

We did get water. There was a house nearby and I could see a well. And we went to this well and we were immediately shot at by a sniper. So we had to lay on the ground, pull the handle of the well… You had your rifle with the sling on and pulled the bucket down for— oh, that took you ages…And when the bucket appeared it had bullet holes in and the water was coming out! So we could fill two water bottles…and then it ran out of water. So you had to put it down again and it took *hours* to do…

The other people were watching where the Germans were coming from and as soon as one could be seen two or 300 yards away: *bang bang bang!* And that kept them out of the way. Nobody passed us. Luck…

They did kill one of our men…When they fire, these 88 millimetres, you can hear it coming and you know whether it's coming near you or not. And this one *was* coming near us, and I dived down some steps belonging to a house and my friend didn't, and he was killed… Well, actually he wasn't really dead when we came up and I had a Jeep nearby, and I got the Jeep and I got some help to put him on and took him to the dressing station.

And…he looked at him, the RAMC man, "Put him down there. He's dead."

I said, "No he isn't."

He said, "Yes, he is."

So I left it. He must have been…That was disheartening.

We got out at 10 at night. During the day our officer came around and he said, "We're pulling out tonight, but you're not to tell anybody if you're captured…We're sending out some tapes from the perimeter down to the Rhine and you will be met at the Rhine where the boats will ferry you across."

So when it came to starting time, 10 o'clock, it was dark and raining a bit. There were hundreds from the perimeter following this tape—and we run into a German patrol. And shots were exchanged, grenades were thrown and everybody scattered and I went for miles until I was under the bridge!

And I thought, *Well, this is no good*. So I found the Rhine.

Now, it doesn't come up to the banks: you drop down and there's a bit of a beach. So I dropped down onto the beach and walked along, back to where I thought the tape was going to be…By this time it's two o'clock in the morning again, and it's dark, and I eventually came to a lot of our people waiting for the boats, the Canadian boats, to come across. And eventually I got over the Rhine…Lucky again. I was lucky all the time—maybe a bit of intuition as well, of course!

Did I ever [get used to death]? I didn't like it…

Yes, I did. I got to put that at the back of my mind, because people were getting killed near you every day. And I decided that, *Poor old Jim, he's gone*, and that was it. Not to think about it anymore…And that's all there was to it, really.

By the time of Operation Market Garden, **Ron Johnson**—*who had been inspired to serve by the Oxford Union debate—had volunteered to retrain as a glider pilot. Placed on reserve for D-Day, he was finally deployed to Arnhem.*

Sunday the 17th [September 1944] was the first day and when the troops took off—both the parachute planes taking the parachutists and the glider-borne troops that were off—I was helping to assemble the gliders…I remember it particularly well, thinking, *Right…the first lift have gone, so we'll be going tomorrow…*

I remember taking off from Down Ampney and we flew over Hatfield…over the coast at Aldeburgh…And as we were flying across the North Sea, probably stretched out a hundred miles ahead because it was fairly clear that day, you could see this stream of tugs and gliders, side-by-side…And then, part way over, there were two gliders down in the water that for some reason had had to ditch—and I don't know whether that was earlier on from us, on that day, or from the previous day, but you see these two gliders down in the sea…

And then we flew over the coast and we could see also that the Germans had flooded the area…as a form of defence…And I remember particularly when we got to Hertogenbosch I thought, *Right, now, Johnson, you really have made it. We're going to get there…*

The landing was straightforward and after unloading their cargo of Royal Electrical and Mechanical Engineers with their equipment, Ron's squadron regrouped at Wolfheze, expecting an equally easy exit.

Eleven thousand went in to the Battle of Arnhem and only 2000 came out. It was one of the most bitter battles of the war that we were involved in—and the Germans lost as many…

During the battle, I'd got a section of 12 men and we were fighting with the King's Own Scottish Borderers…in the grounds of the Dreyeroord Hotel—which became as famous in the battle as the White House. And on the Wednesday night, during the evening, the house opposite our position was set on fire. I don't quite know how, but it was a total blaze and the flames lit up the sky, so it was all quite bright then. And a young lady called out, coming out from the flames in English, "Can I come across please?"—you know—"Help me."

So I was the officer nearest to her and I yelled out at the top of my voice. "Stop firing. Stop firing." I don't know why, if it were Germans, they'd understand me…

And I said to this young lady, "Yes come across now," and she got part way across the road and a machine gun opened up and shot her down. And so there she was lying in the middle of the road and I didn't have any alternative, so I did the same thing again: I yelled out, "Stop firing. Stop firing!" and went out. And fortunately, when I went out and picked her up and brought her back, [the] machine gun didn't open up again…

Her foot had been shot away…When we got her back to the trenches, I handed her over to my sergeant, and he put some morphine in her and took her away to the dressing station. I thought, *Well I was lucky to get away with that…*

Then on the Thursday, we were mortared and a mortar bomb, landed in the next trench to mine and killed the two Kings Own Scottish Borderers who were in that. And…I'd got my helmet on, but all my face was all bleeding from the muck and dust from this mortar.

I remember being a bit concussed but getting out of my trench and going to the dressing station and they spent an hour on me there in the dressing station, picking all the stuff out of my head…

I then went back to my trench and I don't know why, but I got out of my trench to have another look at the one next door…I don't know what I thought I could do, because it was a good hour between. If there were any life they'd have been long gone…Anyway, I got out of my trench and a sniper put a bullet through my back!

So I'm back in the dressing station and I said, "I'm back again!"

And they said, "Not you again, we just spent an hour on you!" That's wartime! It's funny, but…

There I've got my head in a bandage and my arm in a sling and they sent me away then to what is the Hartenstein and down there was a Dr Randall and he put penicillin in my arm and he said, "You are among the earliest in wartime that we're using penicillin on"—and it did the job.

They moved us on from there to another temporary hospital, the Tafelburg. As we drove up to the Tafelberg in the jeep I remember, seeing in through the open garage door, the floor was covered in dead bodies.

And that was when it really dawned on me just how awful, awful, awful this was…

And then on the Sunday the Germans overran the Tafelberg and took us away.

Elsewhere in Arnhem glider pilot **Frank Ashleigh** *was also on a path to captivity. Born in late 1924, Frank volunteered for the Armed Forces on his 18th birthday and to become a glider pilot in the spring of 1943.*

Frank Ashleigh in 2019

Frank Ashleigh as a young soldier

Afterbursts

I was flying a Hotspur glider on D-Day and I heard gunnery instructions coming over the radio. So when I got back on the ground I said, "What's happened?"

"We've invaded Europe!"

Shortly after, I went to North Luffenham, was taught to fly the Horsa [glider] and then became operational. I was joined up with a man named Cummins, "Lofty" Bernard Cummins, who stood six foot four. I was five foot ten, so he towered above me. And we did everything together. We ate together, we slept in the same room…All our training, all our practice flying, everything we did was together. And gradually, a trust was built up between us…I knew, beyond a shadow of doubt, that he would never let me down and he knew that I would never let him down…

Sixteen operations were planned and cancelled. The 17th operation was Market Garden, which was the largest airborne operation ever. That day…It's ingrained in my memory…Take off was bad, because the tug lost one engine on take-off—it had four engines and one failed—and the Stirling could not take off with a glider in tow on three engines. So we pulled off, we released the tug. We turned to port, he turned to starboard, more aircraft went straight through the middle of us…Instead of being second away, as we were scheduled to be, we were last but one.

Frank, too, had a "textbook" landing and the men and equipment he was carrying got safely away.

My orders were "get back to the UK" because you are indispensable: there was only 1600 of us in total…But if you couldn't get back—and we couldn't—you'd take part in the fighting. Two hundred and twenty-nine glider pilots were killed in action… Fighting…

After the Arnhem operation was a failure, we were so short of pilots we invited RAF pilots to be trained to fly gliders…As pilots, they were superb, every bit as good as we were. But as soldiers, they were useless because they'd only had a few days' training, where we'd had six weeks of intensive training. We were classified as "total soldier"…We could use any weapon. Unarmed combat was no problem. How to kill a man with a single blow…Happily, I never had to.

We were sent on a reconnaissance because we didn't know where the Germans were, nor how strong they were. So they called for a volunteer to go. I was in a slit trench with Lofty at that time. The other three were all ready to go…so I made up the party.

We advanced down—this was in Oosterbeek—we advanced down the road using the infantry tactics we had been taught, which kept us under cover most of the way. We got about half a mile, and we were outside a Roman Catholic church, Saint Bernulphus, and everywhere we looked were German soldiers.

We weren't going to just put our hands up, so we dived into the church. We went up a winding staircase. The first level it stopped at was the organ loft and the staircase went on to another level… The treads on the staircase were incredibly narrow, but we ran up them…those took us up to the belfry. There was a very big bell hanging and there was a door on the opposite side. We opened that door, went through it and there was a catwalk—very rickety…and at the far end, there was a very small window, which we opened, slowly. And everywhere we looked were German soldiers. So we opened fire.

We downed a number. And we realised the Germans had no idea where the shots were coming from. So we stopped. And soldiers would sort of walk through everywhere, waiting for us to shoot. We didn't. We went back down to the organ loft, stayed there about an hour, went up the stairs again, opened fire—about 15 or 20 rounds—stopped again. And we did this for four days. By which time we were getting low in ammunition, as you can well imagine. And we had nothing at all to eat…And by nothing, I do mean nothing.

The captain opened the door of the organ loft where we were. There was a German soldier there and he shot [the captain]. In the stomach. And he dived up the stairs very, very quickly. He was badly hurt and we said, "You have got to go down and surrender yourself to get medical attention", which he did.

Now, we were told afterwards he ostensibly said, "There are three more British soldiers up there." Whether that's true, I don't know. If it was, it was probably shock.

Somebody came in under the loft. We couldn't see him; we could hear him. And with no trace of an accent he said, "Gentlemen, we know you're there. You have five minutes to come down with your hands up. If you're not down in five minutes, we will be throwing grenades. Don't try and escape…we've men posted above you and below you on the staircase. There is no way out."

Frank had left his pilot Lofty Cummins in the trench when he joined the recce which ended up in the church. Later, as he pointed out Lofty in a photograph, I asked what had become of him.

He was killed in action the same day I was taken prisoner of war, the 22nd. How he died, I don't know, was never able to find out…

[I only found out he had died] when I saw his headstone in the cemetery about 30 years later. The airborne cemetery is in Oosterbeek and as you come in on the right-hand side, there's an office and in it is a list of everybody who's buried there. And I was going through it page by—*Lofty Cummins*! Bernard Cummins, as he was then, Staff Sergeant Bernard Cummins…

I cried my eyes out. And now, every time I go there, I go to his grave[22] and I salute him.

Over in Italy, **Yoshio Nakamura** *was sent to Europe to make up numbers in the heavily depleted 442 Infantry Regiment comprised of second-generation Japanese Americans.*

I was in Le Havre, France, which is across the Channel from England. Then we were shipped by cattle car. European cattle cars are about a third the size of ours…very, very small…And the reason we were given is that they didn't want to signal anyone that the troops were moving. So we were in these cattle cars and it was very uncomfortable but we made it to Marseilles, in southern France…

---

[22] https://www.cwgc.org/find-records/find-war-dead/casualty-details/2644511/bernard-arthur-cummins/

Thank Christ You Got Here

And we were there until we got a request from General Mark Clark, who was the commander of the 5th Army in Italy. The troops could not move north because there was a Gothic line and every time they tried to advance, the German observation people up on top of the mountain could see this movement and they'd send cannons and mortars down. And so, for half a year, every time they tried to move, they were hit.

So Mark Clark thought the 442nd could break the line, so he asked us to come back…and, so, we went by landing craft from Marseilles to Livorno[23] and then by the leaning tower of Pisa and then up into Carrara…the marble capital of the world.

And then we were to climb this mountain called Folgorito, which to me was almost 90 degrees. It was really, really steep and we were very fortunate that the Italian partisans, who were very, very anti-fascist, were eager to help us. So in the dark they led us up these paths…

It impressed me so much. I'll never forget the climb…There was just enough room for, I think, one fellow to be moving along, walking up there. And one of my buddies, whose name is Nakamura… by alphabetical order he got the [mortar] base plate, which is a huge metal plate…and it's like you're carrying a backpack, except it's heavy…And he thought he was leaning against the cliff—we'd get a break every so often—but he was mistaken: he went the other way, fell off the trail. And fortunately he landed on the next trail, but he couldn't get up, it's like a turtle…

We were able to tell whether we're together by just feeling the backpack, feeling the other person in front of us, and he wasn't there. But we could hear a little whisper saying, "He's down there."

And so a couple of us went down and lifted him up. And fortunately, he wasn't injured…There were others who have plunged off and they couldn't yell. You can't give away your position…We went up to the top and by daybreak we were able to knock out quite a few of the observation posts…

---

[23] This destination name is unclear so it's my best guess

I didn't think I'd make it myself…I promised my God that I would be a decent guy if I ever made it. Because…number one, you're absolutely exhausted going up this mountain and not knowing where we might slip. And then not knowing whether the observation posts would discover us and shoot us down…It was pretty dangerous. And I was probably more scared then than I've ever been, or ever will be. It was just a scary time. But, fortunately, we made it to the top.

Chapter 10

They Ran Out of Petrol

The importance of supplies

Fully functioning supply lines were critical to effective strategy. More than one battle was lost due to a lack of adequate supplies—if not, in fact, the whole war. Although not considered a combat role—to the extent that merchant mariners did not receive service medals for decades after the war—manning supply lines could be incredibly dangerous work. In fact, the casualty rates on many of the delivery routes were far worse than those for infantry troops.

Norwegian **Oscar Anderson** *took part in several convoys, the most memorable being convoy ON 166, from Liverpool to New York, which set out in February 1943. Fourteen Allied vessels were sunk, as well as three German submarines, with a total loss of life of nearly 400 sailors.*

Although neutral, many Norwegian sailors served on Allied ships and hundreds of them died. Oscar had left Norway to earn money as a sailor at the age of 15 in 1936. His siblings and parents remained at home where it was not always easy to avoid dealing with the Germans. As with elsewhere in Europe, he observed that this could be especially tough on the young women who struck up relationships with soldiers.

But you know it's nothing to do with young people, the war. Germans are as good as anybody else. There's no difference. At all.

Oscar Anderson in 2019

And even the colour doesn't matter. We're all the same underneath—and wherever. It's only something happens here [*he indicates his heart*]. That's all, in various people, isn't it?

Norway was occupied by the Germans. They didn't declare war on anybody. But [the ship I worked on] decided to "vote" for England of course, because the ship was American, Texaco…

The one I remember is a very old oil tanker…the Glittre…It was very, very old. We had to carry water to the captain's bathroom in buckets, because there was no electric or pumps…We went off to Manchester and Liverpool.

And then in 1943…we loaded 500 tons worth of fuel for the corvettes that we had as escort…But all hell broke loose, and we had depth charges on deck… When we started going at sea—about two days out—they'd been torpedoing ships all the time and one or two or three were sunk. So it was very, very precarious. And in the meantime, we gave them depth charges. These we had on deck—because they can be regulated, so they're safe onboard but they're regulated [to the] depth when they're going to explode.

But we couldn't give them their fuel, because the hoses we used were just canvas…so they broke. We tried at the side, and we tried aft…We tried all sorts. No way could we get rid of that bloody fuel… If they'd had the correct hoses, like they have now, very strong ones with the reinforced rubber, we could have done it. But we couldn't. The equipment we had wasn't suited…

Anyway, on the fourth or fifth night we got hit…The torpedo came and hit the engine room, and—big explosion—and I was on the monkey island so I saw it all. And of course that immobilised us totally…There was a second engineer and the motorman-engineer, in charge of the engines, and…both of them were killed, of course, because the engine was blown out of the whole ship.

The second engineer, he was so *clean.* I think he was religious as well, and he didn't smoke, he didn't drink. He saved all his money and he didn't spend money on *anything*, wasting it. And the other one, the motorman, he'd drunk every penny he could get hold of. So much so, we were in Venezuela and he sold his clothes and he came home on board, in his underpants. Sold *everything* for drink. So these two when they came to the point they died together. And they also came from the same town in Norway, both of them…

I was midships then. I asked the officer in charge if I could come down. All officers and the steward and the wireless operator and me, we gathered where the lifeboat was…But they didn't want to go in the lifeboat.

So I said, "We've got to go in the lifeboat."

They said, "Well, the ship is floating. We don't need to because it's not sinking."

"We've got to go," I said, "because we don't know what's going to happen…"

So I said to this other fellow—he was Canadian, Frank—"Let's go in the lifeboat."

So he and I went down…We held the lifeboat there and I said to them, "Come on down."

They were very reluctant, but in the end, they finally came down. The captain wouldn't come, so I said, "If you don't come, we'll go without you."

So he came. He threw a sheet down with all the ship's papers and that, and then he finally came.

So I say that I saved their lives, because if we had all stayed on board, we would all have been dead now. Because 10 minutes later they got one or two more torpedoes and it sank like a stone…

And then I said…"For goodness' sake", I said, "get your oars out and start rowing! We can't stay here. Start rowing!"

…And then we had this [friendly] boat after us, firing at us, thinking we could be a submarine because we had no lights or anything! We didn't know anything about that lifeboat…And then all of a sudden a corvette came alongside us and they said, "Don't take anything onboard. Just jump onboard and leave everything, just get aboard, quick as you can." So we did. Left the boat and everything.

And he put full speed on the corvette…English one, this was. They were as poor as church rats, so they didn't give us any food! We had the ship's biscuits from the lifeboats for four days…Everybody's better than the poor English…

Unfortunately, they hadn't got any oil to run the engine…So they used full speed just to get away from all these submarines—they reckoned there was about 30 of them there. It was terrible—a terrible life…

And then all of a sudden the captain on the corvette said, "Come on back and help us to save these people."

That ship that had been shooting at us got torpedoed and sank like a stone and they're all in the water…So I went on the side of the corvette and I helped pushing them on board. I kept pushing this fellow aboard and I saw his eyes roll, and he died in my arms as I was pulling him back on board from the water…

They Ran Out of Petrol

In those days…I'd seen people floating, or swimming, alongside a ship I was on and couldn't stop to take them and help them…It's terrible. It's never published, of course…

There was another grain carrier had built an air deck, like for small airplanes to look at the water for submarines, and one of them, he lost the heart, you know, and he tried to land and he couldn't…So he went back up again and somebody shouted down to us and said, "Come on up and have a look at this airplane! He's trying to land and he can't make it!"

He finally landed on the deck, but he swung around—the bridge was on the side then, it wasn't like it is now in the middle—and he hit that and swung around and back in the sea. And the ship carried on without stopping…

And I saw a big whaling factory—in those days they didn't go whaling, they were used as tanker ships—I saw that being torpedoed, a Norwegian one. And it collapsed like that, hit in the middle. We stood watching that on a Sunday afternoon.

You do in a sense [get hardened] because it could easily be you the next time. Any time.

Oscar died in December 2024, aged 103.

*Navy Cadet **Rolfe Monteith** might have opted to be an engineer but he did not entirely miss out on the action. After the Navy decided to send the students to sea for a few months' operational experience he served in the Arctic, a route frequently subjected to freezing temperatures and where those who ended up in the water often died rapidly of hypothermia.*

His studies would take him home from this service at a critical moment.

My time on [HMS] *Hardy* was precisely four months, the last four months of 1943. And that was because the Royal Navy authorities felt that it was time we had a break from our three-year engineering degree course. And the war was on, so each group at the Naval Engineering College were allocated to a four-month period at sea.

And I had the good fortune of not being sent to an aircraft carrier, or a battleship, or a cruiser. I was sent to a destroyer. And

Rolfe Monteith in Normandy in 2019

therefore, I learned a lot more, frankly, I feel, in the round, of life at sea…

We did convoy—escorting convoys to the Mediterranean for the North African campaign, and then we rushed up north to escort a convoy to Murmansk…It's quite a long run up to Murmansk, because we had to pick the convoy up at Loch Ewe, on the west coast of Scotland, and then we had to go to fuel in Iceland, and then proceed across the top—with German aircraft flying, out of gun range, plotting our course, so that they could tip off the U-boats. So was it an interesting arms-length battle—a hell of a challenge, really…

The Germans would normally fly in what is termed a "clockwise fashion" around the convoy. Unbeknownst to me—I was a midshipman, the lowest form really of naval entity in *Hardy*'s, so I wasn't party to crucial decisions on the bridge, but—suddenly, this German aircraft started to fly the other way.

And what transpired, I enquired quietly and I was told, the commodore who's in command of the convoy—a merchant navy man normally, often a senior Royal Navy man…this commodore had a bit of a sense of humour. He apparently signalled the German aircraft and said, "Welcome. We are totally bored with you flying clockwise. Would you mind reversing it?"

And the German signalled back, "Aye, aye." And he reversed himself and he flew back the other way. One of the curious things about life at sea, and in war!

I was taken off on New Year's Eve, 1943. *Hardy* was directed to join the next convoy to Russia, leaving in the middle of January. And en route, without me, she was torpedoed by the German U-Boat U278. And what 278 fired was the first of the new German torpedoes.

Normally torpedoes are launched and proceed in a direct fashion, and you just hope it strikes the target. The Germans developed a new torpedo—acoustic—so that when it was fired from the tube in the submarine, she listened for noise. And of course, propeller noise is very, very heavily acoustic. So, the submarine just has to fire the thing and it'll find a ship and sink it.

So in *Hardy*'s case—*Hardy* was the nearest one to this torpedo—it blew the stern off the *Hardy* and she sank. And so when that torpedo blew the stern of *Hardy* off…twenty-nine days earlier, it would have been me. Life's rich fabric…

Franklin Medhurst, *who had volunteered to fly for Coastal Defence in order to fight only German combatants, was instrumental in keeping the seamen safe.*

I started my operational flying in Gibraltar on the old Swordfish airplane—it's a biplane, all struts and wires. And we were then doing dawn and dusk patrols to stop U-boats passing through the Straits of Gibraltar. And the only way they could pass through was at night—because they'd be detected easily on the surface and the current from the Mediterranean to the Atlantic was four knots and that's the maximum speed they could do underwater. So…they had to travel at night…on the surface. So we were out on dawn and dusk patrols—but of course we never found one. But…we certainly kept them down if they knew we were about.

That soon ended, because…there were two Swordfish that were flying. The first one packed up with engine trouble—they were quite old—and the second one, when we were out on patrol, had broken a flying wire, which means that the wing was in danger of collapse, and so we had to radio back for an emergency landing at Gibraltar. Well, we then moved on to an American aircraft, the Catalina. Fully armoured, it could fly for 24 hours, over the Atlantic…

[In] 1942, when the Japanese were advancing in the Far East, we were the only nearby aircraft who could patrol there, from Gibraltar. So three aircraft from the squadron—we had a crew of nine, 27 airmen—flew out to Singapore to defend it.

But of course…they were lost, because they were shot down and killed. And so another three—and I was a member of the second group of three—were sent out to what was then Ceylon, now Sri Lanka, to stop the advance of the Japanese Navy. We were flying there and we were detached to places all over the Far East, to the islands in the Indian Ocean, to east Africa, searching for Japanese submarines that were sinking shipping. All the Japanese fleet. And in those 20 or so weeks we lost 33 men and 21 of us survived.

This left Coastal Command so short of pilots in the region that they had no relief. After 1,200 hours of flying, half as much again as normal before a rest, Franklin was sent up to India as a flying controller at a new airfield that was being built outside Delhi at Palam.

[I was in Palam] almost a year I think before I was recalled, and I was put back onto flying and I went to the States—first by ship to New York then on to Montreal at a staging post, and then down to the southern tip of America—Florida—to take a boat out to the Bahamas, where there was a training field for Liberators…

The Liberator was a marvellous aircraft. Beautiful. American-made, and fully armed: four guns in the turret. And so much inside… so much equipment—for detecting submarines, for armaments—that we couldn't carry parachutes. In due course they found enough room for two parachutes and the squadron said the pilots can have a parachute each.

They all refused: a pilot can't jump and leave the crew…

They Ran Out of Petrol

We were highly skilled to do the job—and especially late in the war, when sonar came in…Because submarines are very difficult to detect. If they're on the surface, they have in the conning tower four lookouts with binoculars to sweep four sectors. And as soon as an aircraft is spied, they dive and they can do that much quicker than an aircraft can reach them. So they're very difficult to pick up.

But then sonar was developed. It was a scheme called High Tea—which means if you picked up a target on sonar, at night or in day, and you honed in on this target but when you get there there's nothing there…you immediately realise a submarine had dived. So you had to find it.

So you dropped a sonar buoy where you had believed the signal to have come from. And this sonar buoy would pick up on an underground signal of the propellers of a submarine. And you'd hear this… And if you did hear that, you dropped four more…covering about 40 square miles and you would then switch from one to the other all on different frequencies to see if you could trace the passage of the submarine.

And I would pick this up and trace it and pass it to the navigator who would plot it. And once he had plotted it, such that he knew just exactly where the submarine was, you'd drop a sound-homing torpedo, which would home on the noise and blow up the submarine. Quite a cruel way to die.

But I used to think, whenever we succeeded, of all the merchant men that had been sunk by U-boats—men without defence, cast into seas in flaming waters, because they were sailing in oil tankers. I used to think of that. I'd think, *Well…we've got to stop it some way*. But nevertheless, it was a highly efficient way…

Once the U-boat commanders realised what was happening, they'd try to switch off their engines and sit below the surface or sit on the bottom without making a noise. And on one occasion I think this had happened and there was silence…and then I heard a noise, like a tannoy…voices…And then I heard a thumping, like boots on a catwalk.

And of course, the homing torpedo homed onto it and blew it up. But it's quite weird, that, to hear what was happening under the water from a thousand feet up.

Not long after Britain had voted to leave the EU, I met Franklin in the Staffordshire home from which he had penned letters to the national papers entreating his compatriots to remain in the Union. As World War Two had progressed he had begun to question the sanity of nations "killing their young". Brexit, he felt, ignored the sacrifice of these lives. Franklin died in the summer of 2018.

Upon his graduation as a naval cadet, **Victor Harchev** *had chosen to serve with the Northern Fleet, escorting convoys in the Arctic.*

When we arrived, the liberation of the Soviet Arctic began. We were shelling the enemy's fortifications in Norway. And we were escorting Allied convoys.

That was a very hard operation, escorting the vessels. The loaded transport had very low speed, six to seven knots, which is about 11 kilometres an hour—we could go up to 43, but we couldn't go at that speed; we could [only] follow the transport that we escorted.

We would make two lines…The ship in the front would zigzag, listening…On the left and right there were destroyers, cruisers, and one on the end…

There were many dangers, but the main one was submarines, naturally. The convoy routes were closer to the Arctic Ocean, farther away from the shores of Norway, as Norway was very well fortified. Across all of Norway, there were shore artillery batteries…It was also more difficult for aircraft as the distance increased.

But of course, submarines created the most difficulty and danger. The caravan was passing by and there were constant torpedo attacks. If you heard a submarine propeller, there would definitely be an attack. And you couldn't move away. If a ship got distracted and created a window, then a submarine would sneak in and then trouble was inevitable…

We would go for two to three days, at low speed. The naval caravans were formed at Bear Island and were escorted by the vessels of

They Ran Out of Petrol

the English Navy. The Englishmen led them. At the defined meeting point we would take over and the flagship would belong to the Soviet Army. We would always be a flagship and the commanders of the caravan would be accommodated on our ship.

To maintain communications between our Soviet ships and English ones, the signaller and radio operator from the English flagship would transfer to our ship, while our signaller and radio operator would move there. Usually, we would meet to the north of Cape NordKappe—the northern point of Norway, and closer to the Arctic Ocean. We would meet there, and some of the English ships would go back to Britain, and some would come with us to Kola Bay, to Murmansk and to the White Sea to Arkhangelsk.

A little bit of history. The Northern Fleet out of all Soviet fleets was the least powerful…It was first called a flotilla, and only later a fleet. No one would expect an attack from the north. Sweden was a neutral country. With Norway we just divided the fishing zones…

When it became obvious that in Europe there was a war mess and Germans occupied Norway and started building colossal fortifications there, there was a need to increase the number of ships in the fleet. Because there were not enough ships, there was a redeployment. Three ships came from the Pacific fleet, including my leader *Baku* as well as the *Sensible* (*Razumnyi*) and the *Furious* (*Razyaryonnyi*) from Vladivostok, by the northern route. They arrived at Murmansk—that transfer is a separate story, that was quite epic.

But, ok…The first convoys started arriving in '41. There were not enough ships. Then, the British Navy rented military ships to the Northern Fleet. That was a cruiser, it was called Murmansk, and destroyers, the *Zharky*, *Zhguchy* and *Zhivuchy*. Those were our names. I don't know what they [the British] called them…And more: the *Deyatelnyi*, *Doblestnyi*, and *Dostoynyi*[24].

You understand that there is no war without victims. On January 14, '45, we took over yet another Allied caravan. There were

---

[24] These six aged ships had originally been given to Britain in 1940 by the US, which had taken in exchange leases on several British military bases.

30 transport vessels. Twenty-four vessels were escorted to the Kola Bay to be unloaded in Murmansk, while the other six we were to escort to Arkhangelsk, the White Sea.

We were escorting them in the usual way and on January 16, '45, at 3:45am the destroyer *Deyatelnyi* was torpedoed—one of the ships that were leased to us by the British Navy. The submarine went ahead of the caravan and hid next to the shore, nobody tracked it. When the caravan was close enough it surfaced and torpedoes hit the *Deyatelnyi*. Only six people out of the entire crew [of 200] were rescued...And that was by accident.

Why? Because it was polar night. Darkness. The sea was stormy. The clouds were low. How to lift [the people]...There was a command: "Where possible, save the crew"... One of the destroyers, *Groznyi*... they dropped speed and all of a sudden started firing. The acoustic reconnaissance picked up the propeller of a submarine. That was it... And another destroyer, while *Groznyi* was bombing the area...came and took those six aboard. Just those six survived.

Supply delivery was just as critical in the Far East, where the efforts of the Western Allies in the China-Burma-India theatre were mostly directed at ensuring that China could continue to resist the Japanese.

In 1942 the Burma Road—the supply line into China on which Xu had been a labourer—was cut off by the Japanese occupation of Burma. An alternative aerial route was established, over the Himalayan "Hump". Also known as the "Aluminium Trail", pilots could see the wrecked carcasses of planes beneath them as they navigated their unpressurised planes through the high altitudes. The assignment was one of the most dangerous of the war, killing one in three who flew the route. **Carl Constein** *was one of the survivors.*

Everybody was drafted, you know. All the young people. I had just graduated from Kutztown State teachers' college. And I knew I'd go into the service, so I volunteered. And then for a while I was assigned to be a guard, guarding coal piles in Philadelphia...That was so stupid, so stupid...

They Ran Out of Petrol

I wanted to get out of that…"chicken outfit". So the only thing open was aviation cadets. So I applied and made it, and went through nine months of training and got my license…Texas was one big airfield in World War Two…We trained and were passed after 7 hours in the air. It sounds like not much, but it's a long time when you've been on the ground all this time! Maybe half of the pilots were washed out…

I flew from a little town called Chabua [in India]…Chabua was the biggest base with about eight planes…and I flew three hours over to Kunming, China—because the westerly wind pushed me over—and four hours back…

The most dangerous was take off…It took 30 minutes, flying south, to get up to 10,000 feet…You'd wait your turn to take off, line up. One time I saw a black cloud. The guy ahead of me didn't make it…They were R-2800 engines, not strong enough at that altitude—at any altitude, really. If the engine quit, you crashed. One buddy I played chess with was killed that way. It sounds strange, but you really don't worry about it. You go ahead and do your job and you don't think that you'd crash…

It was not a choice assignment…non-combat, but not choice. Fighters, even, were better off…This is a two-engine plane, the Curtiss commando, and if one engine quits you can still maintain some altitude, but not much. And that was one experience that I had when I was still co-pilot…A pilot on a certain day…when we lost an engine…he lost his composure. And I got close to thinking that I would do the unthinkable: I would get him out of that seat and move over to fly it…That would be hard to defend…

I never got off the base in India or China…because if fellas were allowed to get off the base while the plane was being unloaded they'd get into trouble, obviously. I do remember I used to lie in the field in China, though, and feel the wind on my face…India was a desolate experience…we never got off the base. Ever…[I] made a few [friends], two of whom were later killed in a crash…

I made 96 round trips and was in real danger only twice. But for the most part, the enemy was, of course, the weather. The weather

Carl Constein in 2018

was tremendous. Always…The wind normally blew from the west to east, prevailing westerly. But on one occasion…January 6 1945…the weather switched completely from its current direction and we lost 13 airplanes that day because General Tunner, who was in charge of the whole thing, had a little motto going "The Hump is never closed!"

So…because of him, we lost 13 airplanes that we didn't have to lose. We flew over and back in the worst weather the Hump ever had…Stupid. It made me wonder what pride a man must have in trying to establish a record…putting all those lives at risk…Still, I never had any question about the need for the war, or what we were doing…

Carl died in August 2021 at the age of 101.

George 'Mac' McCrea *was born in the US in June 1922. He knew from a young age that he loved airplanes, and after using his mother's baked goods to entice a circus pilot to let him sit in one, he was hooked. He learned to fly at a government aviation school and following a stint as an instructor he was finally sent into action.*

I was one of a number selected for this special mission that was supposed to be in China—we didn't know it was China, they just said a "special mission"…

They Ran Out of Petrol

First we went from Indiana, to Bangor, Maine…to Newfoundland…to the Azores…and from the Azores across the top of Africa. And I ended in Cairo, Egypt…We opened our orders: they were China…

We made it into India where they took our rubber tanks out and got our plane ready for combat…Then we get orders that we're not going to China, we're going to Burma. Stilwell was surrounded by Japs and we had drop missions, to drop him supplies…

When we first got over there, French IndoChina, the Japanese controlled almost everything…Every plane in the area was pulled in to evacuate the base personnel. Anything they couldn't fly out they put a 55-gallon drum of gasoline in it and put an incendiary bomb in it. Destroyed everything…The men would even hang on to the plane to get out. You couldn't overload your plane. You'd get so many in there, you can't take off…

We were assigned to the fourteenth Air Force, which is the Flying Tigers. Kunming, that was our headquarters. That was the main base in China. We'd very seldom come back to Kunming. We'd get orders: our mission would take us from this point to this point and then from there to another one, then load up again and take it from there.

So…They would usually bring the stuff for you to drop, the supplies, to us, to wherever we were landed. Then we'd…they'd load us in an airplane and we'd take it…to drop missions, to the ground troops. We were dropping ammunition and food…

If we had any big maintenance, they'd send us back to the base in India. Well, we were in India—see, there were no British in China—and we usually stole a motorcycle. You'd time everything, get down the runway…the plane would stop long enough and two men hoist it in and when you get it back into China, scratch your name on the gas tank. And if my name is at the top of the list, that's mine…second, below my name, when I'm not there that's his.

Well, quite a game we had. You could walk down by the officers' quarters—they were *wild* about motorcycles—pick a nice looking one, walk it up the road until you get out of sight…Here in the States,

Afterbursts

I'd taken a little penknife and filed a master key…I used it many a time!

I have, in my log…409 combat missions…I don't know how many of those were, say, the Hump, but the combat mission is usually a drop mission. We hauled the wounded, in Burma and India, and China. We'd land on a little strip and they'd load the plane up with wounded and we'd fly them back to where they could be processed. Seeing some of those mutilated bodies, you'd wonder how a human being could live with blowing up like they…

That was one of our missions.

We moved troops. They'd take a whole fleet of these C47s come in, pick up a whole army of Chinese and move them to another battlefield…

One of our main things was drop missions, supplying the troops. What they would do is put four white—could be blankets, could be a sheet, anything white—four spots and that's where we had to drop the supplies. You're travelling at 130mph when you're approaching it, and you can't wait until you get over it to drop 'em. You have to drop 'em back here because by the time they get out of the plane, you're over the drop area. That's what happened to me, twice. The one time in Burma. You were low over the area, and you pick up ground fire. So I think that's what hit in the engine somewhere…

They would only give us enough gasoline to do the mission. We had no extra. All our gasoline came to us in 55-gallon drums, they would fly it—fly in over the Hump, over the Himalayas.

How many planes were lost in the Himalayas? 900 and something? It would close up on you…Scary…I lost a total of four airplanes in my two and a half years over there. The first one was between Burma and India. That was due to enemy action. The next one was due to weather. And the next one was due to enemy action, and the fourth one was strictly weather…

So within two weeks we were running two missions a day—three hours up, three hours back—and within two weeks I lost [my first plane]…We had picked up ground fire and had a fire in the wheel

They Ran Out of Petrol

well, where the wheel goes up, and I told my pilot, "You've got... maybe a minute, maybe less, to get out of here."

"I'll give the orders to jump," he says. "Anybody who wants to bail, bail...I'm putting it down on an emergency strip outside of Burma. I've got eight minutes, I can be on that strip."

I said, "You've got less than a minute," because the fire was up against the firewall of the gas tank.

He gave everybody the choice of jumping...We had the pilot, co-pilot, aerial engineer and three pushers and a pushmaster[25].

Well, the pushers and pushmaster had no chutes. They didn't carry chutes...I grabbed my chute and put it on—didn't get it completely buckled up, waist buckled, one leg—I didn't get the other leg. I looked out that door and I looked down and all below me was jungle...

I'd never had a jump. That was my first jump. I'd always been scared that when it came to go out that door I might hesitate. But there was no hesitation. The faster I could get out that door...I jumped. We were probably about 7,000, 8,000 feet up...I hadn't opened my chute yet when the plane blew. One big flash...No one jumped. They gambled on the pilot taking the plane in...

And we were always told: don't open your chute if you're up at any kind of altitude because if you're hanging down on a chute, you're a good target. If you're falling and free you're just a speck.

So I fell as much as I could and I surveyed the land—everything that would point to the river, so from wherever I landed, if I went downhill, I would go to the river...I ended in brush. I was three four, five hundred feet from tall trees...

I made my way to the river, *what am I gonna do?* I got a piece of bamboo, put it under my chin, slid in the water that night and went down with the current.

And I knew there was bridges across from India to Burma...Now, the Japanese manned part of the bridges and the Indians manned the

---

[25] Responsible for pushing the supplies out for the drop

others. If I was lucky enough to come to a bridge that the British manned, I could probably get pulled out.

That's what happened [after two nights in the water]. I eventually made it back to my outfit. From there to China. After they pulled me out of the water, [it took] about three or four days. I got back with the outfit and the next day I was flying again…

I was scared one time. The Japanese didn't drop the big bombs. They dropped anti-personnel bombs…a cluster. Well, it would go all over a large area…they could close a field down. We landed at night, or late afternoon, from a mission. And if you land, you don't go out to your plane after dark as you could get shot…So we bunked up in one of the hostels, and a new commanding officer of that base gave strict orders: if the Japanese go over to bomb, everyone will hit the trench.

So I grabbed a canvas or blanket, got in the trench, lay like that. And a plane went over. Now if I'd been alert, I'd have realised that I hadn't heard the buzz of those bombs coming down. Something hit my foot. Well…only thing I can imagine is one of those little bombs. And there's no way you can beat 'em. The slightest movement, they go. I lay over the bank and didn't dare move, figuring how can I beat that?

And daylight came. It was a damn old drunk with his foot against mine!

Harvey Masters *was a signalman but by the time he had been flown to his base in Kharagpur via Bermuda, the Azores, Egypt and Iran, the Allies were advancing into China. A licensed driver, when his unit itself was relocated eastwards, he was sent along the Ledo Road with a truck full of gasoline.*

We worked at a place outside of Calcutta, about 80 miles out…a B-29 base. B-29 were the big bombers and these bombers would fly supplies into China. We supplied communications for the 20th Air force back to the United States…

What happened was that the B-29s moved to China…so they were going to transfer us to China…They decided they needed trucks

They Ran Out of Petrol

Harvey Masters in 2019

Harvey and "Ding Hao" at the end of the war

and supplies in China, so why fly all these guys when they can drive trucks and supplies over there?

So that's what we did…I was assigned a two-and-a-half tonne truck to drive. And the guys who couldn't drive, they rode in the back of a two and a half tonne truck…My truck carried 1000 gallons of 40-gallon drums of gasoline…

So…the way to get to China…You go up to Assam province…a little town called Ledo…south…through Mitchinya, Burma, and then over to the old Burma Road…We drove down there in a 300-truck convoy and we would drive all during daylight hours…Well, there's no guardrails. And they say the mountains are one of the highest mountains in the world…

I remember one time, I'm in this thing by myself and all this gasoline in the back. I'm going down this steep hill, and there's no way brakes are going to do any good. And as I came down there was a little bridge over this stream. And there was a sign up there said "speed limit 10 miles an hour".

And I'm sure somebody put that up there as a joke, 'cos I must have gone 50 miles an hour going across that bridge, and I looked back to see if the bridge was still there. It was still there…

A lot of it…you're on an edge and it drops down…and there was a couple of trucks that went over. And one guy I know, he jumped out, he survived. The truck went down but he jumped out. So you had to pay attention to what you was doing…

We're on a 300-truck convoy, so you think you're going like this [nose to tail], but we're not going like that at all. Because they begin to spread out, and… sometimes we couldn't help but drive at night… and I tell ya, there were times when I was driving at night and there was no truck in front of me and no truck in back of me and I'm wondering…*Did I make a wrong turn somewhere?*. And I say *That's impossible there's no way to make a wrong turn—you can't turn!* but it makes you feel a little eerie there…You know you're in a big truck convoy, but there you are by yourself…

They Ran Out of Petrol

At night we would pull over to the side of the road. We had been issued hammocks…a one-man hammock. It had three ropes on each end supporting it and it had a mosquito net built in. So you strung up this hammock and then you unzipped the mosquito net, pulled it aside, you got in and zipped up the mosquito net. And what we normally did, we would park trucks such that we could string these hammocks between the trucks…and some were in trees, where trees were available…

I tell you something about those hammocks—they were very unstable. And you had to have it strung up just right: if you didn't, it would flip. And it happened to me one night. I flipped, and you're in this mosquito net and you know, you can't get out…You're lying on your face. And, uh, I said a few words, I'm sure!

The only thing I can do is call "Help!" So I yelled for help and some of the guys who were sleeping in the trucks, they came over and righted me up and got me out…

End of the road was Kunming, China, our destination. The transmitters were always out in the boondocks because you have to have clearance for the antennas. So in China we were out—again—a ways from the camp. We could talk to them by telephone…

There's one picture in my album. I'm standing with a Chinese gentleman, a little fella, and his name is Ding Hao[26]…

Well, Ding Hao was a railroad crossman. We had to cross this one railroad to get out from the camp to the transmitter site…and he would stop you if a train came by…All the time I was there I never saw a train come down that track. I don't think a train ever *did* come on the track. But he was a flagman, and he was always there…and friendly. He'd always yell, "Ding Hao!"…a greeting…so we called him Ding Hao…

---

[26] 挺好, or "ting hao" means "very good". During WW2 the Chinese would often accompany the salutation with a "thumbs up" signal that they had learned from the American servicemen.

We were closing up and leaving China…and I was going across that track and I thought, *this is the last time I'm ever gonna see him, I gotta have a picture with him.* So I got out and one of my guys took a picture of me with Ding Hao—and that's my favourite picture…And that was the end of my job in China.

*Perhaps the pithiest observation about the importance of supplies came from **Mervyn Kersh**'s small snapshot of the end of the war in Europe.*

I remember that Battle of the Bulge. I was coming back from Brussels on a weekend leave and I saw the German things, I rushed past them, ahead of them. Then I saw a British Jeep. There were Germans on it, but it wasn't run by the Germans, they'd given themselves up. One British driver was driving. Didn't have a weapon in his hands. They all had their weapons, but they—this peaceful liaison—crowded into a jeep, hanging onto it. To be surrendered. It was the only time that I saw Germans surrendering.

And that's when the Germans, at that time, some were put in British uniforms, and some were put in American uniforms, and they went in between the two armies, through the Ardennes. So the British thought the others were American and the Americans thought the Germans were British. That confused the issue. And they did push ahead, quite strongly, with their best tanks—they had the tiger tanks—but they ran out of petrol. Simple as that.

Chapter 11

Verboten fur Deutsche

Victory in Europe

By the spring of 1945, the Battle of the Bulge had been won and the Allies were advancing into Germany. **Roy Cadman** *was with the British Commandos who first encountered the horrors of Bergen Belsen on 15 April 1945. As with many of his darker war experiences, he only skimmed over what he had seen, but the little he revealed was nonetheless shocking.*

We found a concentration camp...pits 40ft long and 8ft deep. Fresh bodies and ovens...You could go in the ovens where the bodies were, partly burned bodies, still smouldering. The RAF dropped these leaflets and [the German guards] handed it to you with their hands up and you weren't allowed to shoot them—but not the Waffen SS, we were told to shoot them regardless, even if they were wounded... because the Waffen SS were told to shoot everyone...

Of course, the people were starving. And all our medical officers in the whole of the Commando brigade all stayed there for a couple of weeks helping the people that had survived. When I say "survived" they were walking dead. Basically. Walking dead. Three stone in weight. Couldn't stand up. Cos their legs were like...like a stick.

I was glad when they pulled us out and we carried on.

Afterbursts

Ernest Hilton's *imprisonment did not end with the British arrival at Belsen. Three days before Roy and his unit had reached the camp three trainloads of inmates had been sent out to shuttle around Berlin as potential pawns for negotiation—including Ernest and his family, who were on the last and most crowded of these three "lost transports".*

The four of us stepped into that train together with other people…roughly a thousand…But I don't remember anybody getting hysterical.

I think if anybody got hysterical that was my mother when, just before this train started, they brought my grandmother in a bed sheet and dropped her into the train too. That was pretty terrible…primarily for my mother, it must have been the bitterest point in the whole shebang. They could have let her die there, but they brought her…My mother was very upset about that…

But the moment that we were in that train, we must all have thought, "This is the end. We're gone." That was the bitter end of everything…

I don't remember the guards ever bothering with us. It must have been so terrible for them even to see us…when we stopped, they would unlock and we would go out and do our business. Ten days with maybe 70, 80 people in a box car. No toilets…

My grandmother died the fifth or sixth day, from cancer. And we could only take her out when they opened the door, and she was buried in a ditch. But that ditch was marked with something and subsequently, the body—the remains—was moved to Trobitz and buried there. But, anyway, it doesn't really matter: when you're dead you're dead, it's completely irrelevant…

Well, maybe on the eighth or ninth night we were stuck for a long time and my mother saw a farmhouse in the evening with a light, a dim light. And she said, "Take this pan and go to this farmhouse and beg for some food."

So we got there and we rang the bell, and the lady of the farm, she came to the door completely prepared. She had a pile of potato peels and she said, "All I can give you is potato peels."

So we said, "Thank you," and we take the potato peels.

Verboten fur Deutsche

We walked back, we built a little fire—we had a stream, we had water, we cooked the potato peels…And I think that was one of the best meals we had in the ten days. And, you know, Vitamin C—the only good thing in potatoes is the peel. So we ended up with the good part…There's a silver lining somewhere there.

Once we got to a place where the guards and the locomotive left, that's where the Russians picked us up.

Half the train died of typhoid…I don't think I ever got it, I was just decimated. And I was picked up by a Russian doctor and taken to a Russian field hospital. My mother almost had a fit when they took me away. She thought *Now they're going to take him away just when we*…But she was at the hospital the next morning and I was OK…

They created a table on which they could put us, and we all got naked and they washed us and they sheared our hair. That was the first bath we had maybe in a year and a half, actually. We were de-liced, properly. I got sent to the hospital, because I must have looked pretty bad.

My sister and my father were seriously sick with typhoid, and they didn't want to know because the chances are they would just collapse and die. But they both survived. They were out of their minds… The sickness goes to your head…It was terrible…My mother had to take care of me and them. But somehow, they had sufficient immunity to recover.

On our way home in army trucks, we were in Leipzig. Leipzig was the most bombed out city. I was very touched by the damage… We walked through streets, on either side were rubble heaps. There were no buildings. It was all kaput.

I was very impressed, because if it all had been nice and neat and neighbourly, I probably would have reacted very differently. But to see Germany destroyed was satisfying in a way for me, that they had got their come-uppance…It's unbelievable to see what happened there.

And…as part of our repatriation, we were given some sort of ID document, we were given German money. And we came across a restaurant which said: "Verboten fur Deutsche".

Do you get that? That was…the second great moment, after liberation. Here was a place that didn't say: "Verboten fur Juden", it was Verboten for Germans, and we went in and we had lunch. It was probably the most frugal lunch we had but it was a restaurant…

And in another town…we saw a queue in front of a supermarket, or a grocery store. So my mother and I were there and she said, "Let's queue and see what we can get."

And there was a German lady behind me and she talked to my mother and said, "Look, your son has very worn out shoes. Can I take him home and try shoes for my son and give it to him?"

So my mother said yes, that would be great.

And then she took me, and that was the only moment I started to get fearful, that, now, I am being taken by this German woman. Am I really going to get back? And we passed an American station—camp—and there was a black American on guard.

I kept looking at him, trying to say to him, "Make sure I get back this way!" You know, because…I was really worried that this is not so clever. I was obviously still afraid of Germans.

The woman took me up to her flat. She brought me the shoes. They worked. She walked me back and we were all pally pally. It was very nice. And I…I think from that moment on my anti-German sentiment dropped a lot. Because she must have had a bad war, too. There is no German alive that didn't suffer. I came to that conclusion very quickly.

The sense of liberty didn't hit me quite yet.

When we arrived, maybe two to three months later, at this train station in Amsterdam, when we got off the train, which was a normal passenger train, and we put our feet on the platform of Amsterdam, that was the moment I really accepted that it's over and done, I'm alive, and I'm back to live a life. That was the point.

After the war, Ernest was sent to the same school in Switzerland as the teenaged Peter Gafgen, whose father had fought for Germany. The two became lifelong friends.

Nikolai Petrovich, *the pilot turned cavalryman, had made it through Poland and was advancing on Berlin from the west as Germany capitulated. After four years in the war he was a lieutenant in the mounted artillery and still only 21 years old.*

When we entered Poland, we were greeted very well. With flowers and fruits…And Polish women were very friendly to us, especially to the officers…

There was an order from Zhukov against marauding and the punishment was harsh for those who were caught. I was present at one of the military tribunal hearings. A battery commander, also from our regiment, but from a different division, raped a Polish woman. There were two of them…the battery commander and a platoon commander. They went to Lublin to relax but got unlucky…

When they were questioned, the platoon commander confessed, while the battery commander denied it. The platoon commander was acquitted, while the battery commander was executed…Two officers, a sergeant and a captain, were tasked with the execution, both from the KGB…When they brought him to a trench and told him to turn away, he said, "I never turned away from the Germans and I will not turn away—especially from you."

The sergeant refused to shoot, while the captain ran behind him and shot him from behind. The punishment was harsh for such things. There weren't many cases like that…

The parents of those young women asked that he not be punished. In any event, the court didn't take those requests into account…

When we entered Rathenow, my battery's task was to cover the advance of the first squadron that was moving along the street parallel to the Havel River and seize the bridge that the Germans were using to retreat.

I decided [to deploy] just two cannons…one on the left side of the street and another one on the right. I was supervising the left one, while Platoon Commander Vorobyov was supervising the right one. When I shot from mine, the other one was rolling, then the other one shot and I was rolling. Squadron soldiers are running from one building to another, while we give them cover.

We somehow got disconnected from the rest of the regiment and we were counter-attacked by the Germans from the rear with automated rifles. I was thinking *Things are bad…*

At that moment, one of the machine guns started firing at my cannon. I was next to it. Suddenly: explosion. I fell and lost consciousness. It turned out to be a 13-year-old German, from the third floor, with a faust[27] bullet…I quickly recovered, got up…The machine gun kept going and [our] gunner—I don't know, maybe he was scared—could not hit the target. I pushed him away and with the first shot I made that machine gun quiet…

In the last weeks of the war, of course, everyone wanted to survive, and they were cautious—here's one example. In that same Rathenow a messenger came to me and said that Vikulov had abandoned the cannon—Vikulov was a cannon commander.

I asked, "What do you mean?"

I took a scout with me and ran over. When we arrived, we saw him aiming from behind the corner…The Germans were on the one side of the road, while we were on the other. I asked him what was wrong.

He said, "There are Germans there."

I said, "So what? It's not your first time!"

"But they are throwing grenades…"

"Then you go throw grenades too! Do you want to go before a tribunal in the last days of the war?"

"No."

And he continued the battle. In the last weeks, days, everybody wanted to live…

We were trying to reach the Elba. We were stopped. Instead of us, more prepared units went first, with English and French interpreters in uniform.

---

[27] Panzerfaust were single shot anti-tank weapons.

Verboten fur Deutsche

We were pretty shabby and could not meet the Westerners…We had to go back on the other side of the Havel River and we stopped 13 kilometres away from Rathenow. My PO [personal orderly] set up a forester house. We brought the best furniture from Rathenow, tableware from restaurants, and I was settled.

On 9 May '45, in the morning, I was in the forest, in the forester house, which was well-equipped, covered with carpets. I had a German Shepherd…I heard a horn: assembly. So I jumped up, got ready quickly.

The sergeant major entered and said, "Comrade…you don't have to rush…". And because we knew that western Berlin was taken and capitulation was due, I understood—Victory! The Shepherd kept tugging me to line up…Formation: the regiment commander was in front of us, chief of staff, political officer…

Political Officer Kurkovich was from Belarus and he hated Germans. Somebody gave away the information that he was a commissioner and his entire family was executed [under occupation] and anywhere he could, he destroyed [the Germans] unmercifully. So, it was his turn to speak and he said, "We are the winners. Here, you are prosecutors, judges, and executioners. Anything you do here is legal!"

I didn't agree with that…But he was that angry at them…

Victory. I told the sergeant major to lay a table in the forest for the entire battery. They went to Rathenow, brought tables and dishes from restaurants, while we had a lot of alcohol in our battery: nobody drank except for one platoon commander, Vorobyov. He would overdo it. So our stocks of wine, vodka were great…They laid a real feast.

I invited the regiment commander, chief of staff, political officer, all four squadron commanders, battery commanders. We sat down. It was maybe 2pm. The regiment commander made a toast: "To our victory!"

Everybody took a shot. I didn't drink—I [sipped] a little bit.

"What are you doing, son?! It's allowed now. Drink!"

So I did. I'm next to him and to the right is Kurkovich, the political officer. Then Kurkovich stands up. Again, he toasts. I'm again [sipping]…And he's: "What's up with you?"

So, I drank again, a shot. Then it's the headquarters commander's go. Same thing. Then the platoon commander. "To our battery commander." That one I couldn't [avoid]…

I passed out. And then the following happened…I had a motorcycle. I got on that motorcycle. When we had entered Rathenow, I right away seized a nice two-storey house for myself which belonged to a pilot—his wife, Marianna. Downstairs, when you enter, there was a wooden staircase to the second floor… To the right was an old man, father-in-law, to the left, a Polish man…maybe a doorman or servant. On the second floor there was Marianna and to the left I shared space with the orderly and one German Shepherd. So, I told the sergeant major to organise the continuation of the party there.

I didn't remember any of that. At some point everyone left.

Two German soldiers were passing by, infiltrating through the battle formations. They were told that officers there were celebrating Victory Day…So, they broke the window, poured fuel from the motorcycle tank on the staircase and set it on fire…The old man and the doorman jumped out of the windows, started yelling. Marianna was screaming—I ended up at hers for some reason—she woke me up…So, they jumped out, started calling for help. Germans are disciplined, they all came to the house—meanwhile I was still drunk in bed—they came, put out the fire.

At some point, I got up, opened the door and realised that there was no staircase: the staircase was burned, the motorcycle was burned. Meanwhile the orderly was waiting at the entrance. He said a ladder would be brought soon.

Why am I telling you this? For the first time ever I got drunk, and Germans almost burned me alive. That's why vodka never does any good to anyone.

Hans Walter, *who had been falling back as Nikolai galloped into Poland, was also one of those Germans trying to infiltrate Soviet lines and get home.*

I was wounded on 22 April, a so-called "home shot". I got hit by grenade shrapnel. I was just pulling in the [telephone] cable and then a grenade hit the ground, I saw I was hit on my hand. I was brought to the clearing station and I had to wait for all the heavily wounded people to be treated first. Afterwards I was transported to the front hospital in Bad Reinerz [in Poland at the Czech border]…

On the 8th of May I was in the sickbay and the [officer] ordered that we should report at 22:00 in the grand dining hall. That's where he explained to us that Germany had capitulated.

"God save Germany…We will try to transport the heavily wounded soldiers to land occupied by the Americans." But nobody knew where the Americans were at that time.

"Everyone else, get together with the rest of the troops and try to retreat home."

Everybody stood there. They were all used to getting orders. Now that nobody was giving orders, everybody had to make his own decisions.

On the 8th of May a train stood in the train station. Behind it the tracks were already prepared to be blown up. So it departed and we jumped on to it—full of refugee soldiers, everybody heading west. But only to the first corner: there, the Czechs had already blown up the tracks. The first two carriages derailed with the locomotive. You have to imagine—it was at full speed—imagine how great the panic was…

I thought, *What now?*

I got together with a comrade, "We have to get away from here, before the Russians come and take us with them!"

We got away up to the Czech border. We had the idea to get all the way to the Americans, but the Czechs at the border told us, "You have to give up your weapons, everything, stack it up here and then you can pass."

Afterbursts

And then I thought, *Germans without weapons, in a country which was attacked and occupied by the Germans? No! We will take our own route.* We stayed at the Czech border and fled into a wood. There we found a forester's cabin. The cabin was also filled with refugees from Breslau…

We got civilian clothing—because we were in a German area—took off our uniforms, put on the civvies and then the two of us headed west and we got to Dresden without having contact with the enemy…The people gave us food and took us in…

[It took us] about four weeks. We could not always march because we needed time to relax. It was very exhausting. We were in Dresden by the end of July. Dresden was completely destroyed…

At this point I could already use my hand a little, and after Dresden we moved on to Freital. There was a farm there. We arrived very thin and weak. We went to the farmer and were able to work there for four weeks on the fields, and we got food in return. This went well for four weeks, until all people who were not born there had to register with the Russians. And that was the signal for us to move on.

At this point trains were already driving again. Zwickau was at this time the line between the zones occupied by the Russians and the Americans. We got into American territory and thought okay; we've got this far, we will go all the way…

I arrived in Hamburg and had to go to the police. They asked me, "Do you have your discharge papers?"

I said, "No, the Russians do not give out discharge papers."

They told me I had to go to the Bullenhuser Damm because you could get discharge papers there. They again told me, "No we don't give out discharge papers, you have to work for them. You will get food and after a certain time working you will get them."

I had to give my word that I would be back every morning, because I wanted to live at my parents' house, with my parents. I had to go there every morning by tram—and that was the school where the SS had murdered all these children before. But nobody at the time knew that in the cellar Jewish children were murdered…in that school…Bullenhuser Damm. The children were killed in April '45 by the SS[28]. And that was a holding camp for German soldiers after the war.

Leonid Fyodorov *first fought on the frontline with green recruits at the Romanian border. As victory approached, he, like Hans, was not far from the Czech border—but still in combat.*

Of course, the brightest [memory] is Victory Day. We were in the south of Germany—going towards Leipzig, Dresden…We crossed the Czech border…

We had a large Czech village ahead of us which our 49th Regiment was fighting for…The battle started in the morning and they couldn't take over the village. The Germans resisted. Meanwhile we approached the frontline and entered another big Czech village—somewhat distant from each other—and we were offered lunch…But we were told right away that after lunch we would replace the 49th Regiment as it couldn't take over the village.

So, we are having lunch by the road and I'm seeing an officer galloping on a horse, crazy fast. "Where's regiment headquarters? Where's regiment headquarters?"

We tell him that it's in the middle of the village. I didn't even pay attention, it was a common thing during war, probably some urgent message.

But no. Five minutes passed. "Company commanders to the regiment commander!" Kostia Pronin, a very good company commander, we were like brothers…left. He comes back, silent, and we headed to replace the regiment. We finished lunch and were moving nearer and nearer to the frontline. The wounded are coming from there.

---

[28] On 20 April 1945, 20 Jewish children aged between five and 12 and four adult prisoners who cared for them in Neuengamme Concentration Camp were hung in the cellar of the school. Twenty-four unknown Soviet POWs were hung there soon after.

And suddenly Kostia told me, "Liosha, be careful today."

I didn't think much and said, "So what 'today'? What about tomorrow? Tomorrow will be the same."

And he somewhat implied, didn't say directly, "And tomorrow it will all be over."

I didn't even get it—and all of a sudden, we were shelled by mines. I thought, "Right! All over!" But it did indeed end.

We didn't take over that village. We spent a night in a quiet forest. In the morning: "Victory! Victory!"

But the most interesting happened the next day…The night in the forest was absolutely quiet. In the morning, we were lined up. I had a naïve thought…I thought we would line up and march back to the USSR. Not really. We were put on carts and we went south—I realised really quickly as there were signs and the roads were good… Prague!

Prague, OK. We were on the way. And suddenly our Headquarters Commander, Volodin, led the regiment on a different road, the wrong way…I understood that the road was wrong and I somehow oriented myself.

I didn't have a [trophy] watch—the war was over there were no more watches, the Germans learned how to hide them—I just had a little trophy pistol…I'm thinking, *let me try to cut through the forest*…to cut the distance—but mainly to meet Germans and secure a watch, with my pistol…

I didn't tell anyone anything, got off the cart, and left. In the forest I met about 15 armed German soldiers with automated rifles, looking at me like wolves.

"Geben sie Uhr." Give me a watch. "Nein, nein."

…I keep going. Thick forest. Enter a village. Good stone houses. It's about lunch time but not a soul outside—but I'm seeing people looking at me through the white curtains. I'm going towards the village centre…No one at the square. I cross the square diagonally and suddenly I'm seeing a boy walking towards me bravely. We meet at the centre of the square. He stretches out his arm and says, "Hi." I'm shaking his hand and greet him back.

This is what he tells me.

"Do you know what they are saying? These are Germans, they are standing by the windows and saying that you are walking alone and not afraid. And I'm telling them that you have no need to be afraid because they have capitulated."

Boy of seven to eight years…a Russian boy. All of a sudden he asks me:

"Why are you walking on foot?"

"How else am I supposed to walk?"

"We have won!…Let's take their car."

I'm saying, "No, no need." I couldn't even drive.

"Then take a motorcycle."

"I don't need a motorcycle."

"Let's take at least a bicycle."

And we are walking towards the end of the village, he is seeing me off, and he tells me, "My mother and I have been living here for the entire war. I'm from Novgorod oblast. Germans took us away…"

I said goodbye to him. And again, a big group of Germans, headed by an officer, carrying backpacks on bicycles, attached to the back…and the last one, I thought, *I will get the bicycle after all.*

It was the worst bike, huge backpack attached.

"Geben sie Uhr."

"Nein, zu schwer." Heavy.

I don't know how it could have ended, but the officer gave a sharp command…I sat on it and rode to the road. And this is when our unit approached. Nobody even noticed that I left the regiment for two to three hours.

Edwin Ledr, *trained first as a gunner and then in communications, was an artillery spotter by the war's end. He frequently spent several days in the trees directing fire from the guns behind him and was up in some branches when Germany surrendered.*

Afterbursts

On the day of capitulation, the 5th May 1945, [I was captured]... Deep inside of Russia—where, I don't know...They pulled me down from the tree. Five to ten men stood beneath the tree and all of them threw punches at me...I was six to eight weeks in hospital, I could only eat soup and bread...

While I was in hospital, we had the chance to look at Moscow. We were shown around in groups of five. If we went by metro we had a sign which said something like "Prisoner".

And if we entered the train the Russians had to stand up and we prisoners were allowed to sit. The conductor came and said to them all, "Stand up! Stand up!" and to us, "Sit down [*he says it in Russian*]". We didn't even ask for it or want to sit down. No matter if women or men, they had to all stand up...

For four years I was imprisoned in Russia—one year around Moscow, and three in Siberia in the mines, a lead mine. [Labour camp was] a lot of work but I was well...Worked for 12 hours a day, the norm...When I reached the goal for the workload, I got one slice of bread more—instead of one slice I received two—and sugar. I always put sugar on top of my bread, I felt like I ate a piece of cake. *[He laughs.]*

Two times a week we got tobacco to eat. But I never used it...I always gave it to my neighbour. We slept with five men on one wooden flatbed—I slept better than I do now! I used my fur cap as a pillow...

Later on, when I was still in captivity, I became a foreman..."Brigadier" they called me. I had about 20 men under me, and we had to chop down trees for paper, no matter whether it was minus 31 degrees Celsius. We always had to go out of the camp, so we didn't feel like prisoners. Even on Christmas Eve we had to leave the camp to unload the trains which carried peat.

When we were chopping down wood one of us was smoking and then the Russians came (not me, I didn't smoke)...The ones that smoked were punched, but I was never punched. "Back to work!" they said. But he smoked until he was finished...

When I was in Siberia I was given three weeks of holiday in Moscow. I was allowed to go for a walk wherever I wanted—just not on the Red Square, where the soldiers stood. We got a new uniform…a Russian uniform…We got boots, foot wraps…I took a bath in the Volga…When the three weeks were over they took away the uniform and gave us back the prisoners' uniform.

When we were on holiday, nobody tried to run away but when we marched to the camps [from the trains] some people attempted to escape. They were caught, shot, and presented to the prisoners as a deterrent so we would not attempt the same thing…

[We were released] from Siberia to Moscow. We had to stay in Erfurt for two days, and then 19 to 20 men wanted to go to Hamburg and we were taken in by the English. I got two apples for the first time. Four years without seeing fruit, only dry bread—but I was full, I wouldn't say that I was starving. I could have eaten more but I never needed much. I just lived day to day. Only important thing was that I had to eat in the evening—in the evenings, I ate so much that I was full for the rest of the day…

I was probably set free because I couldn't work anymore. I had no strength left. If I wasn't so skinny and weak I would have stayed, like the others…The last half year of being captured I worked in the kitchen. We had to strip the horse meat for the cook. We ate the meat raw if we could…I never knew horse meat tasted so good. Sometimes we also had to slice potatoes. If we did, we also ate raw potatoes. I could eat everything. That's hunger…

I weighed 47kg at the point I came back from imprisonment…I didn't have any teeth left. I had bad hearing. My boss said, "You look like a herring. You have to eat." Then I started eating 10-12 sausages a day. Then I slowly gained weight…

I never…I never…hated [the enemy]. I was never punched. I had food. I had my wooden bed to sleep on, and when I came back home, I stood there and had nothing. No money. No nothing…

When I came home, I found work in my profession straight away. In the meat processing factory—Schrader…I made sausages. It felt so light [to be home]..no barbed wire any more. The only thing that I "missed", that I was happy about, was that everything had been coordinated with a whistle…I didn't hear that anymore. I could stand up as I wanted and I could go to bed when I wanted…

As the war reached its inevitable conclusion, Germans lucky enough to have the wherewithal were running for the borders.

Peter Gafgen's *father, invalided out of the Afrika Korps before its surrender, had been assigned to head the Deutsche Industriekommission in Switzerland. He brokered the "triangular trade" by which the Association of Swiss Industrialists facilitated deals between Germany and the Allies. Notably, the British needed grenade igniters, the most efficient of which came from Germany, while the Germans needed tungsten to which the British had superior access. So, in the midst of the war, agents in Switzerland set up deals which helped the two countries continue to fight each other more effectively.*

His position was a favourable one when it came time to evacuate his family.

[My father] was entitled, because he was a diplomat, to have his family two weeks per year in Switzerland. And my mother was very upset that in '43 we didn't have the two weeks. And she said, "It's not fair…Why didn't he organise that?"

My father applied for four weeks of his family in Switzerland for Christmas in '44, because he figured out, *If they come for Christmas or New Year in '44, four weeks, the war will be over*…If my mother and my father could pay for their stay, the Swiss wouldn't send them to the border. And the money was there; he had stashed the Swiss Francs…

We left on December 31st to be on time for '44, but had a big problem coming to the Swiss border…The artillery of Leclerc was already shooting over the Rhine, so the train stopped in Offenburg— it was supposed to go to Basel.

The train was packed with normal people and with guys that would like to go to the south of Germany, because they thought that southern Germany was a safe place…And on the other track going

Verboten fur Deutsche

north, there was a train with wounded Germans that came from the front and had to be pulled to the north to be hospitalised, because apparently, they had more or less given up the south already.

And we waited…and then at the end a locomotive came and they said, "We are going over the Black Forest into Austria"—which in those days was Germany, because it was annexed…So then we went into the Black Forest. We had some picnic with us, but that was eaten up pretty soon. And there were no windows—there was cardboard, because the trains had been shot at previously. It was cold…Then up in the Black Forest—wonderful countryside, snow on both sides…

And then dawn came. Visibility came—and, of course, visibility came also for the hunters. There was air supremacy of the Allies in Germany. I learned all the different silhouettes of the planes. I could identify the types when they were in the air—the Germans and the Americans and the British…And at dawn in the Black Forest, I saw it was an American…a Mustang. And he flew over the train, very low.

And to the left and the right, you should have seen that, how fast people can move…out in the snow and onto the ground. And the guy returned, looked at the locomotive from up there—*Tak Tak Tak Tak Tak*—killed the locomotive and went home…

We waited. Maybe he comes back…We waited about half an hour in the snow. And then we went back to the train, and the locomotive looked very nice—it was steam and through these little holes, *zzzzh*, in the cold air the steam came out…

So there we were with the train and all our luggage in there and no locomotive. So the guy from the train came and said, "We got to stay put. we will organise [a new locomotive]." So we waited in the train, freezing…And then after a couple of hours the guy came and he said, "You're not getting your reserve locomotive, but we got a reserve train…about three to four kilometres away. Follow the tracks."

My mother says, "You got two arms; you take the two bags. I take the rucksack and I take the other two bags."

I had one bag with my schoolbooks, because my mother had said, "If we reach Switzerland, you go back to school," and I packed all my schoolbooks…Latin and everything. And in the other one, I had the things that my mother had packed—clothes and so on. And we started walking…And after about one or two kilometres I said, "I can't carry two bags anymore." And she says, "Throw one into the forest." So I threw one into the forest…

[T]he train took us to Lindau, but the only border post that was open was between Lustenau and St Magrethen. It was night and my mother went to a hotel near the station in Lindau. And this lady at the reception, she was very astonished, but we looked really in bad shape by that time.

So, that lady said, "Listen, we have this SS guy living on the top floor. He's working at this camp outside of Lindau and he has duty until eight in the morning and [when] he gets here, it's nine. There are two beds. You lie on those beds, you don't undress, you clean up…and you pass my desk at eight or eight five, you got the room." We got up there and we slept—I tell you, we slept. And then at eight, eight-five we were down there at the desk…

And the train came to take us to the Swiss border…We got off at Lustenau and we were the only ones. And we asked, "How do we get to Switzerland from here?"

And they said, "You go through German customs and then walk over the railroad bridge."

Okay. We go into German customs and they look at our papers and they're astonished. A woman and a kid—and by that time it was '45—going into Switzerland…They want to leave Germany. There's something funny about it. So the SS guy there said, "Sit down" and he went on the phone to Berlin—we learnt that afterwards—and he asked Berlin, "We have a Mrs. So and So and her son, and they have a visa for Switzerland…How come?"

And it took some time and then they apparently told the guy, "Yes, Major Gafgen is a diplomat in Switzerland. Everything is in order."

And then he winked to the SS lady and my mother had to go into a cabin. And I had to go into a cabin, and then I heard my mother yelp in her cabin…My mother came out and she told me, "It's impossible. I never thought…What they can do to humans."

Then we went into Switzerland…and there they wanted us to open all the bags…because they felt it was crazy, people coming like that, they must have documents…They opened my bag and there were only books. Which refugee comes across the border with a bag of only books? So he went through my Latin things, looked through the pages—was something hidden?

And then some other guy said, "Is there a code, or something like that?"

And my mother said, "You threw the other bag into the forest??", because that's when she noticed.

I said, "Yes, I threw the other bag, because you told me I have to go to school!"

And the guy at the border control in Switzerland, he also started to laugh…

That's how I checked into the school. They had to clothe me… There was nothing. Just the books!

Chapter 12

All in a Night's Work

The Far East

Victory may have come to the Allies in Europe, but there was no end in sight in the Far East. Full scale war had been raging in China since mid-1937 and across the rest of the region since the bombing of Pearl Harbor in December 1941, which had also coincided with Japanese invasions of the Malayan Peninsula, Hong Kong, the Philippines and Thailand. By mid-1942 Singapore had fallen and Burma was largely in Japanese hands.

With the British having persuaded the US to concentrate its resources on first liberating Europe, the Western Allies turned their attention to the China-Burma-India theatre only once Hitler was on the ropes. Many Western Allied soldiers who welcomed the war's end in Europe with relief were promptly reassigned to fight in Asia. British and Commonwealth troops had been involved in the early retreat from Burma, and British Indian troops were again deployed for the later recovery of Burma from the Japanese, along with Gurkhas from Nepal and West African troops from countries such as Nigeria, all of whom were under British rule. Of the support offered directly to China, most came in the form of fighters, bombers and supply lifts.

Afterbursts

While the reception of foreign forces in Burma was mixed, the Chinese, at least, were appreciative. Claire Chennault's Flying Tigers, US pilots who had resigned their regular commissions to serve under the Chinese flag even before Pearl Harbor, had blazed the trail and ensured a warm welcome for the Americans. As a unit, Chennault's roguish adventurers had had an unusually high success rate defending against the Japanese Imperial Airforce and remain legendary in China to this day. (The British flight from Burma is recalled with slightly less enthusiasm.)

For the Westerners who served in the China-Burma-India theatre, especially those slogging through the jungles, being at the end of the "longest supply chain" often felt incredibly remote. Many still refer to it as "the forgotten theatre". For the Commonwealth soldiers, their very contribution to the effort is frequently forgotten.

Fergus Anckorn *had arrived in Singapore just in time for the Japanese invasion. Already a reluctant solder, he was quite unprepared for war and the behaviour it normalised.*

Now, we were highly trained soldiers. We were the first division that had left this country fully equipped—to the last nut and bolt—but one thing they didn't tell us, ever, which is the most important thing of all: the noise. You're rooted to the spot. Shells and bombs and machine guns, buildings crashing. And you just stand there. *What's happening??*

They didn't prepare you for that at all, the noise. If they'd only said, "Once you get into action, all this is going on", you could get used to it. All this stuff flying around all over the place and all the noises…

So there was I, in action…A lot of people call me a war hero—five days? What did I do to become a hero? I just was there because I had to be there and I had to do what I was told. I made up my mind as soon as I landed out there that I wasn't going kill anybody unless he was trying to kill me, and then I'd let him have it because it's him or me. But to go out wanting…

All in a Night's Work

Fergus Anckorn in 2017

I remember one day in action with the gun there, they found an old Chinese man, an old boy, with some wire cutters in his pocket. So they got hold of him and took him to the gun position officer. "We found this old boy in our lines and he had wire cutters on him, what do we do?"

He said, "I've got no time to deal with that: kill him."

And I thought, *what have you just said???*

And they stuck him up against a tree and there was a *rush* of volunteers to do the shooting—most of them from the cookhouse, who never do anything. "Ooh, I wanna shoot him!" So they shot this poor old devil…

I had to drive an officer up to Seletar aerodrome where there was a water tower, and he was to go up there and observe. And we were driving through Singapore and it was millions of people in the streets—Chinese—and I was going through very slowly and hooting.

He says, "Don't hoot, run them over! They're bloody wogs!"

I said, "What?!"

He said, "Yeah there's a war on. Run them over!"

I thought *What sort of a man could say that?! Why should I run them over? I can drive around them!* No: they're wogs, shoot 'em. It's a terrible business.

But the most time in the war, you're doing nothing…The actual act of trying to kill somebody, it might only happen once a week. All these soldiers are doing something—a job, a fatigue…and it's very rare to get up close and have to fight…You're all busying yourself doing jobs and painting this or cooking that. You're not our heroes, swashbuckling…This is one reason I like the artillery: you never see the person you're killing. He's six miles away. But…all this cut 'n thrust, it never happens.

It happened at Kohima. That was the most dreadful battle ever. It lasted four days and four nights, on a tennis court. Japs one side, us the other. And it was the West Kents and it was on top of a hill in Kohima, and everyone wants the height. And the Japs wanted it and there were six divisions [sic] of them against our West Kents—three battalions—outnumbered about ten to one. And they were fighting all day long and the people were getting wounded and you couldn't do anything with them, you'd put them in a trench where they were re-wounded several times during the day…

And when night came it was hand to hand and some of them hadn't got bayonets, they were bashing each other with spades or hurling rocks at each other. And that went on for four days and four nights, and our people won the day and got them out of it.

Now *that's* heroic. But there again it wasn't heroism—they were trying to stay alive. You know, it's just plain common sense. But this propaganda about "our heroes have done this…"

Aged 98 when we met, Fergus was still enjoying watching the trees and the sky from his flat, but he told me he had no great desire to make it to his 100th birthday. He got his wish, dying in March 2019, just 6 months shy of a century.

Ken Yamada *knew what it was like to fight at Imphal. He had been inspired by his country's militaristic education to become a soldier but* *rapidly had his enthusiasm beaten out of him. After weeks at sea spent kneeling below decks, he arrived to fight in Burma as Japan's offensive was crumbling.*

Imphal was attacked from three different areas…I was initially supposed to calculate supplies, including food and ammunition needed for the Battle of Imphal…I was in charge of this area, calculating and sending the report. But the head [of the unit] reported lower numbers compared to my calculations. They were falsified… This is why the casualties in Imphal began…

The distance [to the storage area from the main depot] was about 15 to 20 kilometres. That's close. But the enemy…the British forces were already there. We had a tough time with them. They came down by parachute…We used a truck—maybe 10-20 trucks. After we transported the supplies, we dissolved…I returned to the storage and then went in the direction of Imphal…At night, we saw light emanating from Imphal, from the city…

We walked for about one week. After seeing injured soldiers retreating, I realised we wouldn't win in Imphal…There were just so many wounded soldiers. We retreated a little. We started seeing the reality but we couldn't go home—there were so many injured Japanese soldiers, people who were sick, so we also couldn't retreat.

The rest is all hell. You want to hear that? It was just hell, every day…Out of 10 soldiers, for example, nine of them died from either disease, starvation or suicide…There were those who couldn't see, some who lost their legs, various situations…More than a thousand soldiers would holler in pain, their voices would be echoing throughout the night pleading, "Help me!"

As soon as they leant on a tree, they weren't able to get back up. That's why many died of starvation. The jungle was so vast…

Because I saw so many gruesome deaths, I decided I didn't want to die that way. The aftermath was awful. I buried so many dead bodies.

Ken and his comrades were being pursued by the British and as he fled he noticed a pathway in the jungle.

A little while later, I noticed the sounds of military tanks and the sound of the British soldiers coming. I then noticed a flame flying towards me.

Have you ever seen a flame thrower? The flames came from the military tank. I injured my arm and I can't believe I'm still alive. There were 20 to 30 thousand enemies. I would have been killed if I ran away. I stayed down a long time. The tank retreated and I continued to stay down and wait…

[My arm] was so painful. On the next day, it was full of maggots. There were no bandages, so I used banana leaves…There was a military hospital but the enemy also attacked this. It was gone. The enemy destroyed it…I washed my wound every day and changed the banana leaves. My bones started to appear…

I ate snakes, giant water bugs. My comrades got them for me… people I just happened to meet who offered me food. In these extreme conditions, the British army dropped parachutes. I would hear them fall to the ground…There were many goodies inside like biscuits and condensed milk…about 10 [parachutes], maybe two or three times. We succeeded [in taking some of these supplies] only once. I realised we couldn't win, looking at the difference in what we were eating. It's amazing how we were fighting a war…

According to the soldier precepts, a soldier must never surrender. It is a shame to surrender. The only thing I thought about was running away…I also believed the rumours that they would cut off your penis. Many ran away and never returned…

We all carried a grenade. People were losing their minds… If someone kills themselves, it's human psychology for someone nearby to do the same…On some days, there were as many as 10 people killing themselves. Their guts were just pouring out. They were totally black from top to bottom. [Their limbs] were all scattered, so we just picked them up and buried them in a hole. It was so hard. I can still remember it now. That's why I don't eat meat. No meat, no eel—it reminds me of the snakes. We didn't have the strength to dig a hole, so we would bring them to the holes made from the shells...

We had to retreat every day because the enemy was coming. Bombs were being dropped every day. You drink bad water and get sick. Malaria...

In the jungle, what one word do you think the soldiers shouted before their death?...Mother. They never shouted father...The soldiers would talk about their mothers, and how they wanted to eat their mum's tofu miso soup, or dumplings. We talked about this in the jungle. They would be shouting, "Mum! Mum!" while dying. They were about 22-23 years old. Just thinking about how they felt...

We couldn't bring back their remains which is one of my deepest regrets. There was one soldier, and there was a big tree and he was lying down and making a soil ball imagining an *azuki* dumpling and stuffing it in his mouth. And after half a day passed, he...That's the reality of war...

I never heard anyone call out for the emperor. They just kept saying, "Mum. Mum..." When I was walking through the jungle, one soldier grabbed my leg and asked me for medicine since there were no longer any army medics. And then he told me to take care of his mother. So I said, "Sure, I will."

Elsewhere in the Burmese jungle, **Art Naff** *was carting around artillery equipment on mule trains. His unit, successor to the jungle warriors famed as Merrill's Marauders, was among the few US ground troops committed to the CBI.*

I was drafted when I was 18 years old...one of the youngest...I didn't know much about the war. It was what you did in those days, in 1944...At that time it was your duty to go...

I went out to Myitkyina, Burma and was put up with the MARS Task Force, the 613th Field Artillery. And then from there on we walked 475 miles over the Burma Road pulling a mule...Of course, the Burma Road was nothing but mud and dirt. I mean, it wasn't a "road", it was just a trail.

Art Naff in 2018 and as a young soldier

The main thing was to stop the Japanese from taking over the Burma Road—because all the east coast, where Shanghai and all was, was held by the Japanese, so China had no way of getting supplies. So if the Japanese could close the Burma Road, then China was isolated...

Well, we were coming down from the north, and [the Japanese] were coming up from the south. And when we got down so far, the engineers had put the Ledo Road in, so they were running supplies into China until we cleared the Burma Road completely...

[We took a] 75mm howitzer on the mule...It took 6 men to dismantle, but they did it in about 15 minutes. One mule had the wheels, another mule had the howitzer, another mule had the carriage and two or three mules would carry the ammunition...We weren't allowed to put [our own kit] on the mule, because if a shell came over and the mule took off, all your belongings were gone, see, until you found the mule...We all grabbed the mule's tail, [even though that wasn't allowed either] cos when you get into doing 20, 25 miles and you come to a mountain, you think, *Oooh!*

I was with headquarters, in communications. My mule had wheels of wire and I would run a wire from A [artillery] battery to B

All in a Night's Work

battery to C battery to headquarters with my mule. And then they would use the magnetic crank phone and say, "Okay; Colonel says fire one at 175 range", and they would fire one, and the spotter would tell them how far they had to come up.

And then, after we'd go through that battle, they would disconnect the wires, leave it there, go to the next. Keep on marching. March another 50, 75 miles, a hundred miles, whatever it was…First part of November, latter part of October, we left Myitkyina and then we walked the whole way down to Lashio…

The only supplies we got was, every three days we got an airdrop for our meals and our ammunition—and anything that we needed came in by airdrop because nobody could get into the jungle where we were. That's why we had the mules: they couldn't get any mechanised things into the jungle…We would get the C rations—which was a can of meat and beans, meat and vegetable hash, meat and vegetable stew—and then cans of crackers and coffee or lemonade, and then you've got one energy "D bar", which was that thick chocolate, which you couldn't break. You had to hit it with a rock or something to break it. That was the energy bar.

And then you're supposed to get a can of either fruit cocktail—peaches or pears or something—and…when that was missing, we would line up and when the [US supply] plane come down and make the next drop we'd go *bang bang bang bang bang*—shoot at him—and he'd go *woooooop*.

And he'd say, "I think the next time I think we give them back their peaches and fruit cocktail!"

You usually kept a can or two with you. We had times that they didn't make the airdrop because the Japanese were there, surrounding the area where we were going to get the airdrop, and we couldn't go in and get it. So we'd call them off and they'd come back the next day…

Oh sure [I was afraid]. The first night that I was in the combat area zone we were to dig a foxhole. Well, when you dug a foxhole, you just dug something narrow and just lay down in it. And then another fellow was four or five feet away from you.

Well, this happened to be a very moonlit night, it's just like a spotlight is on you. You can see everything out there and if anybody would run across, you could see 'em—but it wasn't that. It was that the Japanese, at 1 or 2 o'clock in the morning, would start off with their machine guns. And the only thing you can think of is that you're gonna get hit. You don't know where they're shooting at, they're just shooting. And you don't know if they're shooting above you, or half a mile over from you, but they're shooting.

And…you know how your knee gets to shaking sometimes? Well, I was shaking like that, and the only thing I was thinking of, as I'm laying on my stomach, *I'm going to get hit in the butt!* and somebody was going to say, "Which way were you running?"

But instead, I just calmed down afterwards and I thought, *well this is just a Japanese ploy to try to scare you*, and they actually weren't shooting at me…

The ones that were with the 124th cavalry and the 475th infantry, which we were backing up, they were up the front and had man to man encounters with the Japanese. Being in the artillery…only thing I saw was dead bodies.

Lescher Dowling, *too, was involved with the mule-borne war, serving with the 7th Veterinary Company. At first, he sat around watching as the Company split into three and the two other companies were sent to the Aleutians and then Europe.*

Apparently, they were waiting for something to develop for us. The CBI was kind of slow in getting started and I suspect that we were supposed to have been a rear echelon for Merrill's Marauders, but it took us 72 days to get overseas, because we were on an old freighter converted from coal into an oil burner. Top speed was nine knots. It could not keep up with any convoy, so we were out there all alone…

We had 454 mules aboard. Every morning we'd use a fire hose and salt water to wash down the stalls, and it would all drain to a hatch and drain over the side. All the men would be working and then we'd go on the fantail and we'd see this yellow trail zigzagging behind us—because we were alone, every 10 seconds the ship changed course…Supposedly, it takes 10 seconds for a submarine to line up on you…

We had no idea where we were going until we hit the Indian Ocean and then they sprung it on us that we were going to India. And when we got into the Indian Ocean, we hit a terrible storm and we would go up one wave, and the propeller would dig in, and then we go down the other way and the propeller was free. And the ship was just vibrating…And finally, they shut it down because they were afraid that it would damage itself. And they put out what they call a sea anchor—it's kind of a huge funnel, made out of canvas—and they dragged it behind the ship to keep it lined up so that it wouldn't be broadsided by the waves…for about four days.

[Fortunately] mules don't get sick. They can't, because whatever goes in only comes out one end—they do not have the ability to throw up…Also, mules and animals have a lock in their legs. So it kind of locks in and they can stand for hours…

We came in to Calcutta, going through locks. They said we'd have to stay overnight so they could spend the next day unloading mules using belly slings. Our crew lieutenant said, "These men have been on board ship 72 days. We will unload this boat in an hour and a half."

We did it in an hour and 15 minutes. And that's the last we saw of any of those animals—except for one guy who said he was watching a Chinese pack artillery file by and he recognised one of the mules that was on his team. They were all jewels, hand-picked, and we never saw a single one because they went to Chinese Pack Artillery Units.

Our purpose was changed when we got into Myitkyina. They said, "We don't need any evacuation teams, the Chinese will evacuate their own mules."

What they needed were first aid station for animals, kind of like MASH units. And each platoon was assigned to a Chinese pack artillery as liaison…And so, one by one, the four platoons were sent out to different locations all over Burma to serve these Chinese pack artillery…

When we were going over the Burma Road…we would set up camp and maybe the column is 25 miles away. [The unit's] job was to go into a battlefield and pick up sick and wounded animals and take them out…They'd have two mules, with a long rope stretched between them and then there are clips on the rope, and they would tie about ten mules to the rope. And then they would have two outriders to keep everything going.

And so you would ride into the battle area and pick up sick and wounded animals, clip them on and take them out to the good roads, where you'd load them into trucks and then truck them off to a remount station, tend to them and then truck them back. And so they were trucking them back and forth every day…

They aren't combat, [the mules], they are simply travelling, and all of their problems are from travelling. They had some big Australian horses…they were short on mules and so they went up into Tibet and brought down some small Chinese animals and also they imported some big draft horses from Australia. But the big draft horses have big feet. The Burma Road is littered with all kinds of junk and they'd injure their feet. And once an animal injures the frog, the centre of his hoof, it becomes infected and usually they have to be put down. Fortunately, we didn't have any.

Bob Burke *had been in signals, serving at the tail end of the North Africa campaign.*

I started in North Africa in the combat zone…We were there as a buffer, just in case the Germans wanted to give one last try…We came in on the Atlantic side of North Africa, and Rommel was pretty much running for the northern spit of land…

I guess the Germans were flying home, but the poor Italians, their allies, were there surrendering by the thousands and thousands…We had Italian prisoners of war doing all the cooking for us. Wonderful cooks! And they even put on a play for us, with some of the prisoners being dressed as women…They were happy. Their war was over.

Bob was sent from North Africa to the CBI to help build connections from India to China. He was assigned as a replacement for the

All in a Night's Work

96th Signal Battalion and had to make his own way from Calcutta to Assam via steamship and a narrow gauge tea plantation train.

And we arrived up into the end of the line in the town of Ledo, at midnight, in a combat zone—no lights showing, nobody's stirring, rain is pouring…I was the last person in the world, I felt like…So it wasn't until next morning I found a replacement office. And they gave me an escort out to the airfield and put me on a plane.

The plane had a big cut out in its side—just wide open—and I'm sitting on one side of it and I'm looking at this guy sitting over here and he had one gold earring, which was the insignia of Merrill's Marauders…Well, I had my jacket on my lap. He grabs my jacket and throws it out that window. I grabbed a sleeve as it goes by, and I said, "What did you do that for??"

He needed some excitement, you know? These are guys that have been out there in the killing fields…

From Bhamo to Lashio I headed a team of three linemen who would do the repairs on the [telephone] line that was existing, and this was during the monsoon. Three months of constant rain… Many's the time in Burma I'd have a poncho over me and boots on and shorts underneath that. I'd have to walk about a half mile from where my tent was down to where I was working…and by the time I would get from one end to the other—in the rain—I would be sweating under that covering I had, just from the heat…

I had an 800lb piece of electronic gear right at my cot. It would wake me up if the line was broken for some reason, it'd give me the signal. I'd have to roust my crew out.

And on this heavily raining night they ran up so far, and then they couldn't go any further in the truck, because coming down from Bhamo through semi-mountainous area, the Chinese tanks had cut what they call a "tank road"—they don't go on the nice roads. They got to a good place and they just came through, knocking trees down and everything, to get down to the bottom as quick as possible. So the copper wire followed that tank line.

So my three repairmen had to then slug through the mud there, following the line, and they checked in. If they got Bhamo, they know they're too far, if they got me, they know it's still between me and Bhamo, the break in the line.

And so they were tracing on the line and up ahead they saw, in the shelter of a cliff, a little campfire, and it was three Japanese soldiers trying to keep warm or cook something around this little campfire. Well, they wiped them out, of course—they snuck up on em and wiped them out—and then continued to find the break in the line and repair it…

All in a night's work, ya know. *Tsk.* That's what we get paid for…

And then I was in a retreat, further down at the junction of the Ledo Road and the Burma Road…because a Japanese column was supposedly coming up the trail. I never realised there were so many American units over on the Ledo Road, but all along the road they got word that the Japanese were cutting behind. The road just filled up with trucks and guys with all their gear…It was just a traffic jam all the way up, waiting for the signal…

We could see the Chinese, Chiang Kaishek's forces, sitting up in the hill, and they're watching like it was a show or something. There was just hundreds of guys that come out of the forest around there. I don't know what they're all doing…So that's why they called it Confusion Beyond Imagination: CBI…

About March or May of '45 I was sitting in my tent with my equipment and I got the word from my headquarters back in Bhamo, back to the rear, they said they're going to try and do the first telephone communication between Kunming and Calcutta tonight. Communication seemed to be better at night. Anyway, he said give them some help if they need it. See, I can come in on that line without interfering with their discussions at all, I can just listen to what's going on.

And sure enough, around 11 or 12 o'clock at night there, I'm tuned in and there's a phone call from Kunming to Calcutta. And I didn't do anything, because I could hear somebody in Kunming and I could hear somebody in Calcutta. And they're yelling. And the one couldn't hear the other. There was too much loss in 2000 miles.

So I came in then and I said, "I'm in the middle of this thing. I can pass any messages on." So I passed greetings back and forth… Now, I've seen this written up in books, that first call to Calcutta. General Sultan was on the [one end], and I don't know who was up in Kunming. But they don't mention how it was accomplished. Bob Burke sitting in the middle!

Bob died in February 2019.

Chapter 13

To Survive was a Disgrace

The Far East II

As Ken Yamada had attested, supplies for Japanese troops were severely compromised—in his view by poor management, but also due to overstretched Japanese supply lines. In fact from Ken's account the Imphal offensive, while understocked, was better off than most.

Sueichi Kido, a Nagasaki bomb survivor and later in life a history teacher, observed that one of the many reasons Japanese soldiers were so brutal to the Chinese, besides institutionalised racism, was that they tended to be deployed without supplies. Once they arrived in occupied territories, they were told to take what they needed from local populations.

> The Japanese military is different from the US and the UK military in that once they are deployed, they can never return, they have no holiday. They have to locally procure everything, including food…Such a system was also used during the war with China in the famous Sanko ["Three Alls"] Operation. "To steal everything, kill everything, and burn everything."

Afterbursts

So, to steal everything from the villages—and if you left these, the Chinese would find out about it, so they had to burn everything down and to kill everyone who is a suspected spy for the Chinese military. Many innocent people were raped, killed…This was the kind of war Japan fought before World War Two.

Rodney Armstrong *witnessed some of the mania that this system produced as he fought his way through the Pacific. Trained as a Navy medic, he was spared from dying at Guadalcanal by a bout of measles and then deployed to build a rock garden before eventually being sent to sea.*

I was assigned to join the hospital corps on an escort carrier called the *Suwannee*—CVE27…We took part in a number of battles…Once, a Japanese torpedo hit the side of the vessel exactly at the point where I was sitting in a compartment below the waterline—but fortunately the damn torpedo didn't go off.

So we went along…I wasn't paying a great deal of attention, but somebody said to me one morning, "You'd better go up on the flight deck and take a look around because you're never going to believe what you see."

So I go up to the flight deck…and as far as you could see at every distance—all the sky, all around!—more battleships, more this, more that…You've never *seen* a sight like it. And that was at the beginning of the Battle of Leyte Gulf.

Well, we took on board two fully loaded kamikaze and they bombed our aeroplane elevators so we couldn't take off aeroplanes. And in the end, we couldn't steer…and we went around in circles for a day or two trying to get it under control—and on fire. And the problem was the terrible wounds that came from burning gasoline or the explosions of aeroplanes which had been loaded with bombs and which catch on fire. In any case the ship was a wreck by the end of the battle…

To Survive was a Disgrace

On October 25th and 26th, USS Suwannee's crew suffered numerous casualties.

I'd been very lucky. My best friend had been killed by my side but I had little amounts of shrapnel up and down my back and my arms and on my hand…nothing that incapacitated me from trying to help other people. So, in any case, after a few days of doing lazy circles in the sea, a hospital ship was able to get near us and we unloaded our men—all those of our worst injured.

I came down with terrible infection in all these places where I'd had these small pieces [of shrapnel]. And there was no anaesthesia and no medicine left aboard ship—all used up. So they gave me the choice of which of my friends would hold me down on the operating room table while they…

In total I was in about eight invasions, and the worst ones were in places like Okinawa, where from my ship we fired cannon onto the island and we could see people jumping down into the ocean from caves on the cliffs…The whole atmosphere was permeated by horseflies…It was like having a blanket of horseflies. Of course, they were eating on all the people who had been killed and the air movement would bring this stuff out to sea where we were.

*In the early stages of the war in China **Xu** had helped to build the Burma Road, been caught under a particularly savage air-raid and run away from home to enlist. His unit was assigned to guard a US Army Air Force base in Xiangyun, Yunnan.*

That airport was already old, the Chinese Air Force was landing to the west. When we got to Yunnanyi there were no made-up roads, no fences and no security cordon. Those were pretty tense times. Yunnanyi airport was frontline. There were dozens of fighters.

All our brothers in arms were from Sichuan…[They] weren't happy, they were asking to go to the battlefield, to fight with bayonets. There is a habit among soldiers, which reflects your sincerity, which is to proactively ask to go to the battlefield to fight—everyone wanted to go to the battlefield and fight! Because every day when we were in training, in our minds we all wanted to go and fight the Japanese.

In the end our regiment commander said, "Your request to go to the battlefield…it's well-intentioned, but you haven't thought about another aspect. One of you on the battlefield might kill two or three Japanese. A fighter, if you guard it well, can be much more effective on the battlefield than you can be individually."

So…everyone agreed with this logic: "Many more times effective than one of you alone." Those fighters usually had three heavy machine guns, hey, and several small bombs on the wings…Three, six small bombs.

Xu's home city of Tengchong was occupied by the Japanese and the Chinese ground forces were struggling to mount a counterattack on the heavily defended walled city.

A few divisions went up to Tengchong and all the Japanese in the countryside went back into the city. It was hopeless as attacks failed to get through on the left and on the right. There were huge casualties…

I tell you, the Air Force really was a joint operation…All along the Burma Road every regiment and every division had an American advisor. Once the plane was airborne it was directed from the ground: what direction the enemy was in, how many metres, how many miles…Without ground support they couldn't find the target. So the Americans sacrificed a dozen of them, all consultants assigned to the divisions and regiments. Most of them were lieutenants…13 or 14 advisors in Tengchong.

We couldn't get an attack through, so Yunnanyi sent out bombers, to bomb the city walls. When we loaded the bombs, I was at the front because I was in my teens, early 20s, and it was fun. When [the Americans] were going out to the planes, "I'm driving! I'm driving!" We were messing around, playing. *[He laughs.]*

When we loaded the bombs, I was guarding the front. We used a big truck to pull them to the foot of the bomber's wing and then we used an elevator to raise them up. Some Tengchong people said that the city walls were so strong they must have put steel rods in the bombs. I said I never saw any steel rods, but I did see the bombs. It's pretty clear that since we had to use elevators to lift them, even a steel plate wouldn't stop one, never mind the stone of a city wall.

You can imagine, the weight made it difficult. Those heavy bombers wouldn't take off or go on attack without six to nine fighters protecting them…Why fighter planes? Because their load was so huge they were afraid of Japanese planes coming to attack them…

But the heavy bomber…all around it was glass, only underneath you couldn't see—above, to the left, to the right, everything was visible. The anti-aircraft guns were operated by three people. A fighter was just one man. A bomber had 13 people driving it and it had visibility all around…After the pilot blasted a few large gaps in the city wall, the expeditionary army could get in to start street fighting. They blew three or four gaps…

When it landed and the fighters landed, we were also curious—once the gun was wiped, it was completely sealed with tape for fear of dust entering. The ground crew inspected the aircraft, loaded the ammunition, and all the muzzles were completely sealed with tape.

So, we were curious. After they landed—("I'm driving, I'm driving!")—we'd take a look at the muzzle tape, then: "Today…how many Japanese have you killed!"… It was only on landing that the holes were sealed, if the tape wasn't broken then they hadn't fired. They hadn't killed any Japanese…

Fortunately, the Japanese fighters never came to attack us. We were ready. Those machine guns had two feet and two men could put the feet on our shoulders and fire it as a low-altitude machine gun… Fortunately, they never came. If the Japanese airplanes had come, it would have been tough…

There's something else I still remember. In the plane of an American pilot, China had embroidered a gown for him. Why? Because on the back of the gown were two lines of characters, and what did those two lines say? 来华助战 [I've come to China to help fight] and in brackets were written 美国 [America] and underneath 洋人 [foreigner]…All the guys from American wore this.

Why did they need the jacket? In case they were high altitude fighting and their fuel dried up or they crashed or landed, the civilians would see that this was someone who had come from America to help China fight, otherwise they might mistake him for a Japanese and kill him.

Dick King, *a Pennsylvanian, also served with the US Army Air Corps on the ground. One of 12 siblings, he and three brothers fought in the war, "And, would you believe, all four of us returned."*

I was [drafted at] 21 years old, just a vulnerable age. But I wasn't alone—my God, there was millions upon millions did the same thing. They were drafted and had to go in…And it just happened that I got the Air Corps. And it happened that I was assigned to go to China…

It was a three-hour flight over the Himalayan mountains, [in a] C46…Those guys did a terrific job—because it wasn't unusual at all for those pilots to make as many as 200 trips back and forth over that Himalayan mountain, because everything we had had to come in by airplane! The Burma Road was there…but Japs would always have the thing bombed. And so we couldn't transport anything like we would like to have done by truck…

I don't know how we ever did it. Because, you know, in China, at that time, they didn't have gas, and we were in the Air Corps and we needed plenty of gas. But everything else…food—because we weren't allowed to eat what they had over there, because it was too dangerous, with bacteria and so forth…

I must tell ya, over there in China, everything was very primitive. And we lived in tents…not very nice…I was not in serious danger, but we were always vulnerable to bombings as far as we were concerned. But, of all things—one place, they took over an estate which had a huge house. And by golly we lived in a brick house for a while, and that was pretty much unbelievable. But it was a nice place and it even had a tennis court on there so my buddy and I were able to play tennis once in a while.

To Survive was a Disgrace

Dick King in 2018

That was an ugly time, really, cos we went from our base, where we were staying in that house, to our office area—such as it was—to work, and on the way we would count the number of rough boxes, caskets, that we would see…Rough wood, hammered together. Because plague had hit and just took the lives of so many of those people. That was at Hankow.

But when we were at Liangshan, we needed an extension to the runway that we had. And we had to build it with what equipment we had that was over there—which was practically none, except hard work by Chinese people. There was a long line of coolies going from that place where we were building that runway, out to the mountain, to get rocks to build this base for the runway. You could hardly see the end of it. That's how long the lines were. And these coolies would come in with their "pogo sticks" and a basket on each end with rocks in it. They would dump them on the runway and many times they were too big. So they were broken up by the girls, the ladies, who sat there with hammers and broke those stones by hand. If they had children, they were playing around there.

To roll that runway, to get the stones solid, they had a roller with a shaft going through…and how they moved that, they had straps—which they made, incidentally. Nothing from a manufacturer—and they would have a line of coolies along each side of that long tongue and they were attached to the tongue. And one Chinese would stand there and start to count, "*hai ho hai ho hai ho*" until they finally got that thing to move and roll it down…Those people were mostly small, but they were strong. They were leathery, you know, they were just tough as nails, and… that was their life, that work.

Incidentally when they, that long line of coolies, brought rocks in they would carry a pouch on their belt with rice in it. And one of 'em who was in that group had a wok hanging on them and at the time when they wanted to eat something they stopped along the way, built a fire and made this rice in the wok. When I think about it I can't believe it's that primitive. But work they did…

Of course…when I talk about my trip to China, I like to talk about the things that I have talked about so far. It shouldn't be mistaken for the fact that there was a lot that wasn't very darned nice. No. I don't even want to talk about it. So that's the reason I talk about the…the nicer things. Cos, I felt that, well, I was just darned lucky to be able to do it.

One of the best plane rides I ever had…this one B25, this was right after the war was over. The guns were taken out of the nose and my buddy and I talked a pilot into getting up into the front there where all this plexiglass was around. And so we did, we crawled up through there. And that was absolutely the most beautiful plane ride I ever had in my life. Cos it was like you're riding on a cloud.

Did you feel lucky to get back?

Heavens yes! Oh yeah. Because, you know, we had reports of all the casualties that there were and it was horrendous, really. Goodness. All of our fine young men, just annihilated. Just shot. Killed…

[D-Day especially was] one really sad situation…These virile young men going ashore and being shot down…like you'd shoot a skunk or something... Horrible. It's just no way to settle problems, I don't think. There has to be a better way—and we as people should find that way.

Zhang, press-ganged as a young teenager, had been marched south to join the war effort. He fought numerous battles around the borders with Burma, many during the 1944 counterattack, coordinated with the Americans, which turned the tide against the Japanese in China.

The war at that time, it wasn't easy. And we relied on the support of the English and Americans—their weapons were all cutting-edge—only then could we put up any resistance...

When we came to counterattack...our weapons were all American equipment. We exchanged all our grenades: the grenades made by China, they exploded slowly, and when you threw them, you had to throw them far away. Veteran soldiers waited for a lot of smoke before they let them go, but new solders threw them too near...and then they were afraid to use them. The grenades that came from America, you could use them for close at hand attacks, and even if you threw ten or twenty of them, none of them would have a problem.

In 1944, Zhang was sent with the Sixth Army to attack a strategic point on the Burma Road, Pine Mountain, which had been occupied by the Japanese since May 1943, when their progress into China was halted at the Salween River. With aerial and advisory support from the Americans, it was a turning point in the CBI campaign.

First, Zhang's division had to cross the river, where they assembled overnight.

The next day in the morning, probably around 8 or 9 am, the guns of the enemy opposite started coming at us like firecrackers. When we first went to the firing line we weren't afraid of those cannons, but the sound was loud, and continuous rounds were coming straight at us. We didn't open fire on our side, we were all hiding in the trees...They kept firing until around 9 am, and then they put their boats in the river.

When I was at home I had rowed a boat, but I'd never seen a rubber boat. When their boats got into the middle of the river, the higher ups ordered, "Fire!" When we opened fire, we were firing at people. The boats kept floating, and people rolled out into the water.

So then the information was passed along: "Rubber boat—fire at the boat, don't fire at the men!" So we fired at the boats…That morning, we shot all the boats they put in the river, but most of the people swam downstream. We were fighting until about 12 o'clock before they didn't dare put their boats into the river any more…

Afterwards, there was no way to get across to that side. We'd fought a battle and we couldn't cross the river. Our battalion commander went to Shibanpo. He went to ask the Lisu tribe to tie [a raft], and they eventually sent it over. On the third day, ten men came. But the civilians [who were ferrying us]…one raft could seat a squad, 12 or 13 men. If there were more, they didn't dare cross…

The next day the Japanese—at around 11 o'clock—came and started stealing the civilians' things. Several squad leaders said, "Let's fight them." But the platoon leader said, "I won't allow you to fight. We are short on bullets. We have fewer men and they would be able to surround us easily."

At the time I was young. I said, "If we don't fight the Japanese when they steal the civilians' things, when are we going to fight them?" I said, "I'm not scared. If we're surrounded, we're surrounded." I ordered the soldiers to shoot.

Their orders after they successfully crossed the river were simply to find where the Japanese were going up the Gaoligong mountains, which act as a north-south barrier in the region and cut off their supply lines. The terrain was so inhospitable and sparsely manned that between the key heights the Japanese communicated with signal flags.

The Chinese had been directed to one of the Japanese passes by locals who warned them that the route was tricky and there was a ditch at the foothills where the Japanese entered the mountains. With the monsoon rains in full swing, the Chinese troops could not receive supply drops from the Americans, forcing them to go for days without food.

At the time, the plan was to cut off their advance route, and then completely wipe them out from the Gaoligong mountains. We were

To Survive was a Disgrace

not going to let a single one get away. When we arrived, we couldn't get a handle on the situation. We didn't have any information and so we were defeated, they came out of the ditch and beat us. We crawled to Huangjia mountain...

After about ten days, the unit at Qiaotou ["Bridgehead"] was going to attack us. By that time around a thousand of our men had arrived and our guns and cannons had also all arrived. They attacked us three times and couldn't get anywhere. Their rifles and machine guns were out of range...

We could see people—two civilians, the officer on the red horse and an assisting solder. Behind the machine gun company was an artilleryman...With one shot he hit the hoof of that officer's horse—at the time, we didn't realise that he was a commander. By the next day, a victory report was passed up, saying, "Yesterday you downed their commander." When they said we had hit their commander, everyone was delighted. *[He laughs.]*

About two or so days after we had killed him, they [the Japanese] set Qiaotou on fire and they burned down Hekou ["River Mouth"] village. They were going to retreat—their grain stores, ammunition stores, they were all at Qiaotou...So our regiment commander left the Third Battalion at the upper summit, blocking the way up [and] our First and Second Battalions withdrew down.

When we withdrew to Qiaotou, the Japanese weren't there... *Aiya!* When I tell you this you mustn't laugh at us. That canned food storehouse? They'd taken a hand grenade and blown it up. Some of the cans had been blown into pieces and some were blown open... We veterans were stealing them and the battalion commander said, "Don't take them. They've put poison!"

By that time, those of us who had been soldiers with the Kuomintang[29] didn't care whether or not it was poisoned...In the Kuomintang life was a bit disorganised, usually it wasn't easy to get

---

[29] Chinese term for the Nationalists, who served under Chiang Kai-shek (also "KMT").

some meat to eat, we just ate a bit of old squash, or green vegetables or white cabbage. Ah, it wasn't easy.

After helping to liberate Tengchong in early 1945, Zhang's unit spent months chasing the Japanese in the mountainous region around the Burma borders.

We were again transferred to fight at Mukang on the borders of Mangshi and Longling. It wasn't easy to fight at Mukang. In our squad there was one chap, he was also a Sichuan man, from Luzhou in Sichuan, who had his foot blown off by a gun. I hadn't cried up till then, but…I cried then…

The Mukang battle wasn't over. There were still Japanese around, they hadn't all surrendered yet. So we had to go into Mangshi. Several men from our main army came over. [The Japanese] retreated and one of them hid at the foot of a bridge on a big bend.

When our army crossed the road, he didn't throw the grenade but afterwards, an American car drove up and the Japanese came running out from under the bridge carrying the grenade to blow them up. But it didn't explode. They drove across the bridge. There were a lot of troops and a shot killed him…

They shot him next to the bridge…I still remember, they stopped the car and the officer came over, undid his buttons and cut his stomach open and as soon as his guts came out, they took a photo. I said, "Did you cut his stomach open to eat his guts?" Haha. It was funny.

After taking a lot of casualties by the border at Heishanmen, where the Flying Tigers were sent in to give them cover, Zhang's unit was told not to pursue the Japanese into Burma but to hand over to the New First Army, which was due to arrive to relieve them.

In the end, a fog came up in Wanding early on and they were late in coming. When the fog came up, that side said something and this side said something and we couldn't hear clearly, so we opened fire… Their gunfire and our gunfire was the same…In the end both sides yelled out, "Don't fight, don't fight! Friendlies!" Because Japanese gunfire and our gunfire didn't sound the same. If they had arrived

Zhang in 2016

any later, they would have been cut off on both sides and they would have been wiped out.

After the battle we sat around in that Dai village…Huatian. We carried up the bodies from Heishanmen to be buried, comrades from the battle. Dug a trench to bury them in and gave them a monument. I reckon we buried about two or three hundred men. For everyone of company commander rank or above, they took a piece of bamboo and carved a memorial, to commemorate the person who had died. Platoon leaders and below they didn't bother.

At the time it was the tenth month of the old calendar…The army was moving to Shandong, and we soldiers all turned to each other and said, "Fuck it, we've had more than enough hardship in Yunnan, what are we going to Shandong for? I'm fed up with it!" So we left the force and deserted!

Afterwards I settled in Tengchong. When we got to the beginning of the civil war, I thought it would be better not to go…Bloody hell, to die fighting in a civil war isn't worth it…Fighting a civil war is fighting your own family…

Afterbursts

During the Second World War counterattack, we had such a tough time…I'll tell you something funny: the dead can't complain, but for those who were severely injured—neither dead or alive—it was hard. I still remember fighting at Laifeng Mountain, an old comrade, my classmate, he was injured…One day during a rest I said I'd go check on him. [When] I saw him, his tongue was broken, his teeth had been knocked out…When he spoke, it wasn't clear. The nurse came to feed him some rice. That porridge had to get to his throat before he could swallow it. It made me cry. I tell you, if he had died I expect I wouldn't have cried, but this being half dead and half alive made me weep.

Zhang died in 2018.

Although defeat seemed inevitable even by late 1944, Japan continued to send troops overseas right up to its surrender. **Shigeo Matsumoto** *was one of many sent to China as his country's leadership became increasingly concerned that Russia would open a new front there after Germany's capitulation.*

He was a diminutive individual, considerably shorter than my 5' 3" and slight in build, but sharply turned out in a suit, long coat and shiny black patent shoes. He had come armed with papers, sketches and maps depicting his service and as he relived the traumas of those days, kindergarten music played incongruously in the venue where we met.

I was born in the regional city of Fukushima. I lived there until I enlisted in the military…February 25, 1945. With this notice, I was simply transferred to Manchuria. My older sister came out to see me off and she said, "Please come back. Promise me!"

I then went to Manchuria without anyone knowing…Our troops were sent to the most dangerous area. We were ordered to kill ourselves if the Russians arrived. I got this hand-written material from the Defence Ministry. It says: "Government military order."

I had no idea where I was being sent…In Osaka, I asked about four or five officers where we were being taken: to the south or to Taiwan. I thought something was fishy. I became friendly with one officer, and he—who was a rowdy man—secretly revealed to me that

To Survive was a Disgrace

Shigeo Matsumoto in 2018

we were being sent to Manchuria. I was shocked. I was the only one who knew about it…He said I could not tell the others.

We were told to change from our school uniforms or plain clothes into ragged old military uniforms at the Higashi District municipal office in Osaka. I wanted to find some way to notify Fukushima that I was being sent to Manchuria. We were all taken to the rooftop of the municipal office, locked up there, and monitored by the military officers on our attitude or any fishy behaviour.

I found myself wanting to go to the bathroom. I locked the door, got changed and ripped off the lining of my inner pocket to insert a letter I wrote the day before…The first person who received the clothes I sent back home was my elder sister.

I went to Hakata, which is a port town, and then to Korea. It took one night by ship, but with the US submarines, the sea was closed off. We were given life jackets.

Our soldiers were from three prefectures: Fukushima, Niigata, Miyagi…The volunteer corps were continuously sent to Manchuria between January and August 15, up until we lost the war...It took two weeks to get there, by ship and train. We closed the blinds inside the train, not to be seen from the outside—we were in the dark for two weeks. The train did not stop.

This is Botankou [Mudanjiang], where the main regiment was stationed in Manchuria, and it was obvious that the Soviets would come and invade the area. We tried to build a major shield there to hold a strong position. One hundred and fifty thousand Soviet troops actually entered the area. Against that, the number of Japanese troops working to build a position was just one-tenth...The Russians came in with tanks...

The order to fight until death was already given out in January ['45], but ordinary soldiers didn't know about this. For example, Officer Murakami was the one who sent my death notice—he still lives in Tokyo. They were like dictators. It was almost as though if you didn't die from war, it meant you didn't carry out your responsibility, so of 15,000 Japanese soldiers, only 1,200 survived in the end...There were other commanders who committed suicide [on] August 14 in Azukiyama...It was insane.

I finally understood that Japan had surrendered on January 1 the following year [1946]. I didn't know. Only a few people had survived—and these people's task was to die, in accordance with the order of fighting till death rather than surrendering. So what were we to do? In such circumstances it was impossible to give any new orders since soldiers were scattered everywhere...

A local family who was very kind to the soldiers in Manchuria was all killed and we kept silent about it and retreated south. If they were alive, the Russians would come and ask the family where the Japanese went...

This child [was especially kind to us]. We became very close to each other in the mountains. He brought us water, even though he had to carry it from very far. He was scared of us and didn't talk much at first, but after I patted his shoulder, there was a time he smiled at me, just once...The boy is still entwined in my memory, even today. I

To Survive was a Disgrace

cannot forget him. He was maybe fourth to fifth grade in elementary school…

They didn't do anything wrong. Nothing. What's more, they were cooperative. We killed them all without even thanking them. The man who carried this out died without ever speaking about it. He said he would not clarify if killing them was either right or wrong, he just kept it all vague.

The commander of our unit did it. Our unit had about 20-30 soldiers left and they were wandering, waiting for orders. The unit commander was exhausted from a lack of sleep, he could no longer function both mentally and physically and wasn't able to give out any orders.

After this, we tried to escape from Manchuria to North Korea. We travelled south and all got separated. I saw a small child always following us, hiding behind a large tree, but never approaching us. The small boy was an illusion, he was always watching me…

For the Manchurians, as soon as the Japanese military arrived, they were at war, and when the Soviets arrived there was shooting and fighting. It's horrible. I must say that what Japan did was horrible…I worked for my country—no matter what anyone said, I worked for Japan…I was also an invader…

But even though I became a person of distinguished service, I survived. I returned to Japan. That's unimaginable. We were told to die, and to survive was a disgrace…But I was also a victim of my country. I became a person of distinguished service, and a placard was erected in front of my house—but these were all removed after the war. But now, I'd like that to be acknowledged again. The nation made such fools out of people.

Chapter 14

A Bomb Dropped on My House

Nuclear resolution

Towards the end of the war, Japan was running out of men to conscript. Students, previously exempted, and fathers over 40 were called up. While the official draft age had been 20 at the start of the war, it was later reduced to 19 and by 1944 the country was training boys and girls as young as 15 to fight or provide support.

Even younger school children were used for duties such as demolition to create firebreaks between the wooden houses, cultivating small vegetable plots and delivering public announcements. I heard how classmates played "rock, paper, scissors" to determine which part of the class went into the residential areas and which went to the outskirts to weed fields. On the days the bombs dropped on Hiroshima and Nagasaki this random game determined who died and who survived.

The impact that the explosions had on Hiroshima and Nagasaki is hard to visualise, even when you have visited them. These days they have been rebuilt into bustling and vibrant cities with few physical reminders of the devastation. As I listened to survivors tell their stories at the Hiroshima Peace Park commemoration on the 73rd anniversary of the bomb, it also struck me that the few photographs of the aftermath I had seen had been relatively sanitised. Most were images of a flattened, grey wasteland with the odd remnant of a building protruding from the otherwise featureless landscape.

Rarely, they might show a person or two walking across the grey plains. Only when I visited the Hiroshima Peace Museum did I see victims captured in the immediate aftermath by photographers who had steeled themselves to record people's suffering.

Corpses, however, are the main feature of a survivor's testimony. Corpses so numerous that the living who walked among them became numbed to feeling. Meiko Kurihara entered Hiroshima in the days after the blast trying to find her father, a doctor at the local hospital. As she picked her way around the bodies, it was the carbonised corpse of a baby that broke through her emotional stupor. When she recounted this experience to me more than 70 years later, she still wept.

She told me that she eventually reached the hospital but found it impossible to identify her father, neither among the piles of charred remains in the hospital grounds nor among the living victims whose skin hung from their fingernails "like gloves" peeling off.

Teruko Sasaki was raised by her mother's childless sister not far from Hiroshima. We happened to meet on her birthday, which fell in late August not long after the Hiroshima bomb anniversary, and she recounted her youth over cake at her kitchen table.

I attended nursing school during the war, but it was a peaceful time, at least within Hiroshima city. There was no talk of war…My cousin went to the battlefront, or I heard he was enlisted, when I was working at the hospital. I remember he sent me photos…

When I was at home, I remember soldiers who were promoted and everyone seeing them off together by waving the rising-sun flag and national flag. We would sing songs to give them strength.

I worked as a nurse in hospital in the morning and went to school in the afternoon. I then took a national exam to become a midwife

A Bomb Dropped on My House

Teruko Sasaki on her birthday in 2018

at an ob-gyn hospital within Hiroshima. In April [1945], I was told by the director of the hospital that since I had to look after my parents, I could not die in Hiroshima city. (Americans were dropping bombs and there were enemy planes every day flying over the skies in Hiroshima. The bombings [elsewhere in Japan][30] were becoming very severe.)

After returning home, Teruko was deployed to build a runway.

We all walked four kilometres while carrying soil to an area on the outskirts of Kabe. A group from my village in Mibu town were staying in a facility and at this residence located in the outskirts, on the morning of August 6, I was squatting down in front of a beautiful stream that ran in the area to wash my face. I then saw a flash of light, similar to how it looks when you point a mirror towards the sun.

As I saw the flash of light three times, I thought the children living across from us were just fooling around. But then I realised there

---

[30] Hiroshima was not bombed by conventional bombs, hence its selection as a target for the A-bomb as the effects of the latter could be more clearly assessed.

were no children in the area and just brushed it off. Then at around noontime, I saw a truck loaded with many injured people, their faces covered in blood.

No one knew what an atomic bomb sounded like, so they were saying Hiroshima was destroyed by a bomb…I heard rumours that Hiroshima city was totally destroyed, so I returned to my hometown. Up until then, I was busy carrying soil to the mountains to build an airport. How foolish…

On the day after the A-bomb was dropped, nurses, public health nurses, midwives and doctors gathered and boarded a truck. There were also teams nearby made up of medical staff from Yae town, Minamigata, and Kurazako…Nobody ordered us to go, we all agreed to go together…

We were dropped off just before Yokogawa bridge. We walked across the bridge. As we walked along the edge of the river, we saw dead horses. Have you ever seen how a frog's stomach looks while floating in the water? Humans were floating like this…

We walked while witnessing this landscape. We walked to Eba Elementary School, as the injured were being transferred there. They were all laid down along the Eba line tracks. I nursed these injured people. I was told not to give them water, but they were asking for it. I think people died after I gave them water since they were severely injured and on the verge of dying…I had only worked as a midwife in a hospital up until then and had never treated people with severe injuries…

At dawn, I headed towards Fukuya department store and Kangyo bank where the injured were being transported…Even though we had gone to give the people medical care, we had no idea what to bring. Since the people were suffering from burns, [we used] merbromin for disinfection and baby powder to dry up the wounds… That's the only medicine we had. The government wouldn't send anything else. This was a first experience for everyone.

After the A-bomb…I remember noticing not ashes, but maggots…There were huge maggots feeding on living human beings.

You would find tonnes of maggots underneath a layer of skin, and the patients were all suffering, saying how itchy they were…People's backs were filled with them…

The maggots thrived because there were flies—maybe there were flies, but I didn't see them. I probably just don't remember. It's similar to when flies immediately gather on raw fish…It must've been a few days after the people suffered the burns.

Of course, we removed the maggots—I can't remember what I removed them with—and then dressed the wound with merbromin solution and baby powder. We were the only people who removed the maggots from the injured. It smelt so bad that I wore a mask. But even though I folded a gauze and wore a mask, it still smelt really bad…like rotten human flesh…It was really terrible.

Hiromi Hasai *was a 14-year-old schoolboy when the bomb dropped on Hiroshima. From his home in Hakushima in northeast Hiroshima he had been deployed to Hatsukaichi, a waterfront town about 15k west of Hiroshima.*

In the beginning, there were people who walked from Hiroshima. The first batch of people came in queues and I wondered why so many people were walking here on a Monday. When I asked, everyone said a bomb dropped on their house…their own house. But I thought it was strange since there were no airplanes…If a bomb is dropped, it would [only] affect an area across several metres.

It was past noon [when] the injured began arriving in trucks. At the time, I didn't know what had happened in Hiroshima. I just really remember being scared. The doctors told me since the people would struggle, I should hold them down tightly on both sides—but strangely enough, no one cried out in pain…According to a doctor I recently spoke to, the nerves which are right under the skin must have melted away.

The local factory became an infirmary to treat people's burns. It was shocking. I was told to help people off the trucks since they couldn't walk. I remember how scared I was…Seeing such burns for the first time…Human beings usually notice each other's faces.

Their faces were swollen up and black from dirt and blood. Their faces had melted in areas that were exposed. They were pleading for water throughout the night. The next day, they were all dead…We were told not to give water…Back then, it was accepted wisdom, but today's medicine advises people to drink water. So Japan was behind in medical science…

I found out in the evening that Hakushima was in a dire situation…The skies in Hiroshima were flaming red. It was burning all evening. I had never seen such a fire before…While many people remember clearly what they did the next day after the bombing, I don't remember that well, but what I remember is how everything was so different, I couldn't decipher the roads…I think the train ran up to Inokuchi, and I walked [home] from there. I finally saw houses at Koi station, but there was nothing left on the other side of the residential area. It was then that I realised Hiroshima had been attacked…

My mother and sister survived in Hakushima. My sister was four years old, but she was playing outside with a five-year-old girl. The girl told my sister to go get her doll, so my sister went inside the house with her shoes on. It was then that the bomb was dropped, so my sister didn't get burned…The girl she was playing with outside at the time, who asked her to go get the doll, died instantaneously from burns. The next day, she [my sister] saw her friend's mother and father holding their dead daughter in their arms…

We had a big second house in Hakushima which somehow managed to survive the bombing, so our neighbours all gathered and began living there. It must have been 10-20 [people]. The house was made out of wood, but the fire didn't reach our house because of the huge garden. We put up a mosquito net and the sick were placed inside. Those who were healthy stayed outside. They were waiting, believing their children or families would return from the ruins of the fire.

My sister was there [in Hakushima] the whole time. She came down with stomach cancer when she was 40 and had surgery. She recovered, but developed pleural cancer again at 50. The doctor said it was a different type of cancer, that the initial cancer hadn't metastasised. She was developing multiple cancers from the side effects of radiation. She died at 50.

My mother had been doing the laundry, and the rooftop of the laundromat kept her from exposure to the light from the A-bomb. She didn't develop cancer…

Yesterday, I went to see a facility which exhibits the war from the side of the perpetrator…In Hiroshima, people usually talk from the perspective of A-bomb victims…I want junior high school students to think seriously not just about Hiroshima being attacked, but about whether the actions taken back then were correct.

Back then, it was all about how many enemy generals you killed. That was the highest achievement…It was all about how many planes you shot down. Education [during the war] taught us that this was correct…[Our] military drills involved using rifles, how to polish them—real ones of course. And we were taught how to swim with a rifle, without making the rifle wet. That's what they taught us—and to die for the Emperor, to not fear death…We thought it would save the country.

Such an era has ended…but even now, there are wars which involve receiving rewards for beheading someone, or people becoming heroes for killing many people. Brutality continues. Does humankind have any wisdom?

Hiromi later became a nuclear scientist and, in the 1980s, he returned to Hiroshima to measure the residual radiation levels in the few remaining structures that had survived the blast. When the atomic bombs were dropped, he said, the effect of radiation on the people had not really been considered as much as destruction of infrastructure and people from the blast. His team's finding that even small amounts of radiation were extremely damaging to life contributed to an international decision not to proliferate neutron bombs—high-radiation weapons which can kill people but leave infrastructure intact. He died in 2020.

Afterbursts

From Hiroshima I travelled a day's journey to Matsue to meet **Yoshio Hara**, *taking a bus through countryside so lush it gave me some small understanding of the Japanese passion for their homeland.*

A dapper man in his early 90s, Yoshio met my interpreter and me at the railway station dressed in tweed trousers and a flat cap and driving a classic car. Welcoming us into his home—a privilege quite unusual for my Japanese interviews, which were mostly conducted in public places—he gave us tea in a reception room overlooking the beautifully sculpted garden which he still tended himself.

Steeling himself to relive his A-bomb experience, he told us how, aged 18, he had been drafted as an emergency soldier.

It's what I most don't enjoy talking about…Even when I talk about it now, my heart suddenly feels tight. Activities designed to keep stories alive are painful—it is not something you can talk about with a smile on your face, it is painful. So to what extent should you talk about the truth? There are facets that everyone cannot talk about. There are some things I still cannot talk about now…

Four days before the atomic bombing, I became an emergency draftee [and] I arrived near Hiroshima…Up until then, I was a mobilised student working at a military factory, making shell cases for shooting down planes. They were 77 millimetres, but the B-29s were too high, and the bullets could not reach that high…

Most were usually drafted at 20, but from 1945, 18-year-olds were also drafted. Before being drafted at 18, I was prepared to die… What I heard was that the US Allied forces had occupied Okinawa and now were coming to fight on the mainland. There were airplanes in the sky, and tanks on land…I was a *koheitai*[31], so we had no weapons. I later found out that we were needed to dig holes and jump into them with a grenade [under enemy tanks]. I had no idea. I had just begun training…

This is the draft order when entering the military—not mine, but a copy of someone else's. In Japan it's called an *akagami*…just this simple paper. At the time, they referred to this as the *issengorin*

---
[31] Emergency draftee

A Bomb Dropped on My House

Yoshio Hara in 2018 and as a young soldier

no inochi [32]. If you receive this, it's equivalent to death. People who received this believed it's ok to die. Children today say they cannot imagine, no matter how hard they try--that it's *not* okay to die…

The 114 troop in Hiroshima was based about 4.4 kilometres from Gion. There was an air raid alarm and I heard some type of noise, but it was dismissed and I heard some noise receding. The air raid alarm then changed to an alert warning, and we could no longer hear the sound of the airplanes flying.

The next moment there was a flash, then afterwards there was a blast, as sound travels more slowly—it sounded like *paaan*, not *dooon* to me, like the sky had burst. It was an enormous sound and an intense light. As you can see at the *shiryokan* [archives centre], the ball of light was six thousand degrees, and on land it was about three to four thousand degrees across about 1.5 kilometres.

I was four kilometres from the epicentre. We weren't directly hit and saw the light from a distance. I was in the auditorium, so I survived—our unit had the least number of casualties.

---

[32] A penny postcard of life, i.e. the value placed on a draftee's life

Afterbursts

On the first day I evacuated to Ota River. I saw many injured people there, and many people arrived and the shore filled with people before my eyes…These people looked at us soldiers—as you could immediately recognise us from our uniforms—they begged us to give them water. They also asked for bandages, but we couldn't do anything for them. We didn't have anything. We were totally powerless…as we were ordered not do anything or say anything, nor to respond. They [our officers] told us to neglect them.

It is still painful when I think of this now. I couldn't do anything.

The mushroom cloud eventually faded and at around 11am "black rain" fell, so everyone became drenched in this. This rain contained large amounts of radiation. The soldiers also got wet—when I think of it now, that substance was so dangerous, although we had no idea…

The rain that fell from above was more grey than black. It fell several times…Up until then the B-29s had been carrying out air raids, but that evening everything was in flames just with that single bomb. Just with one bomb! Why? I couldn't understand what had happened. I had never heard of such a bomb.

On the third day, I was somehow chosen by a senior officer to visit headquarters to receive an order…but the headquarters were also destroyed. The castle was destroyed. The trains had been blown away.

Then on the fourth day, I went out to the city for the first time… We had to build roads, and there were corpses all over the place which had to be disposed of. We were the first unit assigned to this. It was the second hell—the first hell was at the Ota River, but this was a real living hell…What we had to do was horrifying, it was inhuman. We had to become machines in order to do our job, like human robots—if we had maintained our humanity, we wouldn't have been able to work. We could not have any feeling of pity…

We gathered the bodies, put them on the truck, and burned them. There were trees in the middle of Hiroshima, so we loaded them, stacked them, put gasoline on them and burned them. Day after day. The smell of this—the entire city of Hiroshima smelled of this, Hiroshima was in flames because of this. Day in and day out. This is how it was on land…

In the Ota River, there were many corpses floating and there were wooden boats that gathered bodies using a hook. The bodies float with the current, so they gathered them, the naked bodies…

I still cannot talk about what really happened—the reality of it… Not even today. I don't think I will ever be able to talk about everything. It's impossible…Not until I die. That is war. War on the battlefront is different. The A-bomb was even worse.

[M]e and three other 18-year-old students—the four of us—since there were no stretchers, we used wooden screens to carry the corpses. We held all four corners and we carried them to the Ota River. We began this work from the fourth day after the bombing, so the corpses had rotted considerably. Their eyes were open, and when we raised them with the screens onto the truck, their bodily fluid would gush out. Our uniforms would become soaked with this. There were no face-masks, so we would cover our faces with towels, but it was too hot, so we just worked without the towels. But the fluid would spurt out, so the soldiers would wash their towels in the river during their break and hang them to dry.

But even so…there was a moment in which [our] humanity was reawakened, even though this is a small thing…Most men became soldiers, so it was old people, women and children, those were the only corpses…Among those bodies, we found a mother who was protecting her child. She was charred while her child was half burnt… Through it all, seeing that mother and child—I saw several of them, I don't remember how many—but…they probably died holding their child in their arms…

For some reason the bodies that were charred were ok, but the ones that were half burnt, they fell apart…The children broke apart. When raising them onto the screen, we tried to raise them so they wouldn't become separated. We did this carefully. Very carefully, without throwing them inside the truck. So we placed the screen on the truck, and carefully placed them inside—that mother and child—even though we were given orders. We were not able to handle them as an ordinary corpse...Other than this, everything else was totally inhuman.

Keiko Ogura's *family had lived in central Hiroshima up until a year before the A-bomb was dropped. Like many other inhabitants, her father felt it was strange that Hiroshima, a military industrial centre, had so far been spared American fire-bombing raids. He knew it could not last and so he moved his family to a suburb.*

On 6 August 1945, a strange premonition compelled him to instruct his daughter not to go to school, a decision that saved her life. In the aftermath of the bomb, her father spent days carrying corpses for cremation. As one of the more able-bodied men in the area, he was always given the heavier torso to carry, looking into the faces of the dead.

During the war I was a little girl but always the teacher says how fearful Americans and the British people were. As a child what my teacher explained was so funny: that Americans, they have tall noses. In Japan, there is a creature, Tenggu—red cheeks, blonde hair and blue eyes...They are like that, but cruel. So, to be good girls, not to be taken away by such cruel people. And they teach us just to endure in case Japan will be conquered or surrender. My brother heard: all children will be killed by stationed army that will come and will kill...

I was eight years old and stayed in Hiroshima, but one of my elder brothers, he was 11. So, nine to approximately 12, those elementary school children had to evacuate into the hillside and he stayed in the temple with around 50 other students—one group, one temple.

Then when Hiroshima was destroyed, they were not told anything and they did not know what happened. But...there were letters—somebody died, the father died the mother died and so on—and the teacher kept them, because the teacher did not know how to tell the children. There were so many—around 48 out of 50 lost some of their family members...

The priest, instead, reported what happened in Hiroshima... The children were sitting down on the floor of the temple and the

A Bomb Dropped on My House

Buddhist priest opened the main door—it's rare to see the main image of Buddha. "What can you see behind Buddha?"

And the children couldn't understand. "What?"

"Behind Buddha: your parents, your sister, your brothers—that are already in heaven."

That was the 15th of August.

And then the teacher delivered the envelopes she got and…the children read. "Oh, my father died, my sister died," and so on.

The children started to cry, all of the children—48. Only two children [were spared]—and one was my brother…He felt ashamed that he didn't lose anybody and that his classmates and children were crying…*I need water to put in my eyes* he thought—to try to cry, imitate.

So…the teacher didn't know what to say…It was so difficult.

Like the bomb—*bang!*—the priest said it. And then what made the children more fearful was *We'll be killed.*

So that day, when they heard what had happened in Hiroshima, they ran away from the temple—escaped—around midnight. My brother told me that they put all their belongings on their heads… and they tried to hide in the hillside, because first they thought *we'll be killed. There is no one who will protect us…*

That's education. "We have to survive—the only way is to get victory." Teachers repeatedly told this to children.

And I remember, during the war, food became shorter and shorter and then it was difficult to get something to eat around the end of the war. And so because of that, what teachers told us was, "Chew…at least one hundred times…"

There is a bowl, a very small portion…you could eat it in only two seconds. Then the teacher just said, "Put that in your mouth and chew." Your hands on your waist, like this, and *one, two, three, four…*

We wanted to eat, but no: "Open your mouth", to check you still have it…It's so miserable, but every day was like that…

And almost every day, we children at night go around "*Hinomi ti gana*"—watch out for your fire, like, five or six [in] one group. And like a *kabuki*...there are two wooden small blocks that make a sound. And we say a slogan—*clack! clack!*—and then we walk saying, "It's okay to kick American and British people. Even though you kick America and England, don't kick the *kotatsu*"—the brazier. Put a stone over it...Sometimes we had a fire [break out in the neighbourhood] and the fire was caused [by] *kotatsu* charcoal...

I was shocked the first time I saw Australian soldiers stationed near Hiroshima. At that time, after the war, I was asked, "Don't you hate Americans?"

But actually, before we hated the American enemy, we needed to find something to eat...What we did is to visit farmers in the suburb places. And we brought our valuables—like kimono and watch and something—to trade. And then the rice was severely controlled, so in the train, policemen...checking whether you have rice or not. If rice was found, that was taken away. Immediately. And then we saw that the women were saying, "This is for my baby. Without eating rice then the milk doesn't come out." Something like that. But the rice was taken.

My mother said, "You are children. They believe children, I think. So why don't you hide [the food]?"

I put some rice or something underneath my sweater...I was so scared...Maybe vegetables were ok but rice was prohibited. The policeman walked by me but he didn't check my sweater, under my clothes.

And then I saw the black market for the first time. After the war. That was so impressive. Always after the war everywhere was so dark, but it was so bright. They have a kind of oil for some light. And I was surprised—there was everything! So many foods! Food Japanese brought in and food from the American base from Yuakuni. And those GIs sold their food—canned food and so on. So many things.

My father bought one. Ten thousand yen for one can that was for soldiers' refreshment—some sweets. My father brought and [we were all] so curious! Open the can…and there: jellybeans and cookies and pretzel-like things…Nowadays Y500 or something…Anyway, we are happy, but father seems so disappointed spending so much money…

But the first time I saw an Australian soldier I was shocked because he was so handsome and quite different from what my teacher told me. I was so afraid and scared, but he was so handsome—*Not so bad!* I thought.

And then with him there was a girl and she had a permanent wave. And until that time, during the war, we did not wear [bright] clothes, [just] blue and dark blue and so on. And she was wearing red and some beautiful design with a skirt—we were wearing until that time *monpei* [work trousers]—and she was holding the soldier's arm.

At that time, I was a child and did not know what that girl meant—later I found out, but at that time I did not know. "Oh, so beautiful. The beautiful soldier!"

And then I was not so scared. But we were told during the war all the girls will be raped…Father was so afraid of that. And my sister and I had to move to the mountainside. Between the borderline of Hiroshima prefecture and Shimane prefecture…

I thought *I am so small!* I was eight, not at all grown up. But if you were cute, you were also in danger. My sister and I stayed I don't know how many days until father said the city will be settled down… That was a very strange experience.

Under the American occupation, Keiko went to work in an orphanage where she looked after some of the abandoned babies that resulted from foreign soldiers' liaisons with prostitutes, a job she greatly enjoyed.

Years later she met her husband, Seattle-born Kaoru Ogura, when she was giving an interview as a hibakusha, an A-bomb victim. He became the director of the Hiroshima Peace Museum and after his death in 1979 she took on his work. She founded Hiroshima Interpreters for Peace, which guides visitors around the Hiroshima Peace Park, and frequently talks about her A-bomb experiences both at home and abroad.

Afterbursts

Retrained from logistics to be a pilot, **Nobuo Okimatsu** *was directly saved by the A-bombs, although this fact was hard for him to reconcile.*

In the year the war ended, in May 1945, I was appointed to the Special Attack Corps [*kamikaze* team]…The training lasted until the end of July and I was to be on the Okinawa mission in August…

When I was told to be a suicide pilot, I felt as though I had been pushed off a high cliff. I think I must have gone pale. I couldn't sleep that night…I sent [my family] a letter, but I did not mention *kamikaze* because they would have been grief-stricken.

Human beings have complex feelings. Of course, I felt pride, but I didn't have confidence in being a pilot. For example, I had 1.0 [vision], not so good…you must be able to swiftly search and find… and you have to be able to hold your breath for three minutes. Pilots have such stamina. It's essential during air battles, which impose a major physical burden. Pilots can see the stars during the daytime— stars actually glimmer during the day and pilots can see this. Only superhumans like that can manage to survive air battles. And the airplanes were not good—the Type-100 heavy bombers were developed four years prior to the war, so I didn't have any confidence that I would make it to Okinawa…

I was prepared to face the end of my life in July: at 3pm on August 15, I was to be in Kumagaya Airport to fly to Kumamoto Airport… But on August 14, one day before, there was a sudden cancellation. At 12pm on August 14, the Emperor made an announcement.

When I listened to that, I realised I had been saved…[Still, I was sad when the war ended]. It's complicated…Firstly, I felt my life was spared, but I also felt sad and sorry that so many people had to die. I broke down in tears. My mother often said that my older brother died for me, so my feelings towards the A-bomb are very complicated…

When the A-bomb was dropped, my mother, who was in Kure at the time, saw a flash of light. A little after that, she said she heard a loud noise. People used to refer to it as "*pika-don*[33]", that's what

---

[33] *pika* for flash and then the sound "*don!*"

A Bomb Dropped on My House

Nobuo Okimatsu in 2018

they called it. The light was visible even from Kure City, 30 kilometres away…My brother who died in the A-bomb was 31. He had quit his job and was at home and just happened to be out in Hiroshima. I don't know where he died. My mother went out to search for his body every day.

SECTION TWO

Children in War

Chapter 15

Our Greatest Treasure

Bearing arms

Many children found themselves directly engaged in the war—in fact, several of those whom I count among the soldiers that I met might today be considered still children. Of the young who stayed at home, as battles engulfed their villages many joined the fighting, making unimaginable sacrifices for their country. In Russia, the "labour army" included children who worked in factories or grew food for the troops, often going hungry themselves.

Leonid Rogal *had watched from his bedroom window the first fires as the Germans invaded Belorussia. He joined the partisans—the Soviet Resistance—aged just 16, a natural progression from the military drills he had undertaken at school.*

I'm from Byelorussia…I still miss it, even though I've been living in Moscow for 60 years. I was born near Rechytsa town, the one on the Dnieper—lovely town.

My first face-to-face with the Germans was when they occupied Rechytsa district. Our soldiers were retreating. Some of the [school] graduates left with the Red Army—the ones who were more fit—and some joined the self-defence group later, the partisan detachment.

Afterbursts

Leonid Rogal in 2019

We were still in the self-defence group, and the school's supply manager—a local resident—and I were on a reconnaissance mission. We arrived—and right at that time, the Germans arrived…Eight people, in full uniform. They were well equipped, they came to the village, left their bikes next to one of the houses, went inside the house and settled themselves in.

The women met them, of course, with bread and salt, and we showed up. Our local people were saying, "Why are you here? Germans are right here, look! Go away!" We managed to get through to the Germans. They were drinking milk, they were given honey… They were peaceful…They were sharing cigarettes…It seemed: Germans, here they are, regular people. After that reconnaissance, [military] units came, also, without any battles or fights…And the impression was that they were not really that cruel.

After those field units, new masters came to establish a new order. Gestapo…and after they occupied Rechytsa, there were anti-tank trenches dug out around Rechytsa, and they started to bring Jews to those trenches and execute them there…Just in our Rechytsa, they executed 2,500 Jews…

Our Greatest Treasure

They invited former prisoners who became their aides, policemen. There was a former dispossessed landowner called Shishov. His house was in the village, a very decent house, and my father's cousin Pinchuk Anton Nikolaevich, with five kids and his wife, had been given that house to live in by the kolkhoz [state-run farm collective] management. Shishov became the head and started following the orders of the Gestapo and German commanders. So, we contacted the partisan detachment once it had formed. They came late at night, took him outside the village, to the cemetery, and executed him.

The Germans arrived the next day...took Pinchuk for having a connection with the partisans. The five kids were executed together with him and his wife. Only his oldest son managed to survive... People were saying that one old man said that he saw from his window how the three-year old boy was running away to the pine tree forest there...A German killed him anyway.

Nikita Siniuk became the new head of the village and again began to collect produce and transport it to the German garrison...Lard, meat, milk, sour cream—everything they could, including schnapps, moonshine. And people were putting up with it. But when Siniuk started walking from house to house saying "Your son will need to present himself and will be sent to Germany for labour", we again reached out to partisans. And they executed him too...

[I joined the partisans in] the spring of '42, and in the summer of '42...my first combat...There was a cart and one policeman and three Germans. The cart was loaded with produce that they were taking away from the villagers. Our unit was checking the perimeter of our camp and we followed them and killed them all.

The Germans, because we killed their soldiers, summoned airplanes, weapons...Started bombing the forest where we had dugout houses. Started searching through nearby forests—but they didn't go in too deep. They were afraid. But they shot at and bombed us three times. They destroyed our entire partisan camp.

They became especially cruel when there was preparation for the Battle of Stalingrad, and during the battle itself. There was a directive to strengthen partisan resistance in the rear and there was a "railway war". We had groups formed which would go to the railroad and blow up rails and train cars.

I was a part of one of those groups…We would start the mission late at night. Two TNT explosive devices and a grenade, just in case. We weren't given anything else—and we wouldn't take anything either, because we had to get over the 200-metre zone cleared from the forest, the so-called exclusion zone between the forest and the railroad. We needed to crawl across it at night.

We picked the nights that were dark, rainy, cold, because there were German patrols all the time. We needed to crawl, lay the explosives, cover with soil and crawl 200 metres back…We would wait for a blast. If an explosion happened, then everything was ok…

Yeah, it was scary, but what could we do?

We had local messengers everywhere, trusted people. My first love was also a messenger, she was in Rechytsa. We had been friends since the 3rd grade…Her parents, in '41—literally, both father and mother—died. They had heart issues. She became an orphan. Her elder brother was in the Red Army and I suggested to my parents to take Zina in. We lived in the partisan zone, in the forest.

Three Slovaks were brought to her to be transitioned to our partisan detachment. The day before, a pal of mine and I went to Rechytsa for messages…I can't forgive myself to this day…We exchanged the messages and left and next day she was taking those Slovaks to the detachment and got ambushed. They were all executed. They were not allowed to be buried for two days…

Later we of course came with a cart and we buried them in a mass grave [bed of honour]. Here she is, Zina. I got this [her name tattooed across my knuckles] when I was in the 4th grade—the first one. And then, I think, in the 6th grade [another one].

My cousin, Volodia, was a messenger and messengers told us a German train was to arrive that was bringing everything to reinforce the fascists. [The partisans] took over that train with outfits, food… seized the station.

Our Greatest Treasure

Time passed, and Volodia was walking through his village... and there was a German patrol walking through the village—policemen and Germans—and a policeman recognised him and told the Germans that he was a partisan. They caught him, [took him] to the Gestapo in Rechytsa. Four days...And he was executed in those anti-tank trenches. This how my cousin died: behind the walls of the Gestapo, tortured...

That's why, for me, Germans are sitting in here, [on my heart]. Generations change. I see Germany as a developed country. The new generation has traces of Nazism, but here [on my heart], there is a German sitting. I can't...I can't...Even though I have nothing against Germany now.

Leonid died on 27 January 2022.

On the other side of Belarus, young **Nina Danilkovich** *also did not hesitate to become a partisan. Above a smart cream blazer trimmed with red and adorned with medals, her eyes brimmed alternately with girlish pride and tears as she told me how, aged 12, she had come to be one of Russia's youngest partisan operatives.*

Within a week, [the Germans] started occupying all the territory and then there were executions...A whole family was buried alive... That's why, of course, the resistance movement began...There were executions for absolutely no reason.

For example, they had already captured Red Army soldiers and they were walked along the highway. We were standing there in Ivatsevichy and one of those captured asked some people for a spoon. "I have nothing. If people around me are eating I will be able to get some food from a pot next to me." Our good friend, Milianchik Ivan quickly brought a spoon for him. Right there, he [Ivan] was executed...

My parents knew that we needed to fight, to do everything to expel the fascists. They didn't force us—and they didn't tell us [my sisters and I]...But we noticed that, at night, Papa is going somewhere, Mama, brother...

So, one time, I followed my brother. He climbed into the barn's attic. So when he wasn't home, I put up the ladder, climbed up there, hid in the hay and waited for him to come…And finally I hear him putting up the ladder and coming inside. Then I hear some metal something…And it turned out he was cleaning a gun. "Why aren't you sharing this with us?"

This is when we told our parents that we, too, would help. And that was actually needed. When the railroad was repaired and [the Germans] started occupying all the territory, there was an order that anyone of 15 years and older had to receive an official permit to go to a neighbouring village. And we didn't need it: school age. That's why our age was worth gold…I hadn't turned 12 yet when I joined…In any case, there were very complicated tasks. Every time it was very serious, very dangerous.

The Germans started cutting back all forests within a 100-metre distance from the railroad, sometimes 200. Trains with troops and machines were going one after another, with literally a 10-metre gap. At night, the movement would stop and in our segment every Thursday—I remember like it was yesterday—a train would "go downhill"…We would dig underneath the rails, camouflage it, the train would be at high speed and there—*bam!*—downhill…My parents did that.

That's why the Germans built guard posts to protect the railroad and there was a guard every 100 metres. We learned about it as our village was close by. German soldiers would come to our house sometimes asking for milk, or because it was too cold. At first, we didn't know why they got cold and they told us that they were guarding the railroad.

Some of them spoke Polish and we all knew the Polish language—and my mama, during World War One, was 14 and did forced labour. She was smart and picked up the German language, so when the Germans spoke very slowly, she understood. And they liked it that a village woman from deep outback who almost lived in the forest understood German, and they talked willingly…So, we were the first ones to learn, and passed on information to our acquaintances in the unit that they needed to be careful…

Our Greatest Treasure

At the railway there was a structure...oval in shape, small windows. The guards were sitting there and shooting around from time to time when they felt like it. Once—we lived close by—he shot around like that with an automated rifle and a bullet scratched the skin from my sister's neck.

We needed to learn how many Germans could be in there and how many machine gun points there were...We had a lot of eggs, and we bought more to take as gifts to the Germans. My mum put the eggs in a basket and we, all three sisters, took turns in going where was needed.

It was my turn. My mama gave me a white handkerchief, basket, and I left. I'm waving the white handkerchief and shouting in Polish, "Jajki[34], jajki". They understand—of course, it's good for them.

I come closer, put down the basket, say, "Present."

He said, "Leave the basket and *geh weg*..."

I told him that I needed the basket, so that I could bring more. They say ok, go there. I approach, there was a cook, round space, little windows...And my task was to report back on everything I saw.

Once...a revolver needed to be passed over, but at every crossroads there were always guards—either Germans, or *polizeis*—and they would frisk everyone. If you have a hairdo, you would even need to let your hair loose...

Our parents knew everything! In Belarus, we had a farm. We sowed flax, there were sheep. We spun threads, made fabric...Mama rolled a big ball of thread around it, so we carried a big ball of thread. Our task was not to let a single German or *polizei* hold the basket, because its weight would give us away. Every second someone could have taken it.

To be on the safe side, we took a very big basket and there was just one thread ball. And 12 kilometres one way, and 12 kilometres back—if we stay alive...If not, then the "black raven[35]" comes for our parents right away.

---

[34] Eggs
[35] Death squads

Afterbursts

So, we went, three sisters...Three of us carried it through, passed all the check points...We had an apron with embroidery—we didn't have much at the time—and we covered the thread ball with that apron...Two of us would carry the basket, as it was heavy, but when we approached the guards at the check points, just one of us had to carry it and pretend it was light.

Every time we approached, we would show the basket right away so that they could see that we just carried a thread ball, nothing else. [Our story was] that we were going to see our aunt who lived at such and such an address and we gave her last name. That's it, and pass through. And the next check point same thing, and the one after that.

And on the last one—I remember like it was yesterday—Ivatsevichy, a small hill, green grass, we're happy that it's the last check point and we passed. I looked: no apron. That was our greatest treasure. I ran back right away. I'm miming [to the checkpoint guards]: the wind blew off the apron, showing the ball again, rolling it back and forth...[I had to go back and fetch it]. We didn't have anything else beautiful but that...

The scariest thing [during the war] was to see the area where the family was buried alive. The second thing was when my younger sister got killed...When my younger sister ran into the forest to pick some berries—wild strawberries—and said "I will be back soon" and she was found dead, all beaten up and with a stab wound in her heart...

Local boys who were walking in the forest found her. They came to our house and said, "Your Larochka is there—murdered." We were suspected, but they couldn't catch us in action, of helping Red Army soldiers...And the rumour was that she didn't give anyone away.

Some could not recall their childhood service with similar pride. Childish idealism met the stark realities of war for a group of Okinawan schoolgirls known as the Himeyuri. Willing conscripts, they were sent into makeshift cave hospitals where they comforted dying (and often abusive) soldiers and held down the injured for amputations without painkillers.

Our Greatest Treasure

Many of the girls had taken their schoolbooks, pens and trinkets with them into the caves, thinking they would continue their studies for a short period until they returned home victorious.

Yoshiko Shimabukuro *was among the 240 students and teachers who were mobilised. Just 104 of them survived the Battle of Okinawa. She met me at the museum she and her fellow survivors had founded, a memorial which depicted the most personal and moving accounts of the war that I came across.*

I was 17 years old when the US naval gunfire started…I was educated on how to wrap bandages and how to help the nurses… Those staying in the school boarding house were mobilised to the Haebaru military hospital as the *Himeyuri* student corps. Those staying at home did not join the *Himeyuri* student corps—but there were people who came afterwards…those who volunteered of their own accord for the country.

When the Okinawa landing operation began and the naval gunfire started, we thought we would be returning to school within a week to voices thanking and celebrating us…since we thought we'd win the war. We had no concern and we were all saying out loud, "Beat them! beat them!"

So we all went with the feeling that we were fighting for our country—we had no thought that our friends would die, or that we would get injured…

When I was on the battlefield, not many of my friends died during my time in Haebaru. During that time, I saw people who had their stomachs blown up, who lost their arms in the battlefield, people being transported, dying without being treated.

I gradually realised [we were losing] when seeing hundreds of soldiers being moved. Even so, the male students came and told us they shot down and sunk enemy battleships—these were lies following military instructions, but I thought that we were always winning. I believed the reinforcements would come and the war would be over soon. I thought we had to retreat [only] because the enemy was in Shuri…I still believed we would win. But if we were captured by the enemy, we were told that girls would be stripped and killed, raped—we were told they were devils.

After I found out we couldn't die by biting our tongues, I was very anxious. I asked the soldiers for a grenade. They didn't have many, only one for themselves and one for attack—just two…We pleaded: if we were captured by the enemy, how do you think we can die without a grenade?

You can die in an instant if you're shot in the head or chest, but you won't die if you lose a leg. So when we were ordered to search for water or food, we would first pray to God in front of the entrance, to let us die an instant death. I wasn't afraid of dying, I was more afraid of being injured and being in pain or being captured by the enemy and being stripped and killed…

If I had had a grenade, I might have used it. But I didn't have one—and I never killed a US soldier. It was only after the war ended that I realised how nice the enemy was.

As well as the 136 who died caring for the soldiers, a further 91 students and teachers from the Himeyuri schools lost their lives during the Battle. Many were killed by the bombardments, while others died of wounds or by their own hands. The youngest were 15 years old.

In the Soviet Union, too, school aged youths were mobilised by the state to support the front, joining women to work the fields vacated by the fighting men. It was a tough job, with limited fertile land available for cultivation and little to spare for those not in combat. **Ivan Kozikov** *was just a teenager when he was sent to work with this "labour army".*

From day one, when the war was announced, we had a demonstration in the village where everyone was saying we would win.

"The war is temporary; we'll be back soon." That's what the men were saying.

They did come back—after four years. But at the time we had thought we would defeat Hitler very quickly. There was massive faith in victory. Massive. We didn't even for a second think that Germany could win…

Our Greatest Treasure

Ivan Kozikov in 2019

I started working when I was 14 years old. Young men were stepping in for adult men, just like women were stepping in for men—and young women weren't just stepping in for adult men, they were more likely to become mechanics…They would drive tractors, harvesters…while young men and adult women took over physically hard jobs. In agriculture, 70% of the labour force was women: I'm scything, and a woman is scything next to me.

Of course, that was a period of fairly hard living. I was constantly sleep-deprived because of the workload—during summers and winters. Why? Because agriculture demands seasonal work. That's why you cannot say, "This I'll do today, and that tomorrow." It has to be done today and only today. There's a proverb for agricultural work: "A spring day feeds [an entire winter]". If you miss this one day, you won't have a harvest. This is a proverb, but it's true.

In January, we tend the cattle. Prepare firewood. Prepare the fields for spring. Then the spring comes. What do we do? Ploughing. Sowing seeds…All that needed to be organised. Some people were in charge of ploughs, others were working on seed sowing machines, some in assistant roles.

Next step is, when some plants start growing, we have other tasks...Fodder preparation for winter—in June. Fodder is essential. Scything. In August, we harvest. Everything that's linked to that. In September—preparation work for future harvest. Again, ploughing, preparation...and, of course, taking care of the cattle that is already switching from summer to winter fodder.

Year after year, we do this work...Sometimes, there was nothing to eat: we sent everything to the frontline. Especially in May and June...because the produce that had been prepared in the autumn was used up by then. All over the country we weren't working all the land, only part of it, and we needed to supply the army, supply the city...In the rear, there was no one but us.

We made attempts to sign up for the frontline. They didn't take us. They said, "No. You are needed here" and that's how it worked out. Later there was even a so-called "shield"—it delayed military service because there was demand for work in the rear, too—and that was the right thing to do, because someone had to supply the frontline. Not just with food, there was a need for clothes, weapons...

Some of my peers left for work at an industrial plant, and they also worked, on machines, delivering multiples of the required quotas... and sometimes [they were only] yay high, while the machines were all the way up to here. So they used steps to reach all the machine gears and do the work...

For the work in the rear, 10 million people were decorated— and 300,000 people with a Medal for Valiant Labour—in the Great Patriotic War. I also have medals like that...Of course, not everyone who worked in the rear got a medal. There were production quotas that had to be met.

While other children clamoured to be involved, **Peter Gafgens**'s *mother was doing all she could to keep him out of the fighting. In Germany, boys as young as eight were required to enlist in the "Jungvolk", Hitler's substitute for the forbidden Boy Scouts, with transition to the more martial Hitlerjugend after two years.*

Our Greatest Treasure

In fifth class, a guy came selecting…to look at the grades, to look at the faces for Aryan people, and he came to our class, and my teacher was Latschinger, and Latschinger had a son in my class and when the visit was over my mother received a letter.

"During the selection your son was being elected to go to a Ordensburg[36]." Signed by Latschinger.

And my mother went to the school and talked to Latschinger. And after that talk she went back home and wrote a letter that she doesn't accept that her son was being sent to a Orden school, because in our family jobs are available which help to rebuild Germany…

I was off the list. And later on she told me she had asked Latschinger, "Why did your son not go to that school?"

So Latschinger said, "Because I knew what was going on at that school."

She got me off the hook two times more…The other time was when I had finished the mandatory Jungvolk—you had to put on a uniform and you had to march, you had to sing, you had to listen and so on…And after I had finished the Jungvolk, you had to go to Hitlerjugend [Hitler Youth], which is the next stage. And my mother didn't want me to go to the Hitler Youth, because of obvious reasons, and she went to the Kommandatura…and she said, "I have a convocation of my son to go to the Hitlerjugend, but….he's a very much an introverted guy and he loves music."

And the guy said, "Well, it's fantastic. We have a lack of people going into the music corps…First step is flute, because we are lacking flute people."

So he sent me to the flute lady and I went for at least two months. And then the flute lady called my mother and said, "The guy has no talent at all. He will never learn to play the flute and I don't know why

---

[36] Schools established by the National Socialist Party to educate youth to be soldiers.

they sent him to me, but…Hide him on Saturday afternoons…and I will continue [to mark] his presence in the flute lessons and get the money."

And my mother says, "It's a deal!"

So from that moment on I couldn't play on Saturday in the streets anymore…One year! Then the flute lesson stuff was finished and apparently she [the flute teacher] sent the report to the Kommandatura that the guy is not the right type to play the flute in the music corps. So…where do we send the guy now? Into the normal Hitlerjugend?

So my mother thought up something…First of all, she dressed miserably. She told me, "When you go to see these guys, don't put on makeup. Put a scarf over your head…Never look attractive."

And the guy said, "Well, now…he has to go to the normal Hitlerjugend service." And after, when you're 16 or 17, they use you in the army [to carry] the flag [or] they have used these children to shoot the planes.

And my mother says, "I need my only son at home. He does the garden, vegetables." Those days, in order to get meat, you raised rabbits—"He is in charge of the rabbits…My husband fights in Africa. I think I do my duty. Is there something which my son could do where he would not be too much involved?"

And he said, "Oh, yeah. Does he like horses?"

And she said, "Well, my husband rode every morning before he went to work. Our family is used to horses."

He said, "Okay. We have a lack in the horse squadron for the Hitlerjugend, and he can go there. After one year, we will see."

And it was the crucial year. So Gafgen got boots, which were difficult to get…I remember they were too big, but silver boots…and I was off the hook again. So I never joined the Hitlerjugend, thanks to my mother.

[Otherwise], I would have suffered like my [half]-brother…He had to do the Hitlerjugend and from the Hitlerjugend immediately he was enlisted and suffered in Italy. And then was sent from Italy into Bastogne, because the Americans were attacking Bastogne and it was the last effort the Germans made to prevent the Allies to go over the Rhine. So, in his Italian uniform, for summer climate, he was sent in a cattle wagon with all his troops, into the Bulge to fight there…in the trenches, in the snow, in the frost and…his body was so much damaged for the rest of his life that he died very early from that exposure.

He was against the system, and every time he came on leave to visit us he was so unhappy and he thought the whole thing was absolutely crazy. Still, he went—he had to.

Chapter 16

Why Weren't You In the Resistance?

Under occupation

Even when directly engaged in the war effort, occupation presented great hardship. Food was scarce—especially in the cities—and even limited forms of resistance frequently elicited harsh reprisals.

After the initial bombardment of Rotterdam, **Max van der Schalk's** *family returned home, where they stayed through the war.*

The early years everything was really rather normal, except my father didn't go to work anymore. And there were lots of soldiers in the street…marching…singing German songs…

There were quite regularly what were called *"razzias"* [round ups]…And the street was completely blocked off…and a combination of German soldiers and Dutch policemen went into every house to check whether there were any sort of fugitives. And later on… every male older than 40 was picked up and had to go to Germany to man the factories—because all the other men in Germany were fighting…

In '44 or so, there was curfew: after 8 o'clock you're not allowed outdoors any more. So we often played with neighbours. We had all gardens that were connected, so it was quite a pleasant time. But also funny things happened.

For instance, next to us lived a judge who was a "normal" Dutch judge, but he was married to a hundred per cent Jewish girl. And so the children had the Judas star on their coats…And I remember that in the war suddenly a cousin of those children, about the same age, came in. And she had been sent out from a Jewish concentration camp in the Netherlands and I was told that I shouldn't talk about it, that I should pretend that she was a very normal girl, who always lived there.

So I was well aware of the "Jewish problem". We knew that all the Jews were picked up, that they were sent and they went to a camp, and they wouldn't come back…But we were all told that these were sort of work camps…I mean…men between 18 and 40 had to go to Germany to work as well…That was part of being totally unfree. But all exterminated? No. I didn't know that they were all…all killed.

That last winter, the winter of '44/45, was called the "Hongerwinter"—the hunger winter—in Holland, and to eat there was very little food left. We also were eating sugar beets…boiled… In the end of the war I was hungry, really, the whole day. But we were glad that we survived. We had an allotment, rather far out, and there we grew potatoes.

But it was tricky, because if you took the potatoes home and a soldier or a policeman saw you, they would confiscate them. So we did that in the evening after 8 o'clock, so in the curfew time. And that was very tricky because if you were caught then—well, my father might have gone to jail.

And we had a sort of four-wheel cart…and that we filled up with potatoes and my brother and I sat on top of the potatoes and my mother with my sister pulled the cart. And my father on his bicycle was number one and if we would be stopped it was just, "No no, there's nothing. There's just two boys in there."

It was a scary sort of undertaking, and once we were home I remember how happy we were when we had these potatoes…for a luxury.

Why Weren't You In the Resistance?

We had those clandestine newspapers...They had beautiful names like *Vrij Nederland*—Free Netherlands, and *Oranje Boven*—Orange Up, and *Vrij Volk*—Free Population. And my sister—she was over 16—was asked whether she would serve as a courier for that. So that also was work after 8 o'clock and my parents were very concerned about it, but my sister wanted to do that.

It was a bit dangerous. But on the other hand, we lived in an area where people had generally front gardens, so if somebody would come, she would dive under a bush.

I think the main point was that the Germans took away the freedom...There was the curfew, and then all the stories about if you were taken in a German prison, how you were tortured...and the Resistance stories—there were friends of my father who were picked up because they were betrayed, often. But often not on purpose, but by somebody who was tortured until they told the names of the people they worked with.

Later on...when I was a student, I heard from all sorts of friends of mine in the university what their fathers or brothers had done in the Resistance. I went to my father and said, "Why weren't you in the Resistance?"

Because I...I would have loved to be proud of him and be able to tell them, "Oh my father did all sorts of attacks on distribution offices and liberated people," and I couldn't.

And I asked my father and he said, "Well, my main purpose in life was to survive—not only me, but your mother, and the three of you...I was asked many times to come and join and I didn't want to do that because that would possibly jeopardise the well-being of my family. So I counted my family first." And I suppose that many people did that...

We were liberated by Canadians and they were followed by Australians[37]...and we thought it was fantastic to have those people

---

[37] He did mention Australians, although I could find no reference to Australians being in Holland for the liberation or afterwards.

there, parading and so nice. And they came in jeeps and I remember I was allowed to sit in a jeep for a while, with five children or so and—Oh! it was enormous. It was the day of my life...

Just before the liberation we got air dumps of food. White bread out of Sweden and margarine and, Oh! Peanut butter! And toothpaste! Oh, it was fantastic. And I was at the time eight years old and I was in the boy scouts, and the police asked all the boy scouts or other clubs with uniforms to help to guard the food that was dumped so that it wouldn't be stolen by everybody, but that it would be collected and divided.

Oh, I never have eaten such a delight as that white bread with margarine on it, and peanut butter. Wow! It was fantastic.

[There were repercussions for some after the war]. And the first ones of course were the girls who were girlfriends of Germans. And you probably heard the stories that their heads were shaved completely, and I saw that. I didn't understand it at all. My mother explained that they went out with the Germans...and they went to nightclubs...and these Dutch girls got presents from them...And that's why everybody got angry: because the Germans were our enemy and you shouldn't do that with them.

But my mother was very indignant about that...She thought it was very undignified that their hair would be cut. And also, she found it very...primitive. Because there was a whole group of people. The girl was tied down to a chair and then a number of guys with razors would cut her hair—and sometimes cut a bit in her head as well and so she often was bleeding a bit...And everybody was shouting and singing...

I remember I had in my class two boys who were children of NSB—National Socialistic Party—and the fathers were of course in the camps. And my mother said, "You should be normal to these boys, because they can't help it."

And my father said, "Yes, be normal to the boys—but don't bring them in the house here."

I found it difficult to understand, so I didn't mix with them. It was only later that one of them became a good friend of mine…So the children of those people also suffered.

Max died on 1 July 2019.

Across Europe, food scarcity was a constant issue. **Maria Anthopoulos** *was the youngest of six children born to Greek parents. Her grandfather had been in shipping and her father and mother had lived in Charleston in the US, where her three oldest brothers were born. (All three served the US in the war, and all three came home). They had moved back to Greece by the time Maria was born.*

After the war, Maria moved to the US to study at Temple University and married. We met in the Pennsylvania house her architect husband had designed for them, styled on a Greek courtyard around an enclosed fountain.

I was born in Greece, November 18th, 1926. I'm quite advanced! I lived a very healthy life—even though I lived during the war. There was no food. Maybe that did it!

Maria Anthopoulos in 2018

I was born in Patras—it's a little city outside of Athens—and then my parents, after a couple of years, they had an opportunity to move to Athens. So that's where I spent most of my childhood and I lived during the war…It was quiet…We were young. Just play, go to school, back at home.

And then, during the war, the Germans came in Athens. They were very strict. You were afraid so much of the Germans. They had no pity for anybody. If they grabbed you—oh!

But the Italians were different, their personality, very different. They would get to the roof of where they stayed, it was an old school, and they would get their guitars and start singing. That was such a pleasure to hear them. On the other hand, if you see the Germans, you didn't know where to hide. They had no pity for anybody. So that makes a difference: the people, where they grow up…They are influenced by their culture, definitely, and they behave accordingly…You would see a German and you would start shaking—and the Italians would go and get the guitar and start singing every night. And many girls married Italians…

Yeah, and then the same time the government had a dictator at the time, but he thought if Greece joins the war, it would be a help to the world. There were sirens going *wooo woo*. And then it would stop and it would go *wooooo* straight. So through the radio they explained that when it goes *woo, woo* it means the Germans, the planes, were coming to Greece, and that we should hide ourselves.

The neighbours, then, said, "Hide where?"

It was a man that was in the army and he says, "I think if we build underground something so we can hide, maybe we can avoid the bombs." And…the older people started organising and building.

But then: no food! We got starvation time…And my mother used to put us in bed not to move around so we can't spend our energy. But a child cannot stay [still]! But it was a winter that came…and it was very difficult. People will come and knock on the door and say, "I am hungry!" Now, if you lived in suburban area where the people can cultivate…But in Athens, nothing. Nothing.

Why Weren't You In the Resistance?

And I had a friend...and her father owned a bakery, and he would bring home bread for the family and I had a girlfriend there, the same age, she would cut from her own portion and bring it to me, a little piece like that. Now that I will never, never forget. It was superhuman.

And she would come there and I said, "Now what am I going to do? There are four persons in the family." So we crack it and divide it.

This we still remember now, my friend [and I], you know. She's in Greece, and we say, "Do you remember that time?"

Yeah, it was...It was very difficult. Very difficult. And then people were coming in the streets and they will go, "I'm hungry!" What could you do?

The only thing the government—I mean, the government was under the Germans—tried to do [was] to feed the children something, but they brought some kind of bread from South Africa. They were delivering it to the children—just a little piece, you put it in your mouth. With all the hunger that you had you would spit it out…

Now…it was the first of the year 1942, and a woman comes, knocks on the door, and my mother had put us in bed so we don't use any energy and said, "Don't move." And [the woman] knocks and she brings a big package, with food. My mother says, "This is food! What about you?"

"Oh, my brother was with the services in Africa…"

So, at any rate, she brought some food. It was delicious! We couldn't believe it. We were eating, we were sharing. My mother started crying and thanking the woman, the brother…But I never forget this, that the woman—her brother sent her something, but she shared it. Now that shows some kind of a quality person…

We had to be in in a certain time period. And one time…I went to the house of my aunt…Somehow, they had more food. The father was working somewhere and they were bringing food, and they used to give me.

So I went there and then on the way back I was walking and then a young man comes and he says, "You have to follow me and go in that house."

I said, "How can I do that, to follow you?"

He says, "The Germans are blocking. You won't be alive very soon."

So somebody—a family—had opened their house and they were welcoming the people from the street to come so the Germans wouldn't get them. It was a fear. So I stayed there about two, three hours…The Germans blocked this particular neighbourhood…The Greek young people had joined together how to protect the other Greeks. This was a well-to-do family; they offered tea to the other Greeks that were there.

So when they gave a signal that the Germans left, said, "You can go home" and I start running, running.

My mother was waiting at the door.

I said, "I'm safe!"

Oh! She started crying, "Oh, you are alive!"

It was no telephone or anything that I can tell her that the Germans blocked the neighbourhood. They were very hard. Very hard people.

Maria died on 24 January 2022.

Viktor Shkadov, *a striking, tall man with head of thick steel-grey hair, was a youthful 84 when we met at the Moscow State University. One of the number of veterans assembled by Nina Danilkovich, he, too, was still supervising students in the Mechanics and Mathematics faculty, of which he had been a member since its first class in 1953.*

As a six-year-old, Viktor had watched his house burn down when the Germans entered his village. His father had been captured at the outset of the war and was conscripted immediately after his release from a concentration camp. The war years were a terrible ordeal for the family the patriarch had left behind and as Viktor relived them his voice occasionally faltered with emotion.

The occupation lasted exactly two years…It was a horrible time for me…Little person. Hunger, cold.

Relatives helped. They would give shelter. But there was no bread. My mother cooked food out of grass and some leftover grains…It

Why Weren't You In the Resistance?

Viktor Shkadov in 2019

was a horrible time—but our mother saved us. All four kids stayed alive...

In winter of '41-42, the German forces were trying to take over Moscow and took big losses: cold, resistance of our military, many wounded. They needed blood for their hospital[s], for the wounded. A big covered truck came to the village and took the boys, only boys, from five to 12, 13 years old. They loaded the truck and took them away as blood donors.

That was a horrible fascist invention. Child donors...[Those] children were kept in decent, good conditions, fed, and were regularly taken for blood collection. People were saying that a child could donate blood three to four times, then they quietly died...Then they were thrown away. If needed, all the blood could be collected in the first attempt and a little person died...

Later, there was a concentration camp, not too far from my village, for child donors. But in my case, apparently, God said "Let him live." And my sister had heard about these measures by the Germans, she hid me at our relatives' house. It was by chance...Later, throughout my life, I kept thinking if that was God's will, I too must do something for people. Something good...

When the Germans had come to our village, in October '41, it so happened that my elder sister was sick. Cold. She was lying in bed. Germans came and asked whether she was a partisan.

My mother said, "No, no, she is sick."

They got her up, took her into the street, put her to the wall, took a machine gun and said, "She is a partisan. Shoot her."

Neighbours came, women from neighbouring houses, started saying, "No, no, she is not a partisan, she is just sick."

And he [the commander] gestured not to execute. Any minute he could have executed her. And, later, she saved me—that was the sister who hid me, when the children donors were taken away.

Based in the Belgian countryside, **Georges Hubaille**'s *family was less concerned with food. His father was a doctor serving the local area. A prominent figure with access to one of the few civilian cars, he was suspected of aiding the Resistance and so the family had frequent encounters with the local Gestapo.*

Their village, Tellin, was liberated by British paratroopers, and among his mementos from the war he showed me a Christmas card that had been sent to his sister by one of the British parachutists with whom she had kept in touch for some years: "I remember—vividly— the long night before the advance on Bure when your father allowed my platoon to rest in your lounge whilst your mother and one of my sergeants played the piano and you and Georges sat on my knees—a civilised break in a rotten war."

Perhaps stemming from his fascination with the bodies of two dead German soldiers, frozen in the cold winter of 1944, and with his father's work, Georges later pursued a career in medicine. We met where he had retired on the outskirts of Brussels.

One day there were some people who came to find [my grandmother] and said to her, "Madame, we are from Antwerp. Is your house empty and would you agree to let it out?"

Why Weren't You In the Resistance?

Georges Hubaille in 2018

There were two couples, one childless couple and one couple who had a small son who was one year older than me. They were Jews.

And my grandmother said, "Yes."

We knew very well that they were Jewish. And they lived there very discreetly—although the little boy went to school.

And one day, the Gestapo arrived.

My grandmother's house was in the main square, and the minute they arrived in the main square everyone dispersed. And at that moment the mother came out. They were in a cafe. They were surrounded. And when they got to the house, they noticed that there was a woman missing. The woman of the couple that had no children.

[The next day] around 3 o'clock in the morning, someone rang at our door. It was the Germans, and the Gestapo. And they yelled, "Open up right now!"

Everyone got up…And I remember it was really like they describe: leather coat, cap. And then I remember that they said to me, "Go to bed, little chap," and then they said, "Where is she, the woman?"

My grandmother was staying with us. Upstairs there was another room with no one in it, and they ran their hands through the bed to see whether the bed was warm.

And at the time we had a daily cleaner who lived in residence. And then they shut us in a room, and said to her—she knew very well that they were Jewish, obviously…"What's going on? Tell us the truth. If you don't tell us the truth, you're coming with us, with all the family."

So she said, "I'm not in the loop. I don't know anything." She played the idiot very well…

My grandmother had made a contract, and one of the Jews had hidden the papers. And they found them. And they said, "Yes, madam, you made a contract."

And she said, "But if I were hiding Jews, I wouldn't have a contract!" That is the element on which everything collapsed.

But if they had said to me, "And you, my boy, you know there are Jews at your grandmother's?" I would have said, "Oh yes, sir!" I was about five and a half.

And the next day there was a truck, with—in front—the father of the little boy. In the back of the truck there was the other man, and then in a normal car there was the mother and the little boy.

And my mother had said to the German officer—not the Gestapo—"Sir, please leave little Roger with us."

And he said, "Madame, we don't separate a child from its mother."

They were…they were deported to Malines, and they were sent on to Auschwitz.

In the final months of the war the family became caught in the middle of the skirmishing between the British and Germans during the Battle of the Bulge. The Allies had advanced through Belgium from the Normandy landings but were unable to press the advantage. The Germans returned just a few months later as Hitler made an attempt to push back and take the port of Antwerp. Throughout it all, Georges' father was still treating his patients in the neighbourhood.

Why Weren't You In the Resistance?

During the von Rundstedt offensive we were very much at the edge of the advance of the German forces—three kilometres away from them—and I was just about to turn seven.

First, we were liberated by the Americans and then afterwards... the 24th December [1944], the Germans arrived in Bure. [That winter] it was very cold and there was an enormous amount of snow. We stayed in the house the whole time.

The Germans simply went past on patrol...They came in the evenings...and I remember that one could hear the tanks passing. And one had to close the windows. Me, I wanted to see them, but I remember my father said to me "Stay quiet..." and I could hear them going, *brrrrrrr...*

When the English arrived, the parachutists, they also had armoured tanks.

They sent an armoured tank onto the road...toward Bure. And there, there was a forest. And my father...he was the only one who had a car...he said to the English, "Watch out. [The Germans] are there..."

We gave them coffee and so on—and my mother took [the tank driver] a cup of coffee and she said, "Aren't you getting out?" and he said, "No madam, I can't, I have to stay at my post".

And they left, the tank and a jeep...

I remember that dad was watching with the binoculars of an officer and at some point there was an explosion...And they had fired at the tank, they had hit it...and they had also fired on the jeep. And then the tank caught fire, the team came out but the driver—he stayed inside. So my mother had given him his last cup of coffee...

At our house we had 45 parachutists [and] my sister said to me when they went out they said they were going "on patrol"—but, no, they were going to fight. And when they came back, my sister said to me she counted them back in. And one could see who was missing.

After the fighting at Bure they had to leave. They were very, very unhappy…They said they had fought; they were exhausted…And then on the day of their departure they were about to go, and then someone said, "We're not going!"

Oh! Cries of joy! Songs! My mother sat herself down at the piano and played *A Long Way to Tipperary*. They were so happy that they were staying on.

They stayed another 24 hours. And then on the day of their departure they said their goodbyes again and thank you and so on. They had to run to get in the last truck…

In Tellin there was a school for girls, with nuns. There were three nuns and there was one who was pro-Nazi, pro-Germany. And she was killed, randomly.

The priest of the village parish, announced that at the Sunday mass "Sister So and So was killed during a bombardment," he said, "and she was killed by her friends."

In all truth, he said that…

Chapter 17

Je Suis Mort!

In the crossfire

*When I met him, **Jean-Pierre Offergeld** still lived in the valley where he was born in 1931 and where his German ancestors had arrived to set up a trading business several generations before. He was an elfin man just slightly older than my father, who came with me to our meeting, and his kindly face frequently crumpled into tears as he relived the traumatic final months of the war.*

He had just turned teenager when his village got caught in the crossfire between the Germans and the Allies. Only 30 kilometres from the German border in northeast Belgium, the territory had often changed hands, with the final occupation spanning Christmas of 1944 as Hitler made a last-ditch effort to re-capture Antwerp.

He told me his story in French, occasionally breaking into English as he recollected his encounters with soldiers.

On the 16 December the Germans arrived…They came to our house. They installed themselves there. Three came at first…They shouted out [*in English*]: "No Tommies here?"

My mother shouted out, "We are civilians, here in the basement. There are no soldiers."

Afterbursts

Jean-Pierre Offergeld outside his childhood home in 2017

They came down and they were three Germans—dressed as Americans, but they had nails in the soles of their shoes. The Americans never had hobnailed boots, they had very soft-soled shoes. One never heard them marching…So even before they appeared we had been saying to each other, "They aren't Americans, those are nails!"

And then the Germans all arrived and occupied the house and they fought all Christmas night long to take the barracks back…

We were sheltering in the basement. They brought into the basement a German officer who was wounded. They made him sit. They chased my grandfather out of his chair—he had an armchair, he was 73—my mother cleaned and treated the wound and when morning came the soldiers came to fetch the officer and took him away and the officer said, "Good luck." And on [the armchair] there was a cushion, and on top of the cushion he had put a grenade which was almost unpinned and if he had moved just a little, it would have come out and we all would have been killed. My father took the thing and exploded it in the garden.

Je Suis Mort!

And then life had to adapt to the Germans again. There was nothing to eat. There was one baker who continued to make bread, and one farm a bit further away where they continued to tend their cows and get milk. The fourth child, my little sister Francoise, had been born a few months before in June. She was six to seven months when all this happened. She needed to be fed with a baby bottle with sugar and milk.

My father had had to hide because the Germans were looking for everyone in the Resistance to kill them…I was the oldest so my mother told me, "It's up to you to go and get the bread and the milk."

So I set off for the baker, and there were bombardments, so I knew where to take shelter on the way. And to go and fetch the milk, which was a bit further, the same…

On one occasion…I went to fetch bread. The Americans, to hold off the Germans, had put the parachutists—it was the 82nd division—there in their foxholes. I came back with my bread and there was a big American there in a hole…It was cold…He saw me with my bread and asked for a piece. And I said to myself, "I'll give him the bread."

I went back to the baker and luckily there was still some bread left. I came back with a loaf and passed not far from him and he indicated *I'm thirsty and cold…*

I took him with me, back to the house, and on the cooker my mother had made some soup, a big casserole. And we gave him some and he went back…As he left, he hugged everyone. He hugged my mother, saying, in English, "I would not like my mother to be in your position right now," because he knew what was coming. And then he left…

That's how we lived.

The priest of Vielsalm came to find us in the basement and gave us absolution. He forgave our sins: "If you die…you have been absolved…"

Occasionally there was a bit of sunshine, but it was very, very cold. And the Americans, when there was a bit of sun, went to bomb the Germans next to St Vith…a small village 20 kilometres from here which was razed to the ground. And then one day we were in the garden, my brother and sisters and I…we'd made a slide in the snow. I saw the planes turn above Vielsalm and then I saw bright spots which came out of the planes—and I said to the children, "They're bombs!"

We threw ourselves into the basement. And they bombed Vielsalm…And then things were very bad in Vielsalm…the Germans said, "No one is allowed to live in this area, you all have to leave."

My mother and father spoke a bit of German and explained that there was a baby and the old people: my grandfather and great uncle and my great aunt, all over 70 years old, and it wasn't possible. There was snow; it was very cold.

Nothing could be done; we had to leave. We left on foot. My mother pushed the baby carriage and I pulled a little cart too. The Germans pushed us towards the east…all of this under bombardment…

We passed two villages with no room for us…At the third village, 20 kilometres away, a farmer welcomed us and installed us with some others, and we lived at the farm for several days with some Germans, who cooked with us—and we slept on the ground. Everything had been bombed…

Then the lieutenant-major of the Germans, the boss, moved into the farm and said, "Scram, civilians…"

My grandfather and my uncle went looking in the village and they found a farm which would have taken us, but there were too many of us. So we stayed in the basement and slept on a pile of potatoes…

My little sister, we fed her snow, melted—there was no more milk left—and into that my mother put sugar from a packet she had taken. We didn't know how to change her so she was one big sore…It was appalling…

At some point I said to my father—we were in the basement and the Germans were upstairs—and I said to my father, "I'm hungry."

"So go and have a look," he said.

I went up the stairs and in the farm kitchen all the Germans were sitting around. The farmer was sick and he was lying down, and there

Je Suis Mort!

was a ham bone on the kitchen table. There wasn't much left on it. I said—[*he gestures, as though toward the ham bone*]—to a German and he said, "Sure," and he put me on his knees and I ate.

At that moment, into the corner, dropped a shell…They were killed all around me—the farmer, the Germans…all had turned blue, black. I had a small piece of shrapnel in my hand but it was nothing, really. I threw myself down the stairs into the basement yelling, "Get out of the way! Je suis mort! [I'm dead]"…All the people laughed.

Then maybe a day passed…and the Germans said, "We need the cellar—you have to get out."

And they chased us out and we crawled, because the Americans were firing—it was passing over our heads…And after we had gone about two or three hundred metres we came across a shelter in which was a German with a machine gun, looking out for the Americans so that he could shoot them.

He saw us and felt sorry for us and made us come in. My father had gone looking for the cart and the sleds in the burning farm, and he brought them…And the German and my father cried. They fell into each other's arms…and the German cried, "The madness! The madness of war!" [*He weeps*].

We couldn't stay there. We continued, crawling, and we arrived at a farm which was still standing and there we asked the farmer whether we could go in. There were a lot of us, and the farmer said, "No—there's no room left."

There was a manure pile with a little roof over it. And my father said, "On the manure it won't be cold. We'll all go and lie down, one against the other on the manure, and wait."

And wait for what? It was night. We prayed…We thought we were going to die…And then at some point my mother called out [*in English*]: "Women, children here!"

The Americans had arrived…all dressed in white. They had bed sheets on them so that they couldn't be seen in the snow. The Americans took us. They opened the door of the farm and pushed me in first, with my brother—and there in the farm were 70 Germans, who raised their hands.

They surrendered. If they had resisted, we would have been wiped out...But that was normal on the part of the Americans...they were protecting themselves, too, no?

When the Americans invaded the Ryukyu Islands **Zenichi Yoshimine**, *too, was a young teenager. He met me at the Okinawa archives in a dark room where I was watching documentary footage of the Battle of Okinawa and its aftermath. After the reels finished, he shared his own experience in halting English.*

I was twelve years old when Okinawa began. At that time the government told us to leave for mainland Japan because maybe, after, Okinawa would be a battle place. So we are trying to go to the mainland, but we couldn't go, because after five or six boats left and arrived in Japan's mainland, the last one was sunk—the *Tsushima Maru*. After that, we had no transportation...

We lived in a cave near Shuri Castle and [then] moved south because the Japanese soldiers said, "Beasts are coming. Get out."

Zenichi Yoshimine in 2018

Je Suis Mort!

That's why we left…"*Kichiku beiei. Kichiku* [Americans and British are demons]." They told us again and again…[the Americans] would cut our eyes, noses…and then kill us by war tank—but part of that is true. In Mabuni, war tanks went over the bodies…But war makes humans crazy…

I think we left around end of April 1945…The three of us were very, very lucky that no one was killed, because only 13 people remained alive from over 60 [of our village]…Around six before dark, we just get out from caves and look for food, water—but American ships saw that, they came and killed everybody…They attacked from sea, land and air…Beyond Mabuni is all ocean, no place to go. That's why the people were all killed there. I was surrounded by bodies, all over.

He pulled out some photocopies.

You've never seen this…"Jap-hunting license"…Americans, issue this kind of license? Never…

They dropped this [information leaflet]…about eight million pieces, all over…This means United States makes war according to international law. That's not true: they killed everybody.

They made an announcement around the 20th June: "Finished. War finished, just come out." But [the people] never go out [from the caves where they were hiding]. You know why they didn't go out? Wrong education: They are not human beings. They are beasts, monsters…We didn't know any Americans at that time, so we didn't know…We never go out. That's why American people killed everybody…mostly with fire [flame throwers].

Maybe 23rd or 24th [June] Japanese soldiers made an announcement: "War finished. And American soldiers never kill you—just come out. We'll give you water and food."

Still, no one went out. Our area was all dead bodies. Still this Japanese soldier says, "Please go out before dark, otherwise they will use gasoline and burn this area."

That's why we went out. We saw many people burned and killed…so we don't want to die that way…

Somebody called, "Come over, come over here."

So we thought the Japanese soldiers were trying to save us. So, go out and another soldier picked me up—with big, big hands…I looked up and found it was an American soldier and they were smiling. At that time, I didn't think I would live, but we could not get away. I thought we would all be killed.

On the top of the hill the soldier said, "Wait here." I found about 15 or 18 people there all wounded, with bandages. So finally, I thought, "So many people, alive!"

The young soldier brought water and put it in a cup. He drank first and I thought it was safe, so I drank it. At that time—water! Aaaah, that taste!

So that young soldier brought a little bit of canned food and sat in front of me and opened it. The smell—it smelled like heaven! I forgot everything…My mother said, "It's poisoned." He picked up a spoon and gave me some.

Ooh, that taste…I've eaten famous food—escargot in Paris—it never tasted like that. That canned food tasted like heaven…Then he brought cake, chocolate.

We all ate, because we hadn't eaten anything for about three or four days—no drink, no water…So we ate everything. Then, in front of me, the mountainside was all bodies.

Zenichi died 12 May 2021

Choho Zukeran *came from a long line of Okinawans. His ancestors had been involved in trading with China for the Ryukyu kingdom, but a couple of centuries back they had been demoted and moved from Shuri, where the castle was located, to the countryside to farm. We met in the village where he had been born in 1932, the 13th generation of his family to live in the area.*

As he told me his story, Choho followed a map of his family's flight across southern Okinawa between May and June 1945.

Around 1944, Japanese soldiers forced all the students out of the schools, even in the countryside…School classes were hardly held. The students were mobilised instead to help build caves for the

Japanese military. We dug caves every day. I was about 12 to 13 years old. Men would dig using shovels and picks while women had bowls for transporting...

In 1945, the situation became increasingly severe. All young people over 16 years old were mostly summoned to serve as young soldiers, and students were called to serve in the "iron-blood" army.

I dug caves. The younger students in first to third grade couldn't dig caves so they were in charge of digging [trenches]. This area is comprised of [limestone] so while it's easy to dig, the caves would easily collapse, so to prevent them from collapsing, we would cut down Ryukyu pine trees and make a frame. The younger students were in charge of shaving tree bark.

There were eight soldiers deployed in my home. During the daytime we would receive imperial education, help the military, and at night, we would return to the farm to dig potatoes and do weeding.

I had 12 siblings...Since the sanitary conditions were poor, five of my siblings died under five years old. During the war, four of us lived together, including me and my mother, my younger brother and one older sister.

My father died in 1945...He fell ill after being tortured by the Japanese military...My father was the first person in this area to graduate from school, so he was able to read books and write. That's why he was held, under suspicion that he might have books about socialism or may be involved in spy activities...But my father was an earnest farmer, so he fell into a depression, and he left our world. He was 49 years old...

On March 31, 1945, the US air raids began...We spent most of our time in the caves. They called it the iron storm. You can't survive unless you're in the caves—if you walked outside, you wouldn't last even five minutes. On May 23, a Japanese soldier came and told us to leave the caves since the Japanese military was going to use them. My mother said this was our cave and she asked for the soldier's mercy as women and children, especially, had no place to go to.

Afterbursts

Orders from the military were orders from the Emperor. They said they would behead anyone who resisted the Emperor's orders, but my mother pleaded on her knees and begged in the rain. She apologised and pleaded, "Just give us one day, and we will leave tomorrow." And so she was granted permission.

She prepared for us to leave...a handmade bag and a backpack with enough goods inside for each of us to survive. She packed all the basic necessities including money, potatoes, rice, sugar, salt and miso. She also put in *kanpan* dry biscuits and canned mackerel, and protective hoods she made out of old clothes stacked together.

We went to a distant relative's place in Tamagusuku, Maekawa, but they were also forced out. We then tried to go to Itokazugo, but we couldn't enter because the *Himeyuri*[38] corps were there along with the locals, and they didn't accept people from the outside. There was a big rock in between Funakoshi and Itokazu, so we hid under there for about three days.

The Japanese military was putting out false propaganda that they would chase the US forces away, but the US soldiers kept coming and Shuri Castle fell. There was information that the US forces were right nearby—they landed in this entire area of Kadena, Yamitan, Ginowan...The fighting lasted for about a month, but after the Japanese military lost this battle, the commanders had already fled.

So...because they lost, the armies were no longer organised—the moment the organisation is dismantled, the soldiers become abandoned. The abandoned soldiers who had nowhere to go drove out the weak citizens and stole all their food. This is the reality of the Battle of Okinawa...

[On this paper] are the Japanese military's rules of war from the time. They imply that if you are captured alive by a US soldier, you must commit suicide, rather than being shamed...So many people committed suicide. There were also group suicides...We were told

---

[38] Girls from the school attended by Yoshiko Shimabukuro and conscripted to nurse the IJA

Je Suis Mort!

there is nothing more shameful in this world than for Japanese citizens who are children of the Emperor to be caught by the beasts, so we must die rather than live. That's why everyone had a grenade… We had our own hand grenade and said we would commit suicide if the US forces came.

We somehow managed to break through and not commit suicide. My mother's elder brother and his wife said since Japan was losing the battle…since we were going to die anyway, they wanted to die in their home. They wouldn't listen.

When they tried to retreat, there was a naval bombardment and my aunt was immediately killed. My uncle had shrapnel all over his body and couldn't walk from blood loss…He committed suicide… There was a 13-year-old boy carrying a three-year-old girl on his back…fleeing with us. The two were hit through the heart from behind…In this area, both sides of the road—and in the middle of the road and the houses—were all filled with corpses. It was June, so the smell of rotten flesh was gruelling to the point of being unable to breathe. I rubbed mug wort leaves and held it to my nose…

I heard a baby crying in the farm fields and when I approached, I saw that the mother was dead but the baby was alive. But there's nothing we could do…The baby's voice still echoes in my ears.

In a war…people lose their humanity.

Back then, in the countryside, there were concrete rainwater tanks. [These] tanks were destroyed from the bombs, and three Japanese soldiers were hiding in them. Up until then, the soldiers had all driven us away, but a Japanese soldier beckoned us over. I thought it was strange, but we went inside and he treated my mother's wound [from a bomb fragment]. As an expression of gratitude, I gave him some bread. He was very happy.

Then in the evening my backpack was gone. So the soldier called us not to help us take shelter, but to steal what was in our backpack… People will do anything in order to survive.

There was another naval bombardment, and my elder sister was buried alive…luckily, we were able to dig her out. We then went to

Bushichan, which is now a golf course, but we were told this is the road to captivity. We still thought it was shameful to be captured due to what we were taught so we returned to Mabuni on the east side of the [Okinawa Peace] Museum, arriving there on June 19. It was raining…

On the morning of June 20 at 6:30am, about 300 metres north on top of a hill, we saw about 100 US soldiers naked from the waist up… but strangely enough, not one bullet came our way…Since March, there wasn't a day when no bullets were fired, so everyone thought it was strange…

From there, we saw a middle-aged Okinawan man walking towards us carrying a white flag. This was, again, strange. Everyone had been driven into a corner, ahead of which is a cliff 30 metres high. Under these circumstances, it was difficult to fathom why the attackers[39] would be holding a white flag and heading towards us.

While everyone kept a distance from the man, he told everyone to be reassured. The man said he had become a hostage of the US military. While holding the white flag, he said he would guide us. He said we would be provided with clothing, food and a place to stay at the detention camp. The man said he would guarantee our lives and asked the men to strip down just into their underwear, and women wear what they have, and leave all our belongings behind.

While we were receiving these instructions, three Japanese soldiers who were hiding took out their swords and shouted out, "Traitor!" and beheaded the man.

For humans to behead a living human is horrific. Blood splashes… It's a hell that mere words cannot describe. The women were speechless and were shaking in fear and the men were just dumbfounded. Another citizen who tried to take his clothes off was attacked by these men and slashed…

The US soldiers were also watching this with binoculars. They had tried to help us by dispatching an Okinawan man, meanwhile, Japanese soldiers were murdering their own people…So the US

---

[39] The Okinawan man was representing the US military.

Je Suis Mort!

soldiers gave up. Then, about five to 10 minutes later, there was a naval bombardment…This is when nearly 20,000 people died. In the end, everything was burned down with a flamethrower…

While almost everyone died here, we descended the cliff. I don't know how…I think I must have descended using a vine. I must have jumped into the sea midway. You can manage to do something like that when push comes to shove. I must have been frantic enough.

After I had descended, there was nothing, no food. After a week, I would hear voices from the jeeps yelling, "Come out, come out!" three times a day…They would yell, "Come out…Don't worry, it's ok, there's food."

In the beginning, since I was brainwashed, I thought, "Never." But then from the third day, I started thinking, "It's ok to eat something before dying."

After a week, since you're always wanting food, you start hallucinating that you're eating—but then realise you're not. And when you're called out to in a gentle voice, you naturally start thinking maybe it's ok…So after a week, I finally decided to come out.

There was another boy who had injured his leg badly, and there were maggots. And the medical orderly picked away each maggot one by one, placed a gauze on the wound and was treating the boy. And I thought: these people even try to save someone like this. So I was reassured.

The military and civilians were separated and they provided food—a lunch box that the US soldiers ate. We had never seen or eaten cheese before. Butter…I thought, *how can we eat something that's rotten?* and spat it out.

Since we were civilians, we were taken to this detention camp. Some teachers who survived started a school. Since we were still influenced by mind control I hardly went. Instead, I was busy visiting the US soldier buildings and received goods and food from soldiers. But one teacher convinced me.

It was here that I was finally released from my mind control. As a result, to see the reality of Japan—which I had so admired and aspired to fight for—versus the US's esteem for human rights, freedom, democracy...I was clearly able to understand the difference between militarism and democracy...what the source was for Japan's erroneous policy.

Why did we have to be forced out of our own caves when we cooperated with the Japanese soldiers?

I thought they were the perpetrators, but in reality, they were also the victims. The soldiers who murdered the Japanese citizens—all of them were victims. The real perpetrators were some politicians and the military industry. It was this group of people that started the war and profited from it. They exploited the Japanese military, and the citizens suffered the most.

Indoctrinated throughout their education, Japanese were expected to sacrifice their lives for the glory of the Emperor and children were no exception. **Shigeaki Kinjo**'s *experience of this was particularly horrifying.*

In a coffee shop near his home, jazz playing incongruously in the background, the diminutive 89-year-old recounted his teenaged experience of the war. As he talked, his train of thought was unclear—almost as though his mind could not endure the details of his ordeal.

I was born in Tokashiki Island, Kerama, Okinawa on February 12, 1929...[My father was a] farmer...

Before the war, it was militarism...We had to sacrifice our lives for the country, for the Emperor...that was how I was educated.

We were terrified of the *kichiku beiei*, the American savages. We were educated to believe terrible things would happen if we came face to face with an American soldier. If we were captured by the demon-beast, our heads would be cut off, our nose would be shaved off...So it's better to take one's own life instead of being captured and murdered...

We were in Aharen village in Tokashiki island...The [American] soldiers arrived on the south side and we were driven into a corner... The Japanese military was there so we were cornered in one place.

Je Suis Mort!

Shigeaki Kinjo in 2018

We lived in fear of when we would be murdered by the *kichiku bei-ei*…I believed this—but when we met them, they were very polite. It was the Japanese soldiers who did brutal things…

The mass suicides took place after we fled to Nishiyama, in the north, where the Japanese military also fled. We weren't always moving with the military but were under their control…There's a process to the mass suicides. Our village leader led with "Long live the Emperor!" The villagers gathered and helped kill their families and others. It was a clear order from the village leader, a former soldier, to die heading towards the enemy shouting "Long live the Emperor."

Relatives would kill their families. Adults would do it to the children, since children can't die by themselves. They used sticks, people who had short knives would use them for stabbing, it was done in many ways…We also had a short knife…Me, my older brother, killed our family…

The reason that my older brother and I couldn't die ourselves [was that] we had to help our family commit suicide—my parents[40], younger brother and younger sister...And my elder brother and I survived...

After the war we found American soldiers helping...They actually released people who were injured and cared for them...Japanese soldiers and Okinawans.

That was totally different from what we were led to believe. They weren't brutal...They were very humane...They gave food to those who were starving. It wasn't about if you were an ally or enemy... They were treating the injured out of love.

---

[40] Shigeaki's father had in fact died earlier on during the war, so Shigeaki and his brother had the responsibility to kill their mother and younger siblings.

Chapter 18

You Learn to Catch Very Quickly

Incarceration

Being a prisoner during the war was a desperate experience, with food scarce but maltreatment abundant. For soldiers, this was in contravention of the Geneva Convention. Excluding Russians, vastly greater proportions of POWs died under the Japanese than the Germans. POWs were put to work across occupied territories, often in extremely harsh environments.

Concentration camps were another level altogether of inhumanity. In many cases, as an antidote to the brutality, the prisoners attempted to carve out some sort of "normal" life within the constraints of an otherwise unimaginably hellish existence.

__Ernest Hilton's__ father had opted to move his family to Holland to escape Hitler's persecution of the Jews, but this did not save them. In 1941, they were called to present themselves at Westerbork, a camp which had originally been established to house illegal Jewish immigrants fleeing Germany.

We were one of the first to be called up to move to Westerbork… Nobody actually came with a machine gun and trotted us to the railway station. Before we left for Westerbork, my mother made salted eggs…a lot of eggs. That way they don't spoil so you can take them and you could eat them weeks later…

When we arrived in Westerbork, it was 1941, two months after my ninth year. All I know is that I was quite nervous, and my mother knew that I was very keen on liquorice, and she gave me a handful of liquorice—or a bag—and we went into this hut where there was a family with a small two-year-old child.

And they talked and said how they were going to move the available facilities so that we can move in there, too. And I was eating the liquorice…like nerve pills…

Dutch Jews started to come behind us, and the camp became a much busier kind of place. And then, there came a day when the first transport was organised. And the Commandant ordered all the inmates to line up and to come in front of him and he would say, "You go on the train and you stay here."

And we came as a family of four and our neighbour was also in this camp. His name was Jup Weiss, Joseph Weiss, and he was the Jewish representative of the Commandant. And at that time my father was already hired to be an administrator and my mother was a barrack leader.

So Jup Weiss said, "This is the family Herz and Mr Walter Herz is the administrator and Mrs is the Barrack Leiter."

And then he looked at us and he said, "Well, in that case, you'd better stay here." And after that, every week there was a trainload—not passenger trains, goods wagons, where they closed the door *[he thumps the table]*—and the train left…

They said, "Don't take too many goods with you because you don't need it."

The people who shared the family house with us in Westerbork went on one of the first transports. And I never forget this two-year-old child that tried to talk to me a bit…

When we got to Belsen, guess who received us? Jup Weiss. He was the headman again in Belsen, the representative of the Commandant.

You Learn to Catch Very Quickly

Belsen was not one camp, it was many camps, and we were in a camp called Stern Lager...Once in a while they would bring these big heavy jugs that farmers use for their milk and they would distribute this only to the children. And my mother said to me, "Go quick to where this lady is handing out milk and say, 'Madame, je voudrais un peu du lait.'"

And that's the sentence I learned in French and I got a cup of milk.

Because the food we got was delivered in these big 50 litre thermal containers. One was a slice of bread and an ersatz coffee. So: hot water and a piece of bread...In the evening we got a soup made from very little nutritional value—swede. For a year and a half or more we ate this terrible...It's not even much carbohydrate.

Protein didn't exist except where you got a red cross packet and you got canned sardines. This is what my mother called "the iron reserve". And towards the end of our stay in Belsen...I stopped eating completely. I didn't even want to eat any more. I think I was so thin that I didn't really have the strength to digest it...I was in pretty bad shape, nutritionally...malnourished. I was very, very small and I wasn't growing...

Originally it was just German army people that were the guards, but seemingly they were conscripted to go and fight instead, and they took German prisoners—criminals—and made them quasi-guards. And they were known as kapos, and the kapos were pretty brutal to the inmates, just because they had some power. And I remember towards the very end we had one professional nurse in our barrack. And one of the kapos got sick. And she killed him with an injection of air...

On a daily basis we did play, a kind of stick ball. I don't think we actually had a ball. Maybe we had some kind of paper crumpled... Anyhow, we played, we walked. We watched the planes.

He said he daydreamed that the pilots might drop on him a cheese sandwich. By coincidence, a veteran who had flown with the RAF over Europe had described to me how the young aircrew, huddled in sheepskin jackets against the cold on long unpressurised flights, would travel with a snack of sliced bread kept under their armpits to prevent it from freezing.

When the planes came, we were not allowed to be outside. The Germans didn't like us to stand there and quasi "enjoy" their country getting bombed.

As much as I liked the Air Force bombing Germany, I was quite aware that a lot of people are dying each time these swarms of bombers arrived. I didn't cry or bleed heart, but I was aware that this is worse than still sitting in a concentration camp, actually. Being bombed is practically a death sentence…

I don't remember that my grandparents spent any time in Westerbork…I think they were being hidden…And it worked, but didn't last. So they came to Belsen…

That was a big to do. Because it's one thing that we were in there, but for them to come at the end was a real tragedy…He went into a man's barrack, she went into a female barrack. I don't remember seeing them much…

My grandfather died in Belsen…We got a cart with a horse to take the body to the mass grave, so we could walk behind it until the gate—but not to the grave, of course. My grandfather had a casket, and there was a certain process, semi-decent. Instead of just throwing you into a cart.

But the camp next door, I could see every morning the dead, naked corpses that were lying there…piled up outside…and they would throw the bodies up into this cart. That was what we did, we watched them throw the bodies…The people that were alive took whatever clothing they had and used it, because everybody had limited stuff…

My father had a preferred job in the kitchen, which was more or less opposite our entrance, you could see it. And he stole a pack of butter one day to bring to us, and he got caught. So we didn't get the butter and he was put into solitary confinement. And so the next afternoon I stood by the gate and this officer came and said,

You Learn to Catch Very Quickly

"I come to tell you that your father has been released, and he's in good shape."

It sank in that my father must have gotten away with something that they could have killed him for, and they were quite easy on him. I think...Since he was a soldier in the German army in World War One, and since he looked like a Nazi *[he laughs]*—sorry, but he had blue eyes, he was blonde...he was quite Aryan looking—he must have said, "Look I'm from Munich, I was born..." Between two men you can talk, but if you've got a hundred, they say, "Kill him."

I never asked him what happened in this overnight stay.

But then he was taken to the miserable job, which was digging out roots from cut off trees for fuel, which is hard work in the winter. That's why most people died of malnutrition in Belsen. The camp did not have a gas chamber or anything, but most people died there out of malnutrition.

Yoshio Nakamura *was also imprisoned based on racial motivations. After Pearl Harbor was attacked, the US government became paranoid that any ethnic Japanese in the US might be a spy. In panic, the authorities moved to lock up Japanese Americans living on the West Coast, which was much of that immigrant population in the US at the time. When the Japanese Americans were eventually allowed to serve the US, their dedicated unit in Europe, the Nisei 442nd Infantry Regiment, became one of the most highly decorated in US military history.*

I was born in Rosemead, California, and I spent my childhood in Rosemead and El Monte. And then I was incarcerated when I was in the 11th grade...

We had a truck farm, small things like beets or carrots, broccoli, lettuce, berries. I was on the farm when my neighbour friend came over to tell me about the [Pearl Harbor] bombing.

And, you see, we have Japanese faces...There was a sense of... hysteria, you might say...People were very, very scared and so anything that was said about the Japanese Army or the Navy, etcetera, they painted that same thing on us...

Afterbursts

On February 19th of 1942, President Roosevelt wrote an executive order 9066 that authorised the military to do whatever was necessary…And General DeWitt, when he was told that there isn't one instance of Japanese-Americans doing anything wrong, said, "That's the very reason. Get them out of here. They just *might* do something."

The first act that was made in the Selective Service was to make us American citizens 4-C, which is enemy alien, and that made us ineligible to serve in the armed forces. You couldn't volunteer.

The Japanese-Americans who were in Hawaii, they felt the attack as much as anybody else, and many of them wanted to volunteer and they were turned away—and in fact, the ones who were in the service there were disarmed. And some of them were then discharged, and the young people who wanted to do something, joined something like the CCC—the Civilian Conservation Corps—to build roads and repair things and they thought that was the best thing to do for the war effort.

And eventually the President was persuaded that we should be allowed to serve. So they asked for volunteers to form the Hundredth Battalion, and when that happened it was mostly in Hawaii, I think 10,000 people volunteered for about 2,000 openings. So there was a great sense of loyalty in the Japanese-American community, particularly in Hawaii…

I was interned in the Tulare racetrack. One of my friends brought me one of these executive orders that were posted on telephone poles, in which it says "All persons of Japanese ancestry, alien or non-alien"—it didn't say "American" and "born in America", no, it said "non-alien", and we were to go somewhere…

Well, my friend took our family to Pasadena, where we were put on a train. And I don't remember too much about the trip because all the blinds were put down and so I didn't know where we were going…It took a while, and I just remember there were mothers with their small children and we could take only what we can carry.

And when we got to the train station, we were getting off, and—my gosh! I mean, there're all the soldiers lined up along the street, and there were bystanders wondering what's going on, like it was a parade or something. And here these families, carrying what they had and walking down from the train station to the racetrack.

It was a fair distance, and you could hear children asking why all these men over here have guns and where are we going, and all these kinds of things. It still rings in my head...

But when we got to the racetrack, we noticed that the entire ground was surrounded by barbed wire and they had erected guard towers and there were soldiers up there with guns and searchlights.

And so we asked, "Why do we have those things?"

And they said, "Well, it's for your protection."

But the guns and the searchlights were facing inward...

We were in this compound and they made living quarters out of these horse stalls...We had a small portion of a horse stall for our family, little cots inside. And...I just remember it was getting warmer—we got there in May and by June it got warm and the horses were there before us—so it got kind of steamy, and the aroma wasn't exactly great.

And that's where my friend came to visit me from El Monte and he just couldn't believe it. First of all, he had to go through the checkpoint and describe why he was there, and we were in this room and had to talk through this, kind of a grated window...And so he was so shocked...He knew I was innocent and it affected him so badly that he said he couldn't talk about it for 30 years...He couldn't even mention this to his friends, what he had seen. So, here I was, trying to reassure him that "I'm okay", you know, but it was just beyond his comprehension that someone was being punished for something he hadn't done...

Well...from there we were transported by train to Phoenix and by bus to this camp south east of Phoenix near Sacaton, and it was a part of an Indian reservation. Dusty mesquite and saguaro cactus and all these barracks...Just a bleak environment and several of us felt we really should try to make it fairly normal by organising clubs and activities and having a constitution and all this, keep our spirits higher and concentrate on things that are fun...

Afterbursts

And because so many of the people who were interned were pretty good at farming, fortunately there was some water that came in and these guys made the desert really bloom with a lot of vegetables and things. And this was so successful that some of these were shipped to other camps…

And fortunately, I had a fairly positive attitude…Because there were others who were so humiliated by being imprisoned, even though they didn't do anything wrong. The shame of being incarcerated was too heavy for some. They even took their own lives, and some of them got very bitter…And I'm just lucky that I'm one of the people that felt I could learn from whatever experience I had.

My father became really just a shadow of himself…He had nightmares and he fell out of his bed and he developed sort of a palsy…He never was whole again.

Fergus Anckorn *had arrived in Singapore just as the Japanese attacked. He was wounded, survived the massacre of all the patients and medical staff in Alexandra Hospital where he was recuperating and interned in Changi.*

While Fergus showed me photos and drawings made by a fellow POW, he described the people he had encountered during nearly five years of deprivation, their deaths a footnote to the memories they left.

When I was first a prisoner in Changi we had a chap whose name was Foster-Haigh. He was a singer—he was a priest actually, a Roman Catholic priest—and he was on the BBC as a singer under the name John Foster. And one day he said, "Would anyone like to learn Greek?"

"Ooh", I said, "yes, I would!" Because I had Latin. So he was teaching us Greek so easily and in five weeks, he suddenly died[41]…

I had another particular friend [in Changi] called Reginald Renison. He was a concert pianist. He had played all the top concertos backed by the Boston Symphony Orchestra before he was

---

[41] Foster Haigh, Renison and Martin all in fact died in 1943 and are buried in Burma.

21. And as there was nothing much to do in those days, he decided to form an orchestra—and a lot of the officers were there, because they'd brought instruments with them…Of course, we had "theatres" there and a grand piano and all the rest of it—and he wrote out the scores for every single man in the orchestra on a back of an envelope, and then they rehearsed it. He had the whole lot, written, without touching a piano.

And I remember…he said to me, "I'm going to rehearse these oiks today"—because he hated the officers, but there they were—and he said, "would you like to come?"

And I said, "Well, can I? I'm only a gunner."

"Of course! I'm the conductor!"

So we went there and they were all, the orchestra, they've got their cellos and they were smoking cigarettes, chatting away. And we walked in and after a bit he tapped the thing and they all stopped talking—he was a signaller, lowest of the low—and he said, "Gentlemen, it is the custom when the conductor comes in for the orchestra to stand."

And he walked out, and he walked back in again. And then [they] get rid of the cigarettes.

And he ended up doing Rachmaninov Number Two, which is my favourite, with full orchestra as well as an underneath symphony orchestra and he'd written the whole lot right down to the percussion. And he died six weeks before the war ended. It's sad. What a wonderful man…He could play any single classical piece you'd mention…

I know, that if you want to learn something in a prisoner of war camp, whether it's astronomy or navigation or Russian, there's always an expert.

From Changi, Fergus was transported to Thailand to labour on the Death Railway. After its losses at the Battle of Midway, Japan could not defend the sea lanes around the Malayan Peninsula and so it planned a railway from Thailand to Burma to supply an invasion of India. Construction of the railway was undertaken by POWs and conscripted Asian labourers, with over 100,000 people dying as they cut the route through inhospitable jungle. The supply line was redundant before it was put into service.

When we went up to Thailand, Banpong, we had to unload the trucks—two hundredweight sacks of rice and they would put it on your shoulder and I couldn't move. I couldn't get my foot off the ground, especially as I had a string round it [due to an earlier wound], and [my good friend] Lester Martin took it from me and went and emptied it and then spent the rest of the morning taking it off other people's shoulders. And he died eventually of dysentery about eight months before the war ended…

Here's [a sketch of] a man getting his leg cut off, and that's in my hut, I was sitting here. There's the leg coming off. This is [Captain "Marko"] Markowitz and that's [Colonel "Weary"] Dunlop. I carried it out and buried it. And the next morning this fellow who'd had his leg off said, "That dog's got my bloody leg!" And a dog had dug it up and was off with this leg in its mouth.

And we got after him and got it off him and then I buried it again, deeper. And that man made some bamboo posts round this little gravestone—my leg's in there"—and every morning he used to put flowers on it…

The other thing was, the Japanese had had orders that if an Ally put one foot on Japanese soil, first job: kill every prisoner of war, without trace. And they showed them how to do it. They could get us into a cave and then put flamethrowers in. Or they could march us out to sea and machine gun us. And in my camp, we had to dig a trench right round the camp—a moat, 20 foot wide 20 feet deep, so that we couldn't get out—and they were going to do us in there.

And if only I'd known I'd have given up trying to survive, if I'd known I was going to get killed anyway…

We only had one card ever and that was it. But being Japanese they wouldn't let us write on it, it was printed: "I'm well/I'm unwell/I'm working for pay". All that stuff. And they let us sign our signature, that's all. And my parents had been told I was killed in action and they knew nothing more for two years. And then my card turned up—used to take a year to send a card.

And my mother said—when they'd been told I was killed—she said, "Well I'll send a card every week in case he's not."

They were allowed 25 words. We used to be so angry when we got them. They all started off: "My dear boy I do…" Oh, tell us the war news, for God's sake! Wasting words…

And then my card turned up and my mother said, "He really is dead. That's not my son's signature."

And she must have taken herself off to bed, my name not to be mentioned, and then ten minutes later she was screeching the house down: "He's alive! He's alive!"

She'd spotted the shorthand—she was a good shorthand writer—she'd spotted it. Because when I was a baby they'd called me Smiler. And on my signature I'd worked into it *Still smiling…*

Fergus suffered extreme abuse at the hands of his captors on the Death Railway. He had nightmares for some 60 years after the war until he visited Singapore with his son and achieved "closure", he said. On another trip, he photographed his daughter standing next to the hospital bed in which he had lain as the wounded around him were massacred.

More amazing still than his seemingly casual account of revisiting a traumatic past was his story of running across one of his former guards at a reception at the Japanese embassy in London. I asked him, "Was it not strange for you to see him?"

Sounding baffled by the question, he replied:

No. I just said, "What are you doing here?"

The war's over, I've got no bad feelings. It's all over and I was only too pleased to see him…

I was on a show on television called Hard Talk. And the last question he asked me was, "Do you hate the Japanese?"

And I say, "Not at all. I hate the war." If there had been no war I would have never seen the Japanese…They were in it the same as we were. They were nasty with it, but as soon as we knew the war was over, I said, "Let's…forget it. It's past."

Born in 1931, **Gustaaf van Beers** *was the third generation of a family of Dutch settlers in Indonesia, at the time the Dutch East Indies. His father had been born to the Chief Justice and was a plantation designer. He was close to his grandparents, learning from them a love and respect for animals and life. His idyllic childhood was shattered by the war.*

Well, as a child, I lived in a paradise. We had a beautiful home. We had servants, large property and I had all kinds of animals: sheep, rabbits, pigeons, dogs, fishponds…Yeah, it was ideal. Schooling… until the fourth grade.

And then the war broke out. Pearl Harbor…And several of the neighbours came to our driveway. And they asked my father, "Mr van Beers, what do you think of Pearl Harbor?"

And I hear my father. "Ha, ha, the Japanese think they can take Netherland East Indies—impossible! Seventeen thousand islands and the Indonesians will stand behind us."

And I was standing behind my father—and I loved my father, I had great admiration—and I thought, "Dad, I love you, but it will be totally different."

And two months later the Japanese invaded Indonesia, the Netherlands East Indies, and within days he was arrested, thrown in a camp. And that was very traumatic…I saw that he was hit! hit! hit! up to a truck with all the men in our neighbourhood and we didn't know where they were going to, whether they would be slaughtered…

And that was it. The family was devastated, no income. And shortly thereafter there were many, many *razzias*. My older brother was arrested and thrown in prison. [He was] four years older…14, 15…The Japanese threw everybody they thought could be a danger, or to crush the family structures…many boys were thrown in prison.

And very early on already, many died for the misery, away from their mothers—because the fathers were in the camp. Bad food and no food. But my brother survived, but after the war suffered badly from post war traumas.

And shortly after my brother was thrown in prison, the Japanese announced…all children nine years and older must also stand there to be taken to prison. And I thought *No way!* so I fled, and those were very traumatic days for me…fleeing as soon as you know that the Japanese came…I then run away into the rice fields and I was hiding there until it was pitch dark, and it's very dangerous, because then the snakes come out. Very traumatic. And it happened a few times…

But I remember also that about ten o'clock, say, they banged on the door and it was frightening. And our house was full of people and I slept in the lounge. And they said, "Who is that boy?"

And my mother said, "Well, that's my son."

"But he's older than nine."

"No," my mother said. "No, he is not. His father is very tall." Which was not true.

So they argued, argued, argued, and they left, leaving me behind. And that happened two times, and I remember that I was so frightened that I peed in my bed, from fear. I was constantly haunted by fear…

There were very serious rationings…I was hungry every night and I still hear myself saying, "Mum, I'm so hungry. I can't sleep." And it was awful for the mothers. And you know if there was starch, she gave me a little bit of starch, but it didn't really fill my stomach.

They were very traumatic years…

My father was released from camp and we were so glad that daddy came home, and we collected flowers—and of course there was nothing, dandelions and things like that—to welcome him.

But when the Red Cross came with him on a stretcher we all ran away, because a monster was brought back. A monster! His eyes big, his legs elephantiasis, and his voice was totally different. And my mother had a very difficult job to handle my father…because he had fits of anger, you know. And my father never recovered…And we… We lost everything.

Afterbursts

Gustaaf pushed himself to overcome his childhood deprivations—notably the shortfall in education—and became a renowned international economist, returning to Indonesia to work on the country's development.

He died in May 2020, a man inordinately proud of his contribution to economic development in Indonesia and emerging markets—and of his "remarkable" grandchildren.

Christopher McDouall's *parents had met in Beijing where his father was a missionary running the main Anglican Church and his mother had gone to be a missionary teacher, having abandoned hope of finding a young man to marry in the slim pickings that remained after World War One.*

I had no sense of [the war] until 1942. And, as I recall, somewhere around September, October '42, we had to leave our house—we had a big house that went with my father's job—and go and live in a single room in the British Embassy, or consulate, and we weren't allowed out of the compound. And we stayed there 'til March of '43 when we were removed to Weihsien. I was six…

One of the vivid memories…I know that the Japanese did this to everyone: they made you walk from wherever you were to the train station and they got all the Chinese out to line the streets, to demonstrate to the Chinese the humiliation of the Westerners. And I can remember feeling really, really bad about it as I trudged to the station towing a little wagon which had my toy train on it…It was a very unpleasant feeling even for a six-year-old…

Weihsien had a main block, a church and a whole lot of single room terraces…And my parents and I were allocated one of these. I think it probably measured something like 10 feet by eight, in the room…my parents had a bed each and then I slept on the trunks [of our belongings] in between my parents' beds…

So that was March '43. And I think that there were initially 15 to 17 hundred people in Weihsien, from lots of races…There were lots of professionals, teachers, doctors…So life was organised for children…

You Learn to Catch Very Quickly

There was this big church building which was used as a place for schooling. So I was taught Latin by a fierce woman called Molly Rudd, who walked with a stick and had vibrant white hair and there was Cub Scouts, and I remember once they arranged a camping weekend for the Cub Scouts within Weihsien. But if you're seven, that's exciting…

The food was very scarce. The staple there was a grain called *gaoliang*…It's cattle fodder…And that grain was used to make bread and porridge and cake and…everything…The Japanese did bring other food in—fruit and meat and things like that—but in very low quality and very small quantities. So we were all malnourished. In the three years I was there I didn't put on any weight at all, so when I came out aged nine, I was still the same weight that I had been when I was six. So you got used to being hungry all the time…

And of course, the climate is quite harsh, very cold in winter, and pretty hot in summer. And so every one of these rooms had a little coal fire stove—but they only gave us coal dust, not lumps of coal. And so what everyone did was to get the coal dust, mix it with mud and make it sort of cake. And then you had to dry it before it would burn.

So one of my memories as a child is helping my father to make little briquettes of coal dust and mud—which is very cold. We had to do it in the winter with cold water and then they took a day or two to dry out and it was a job to get the stove going and all that…

[Liberation] was 72 years ago yesterday, but I remember quite vividly because we were actually in a Latin lesson—with this fierce woman Molly Rudd—and we heard an aircraft overhead which came lower and lower. And school was abandoned, everyone rushed out. And there was a B-29. And then it climbed up higher and seven parachutists came out.

They were all Americans…One was a Japanese American, who could act as translator. And the troops guarding us were third rate troops. And they just surrendered and the Americans promptly rearmed them and said, "Right, you're now working for us." Because there were major irregular Chinese armies in the area.

Afterbursts

In fact, one of the memories I have, as an eight-year-old…We had some Red Cross Parcels get delivered to the camp…And as an eight-year-old I used to collect empty tins. And then I heard that the Chinese militia around wanted the tins to make bullet cases with, and there was a heap of earth inside the wall and if you were lucky you could shout out and there'd be a Chinese standing in the *gaoliang* the other side, they being shorter than the crop. And you could barter the tins for eggs. And, in fact, I managed to do this on two occasions. And one time I got five eggs and one time I got three.

Now, if you're hungry and you're eight, satisfying your hunger involves learning to catch—you learn to catch very quickly. So, I caught all eight eggs…

Then we were liberated on the 17th of August and maybe a month later we were organised onto trains go to Qingdao. And from Qingdao on an American troop ship to Hong Kong. My father went back to Beijing to try and rescue his life's work.

When we had to vacate the house, my parents put their most valuable possessions into trunks and with the servants buried them in the compound, saying to the servants, "Look, if times get tough feel free to dig them up and sell them." But they didn't, so my father got back there, the servants found him, said, "There's all your possessions."

Christopher's family eventually made it via New Zealand to the UK, where he did his National Service with the RAF, graduated from Cambridge University and became an engineer. He died in November 2017.

Ron Johnson *had been caught at Arnhem—and while the battles there had been harrowing, his worst experience of the war came when he was captured.*

They decided, the Germans, that they would move a lot of us away in a hospital train. And the hospital train was cattle trucks, with dirty straw on the floor, and we were locked in there for four days and three nights, just on bread and water.

You Learn to Catch Very Quickly

And that was the low—without any doubt—the low point in my life…Just like an animal, you know. Really awful…Having been in battle for a week, nothing to eat. Hardly any water, because there wasn't the water there…

We were lucky to be [imprisoned] in a castle, [Spangenberg]…I remember we went through Hanover station on the way. As we were taken across there I thought, "They don't look very happy with us, these German civilians."

You know, if we hadn't got the armed guard with us, they would be attacking us—and in a way you couldn't blame them…because they were being bombed night after night by the Royal Air Force… And as we went through Munster in the cattle truck, we could see through the slits the desolation the Royal Air Force had brought to their cities. And of course, it happened to Dresden as well…So, understandable they didn't much like us.

That was September 1944, and we were in there through Christmas time…During the time that I was there we had two halves of a Red Cross parcel. Earlier on they'd had quite a reasonable supply…At one stage they were getting, I think, a parcel a week, but they'd all dried up by the time I got there. We were very short of food, hungry all the time…

Two things stuck in my mind about it…For the first time in my life, I heard opera. We had with us George Lascelles, later the Earl of Harwood, and [the] love of his life was opera and later on he became director of Covent Garden, and he'd had sent to him, through the Red Cross, records…and two evenings a week he'd put on an evening of opera. So, at 23, I was introduced to opera…

The other thing is that I'd never played roulette…It was far from a holiday camp, but on two occasions, I remember playing roulette. We had house money inside the camp, which was debited later to your Army pay that was back in England. You did have some money that you'd spend on a sort of rough beer. And, no—we were hungry, I can tell you that. You didn't think about anything other than food. And the Germans were hungry, too…They were in a bad way, no question about that.

Oh, another interesting thing…They put some water in the moat at Christmastime and the Scots that were in there had managed to get some curling stones sent across, so they've put some water in and frozen it and for the first time ever I had a go at curling.

Sounds funny, doesn't it?

Ron and a comrade escaped in April 1945, as the Germans marched the POWs towards the Russian front line. The two spent eight days hiding in the hills with just a few biscuits for sustenance until they were confident that they could come down and meet up with the advancing Americans.

Frank Ashleigh *and his men had been cornered up a church tower near Arnhem. They were given five minutes to surrender.*

In those five minutes we made our weapons useless by breaking off the firing pins, and we surrendered. I managed to communicate with one of the Germans that we hadn't eaten for four days. Ten minutes later, plates of food were brought out to us.

"Don't worry gentlemen. It's not poisoned…We'll eat a piece of food off your plate. You choose the piece."

So we each chose a piece of food—a different piece…They ate it without trouble at all…And we had it with no problem either! And then it was off to interrogation. They pushed us into a truck and drove us over the bridge, which by then was entirely in German hands again. There, I was presented with a dummy copy of the Geneva Convention.

Now, we had already been briefed in the UK, "You give your name…your rank and your regimental number, and that is all…"

[The Germans] said, "If you'd like to read the Convention, you'll see for yourself that you are permitted to reveal the name of your commanding officer and the location of your unit."

I gave my rank, my name and my number, and that was all I would say. This went on for three days, and they realised I was not going to talk. And they put us into a train and took us to a prisoner of war camp. And we stayed there from late September until early January.

By this time Allied forces were advancing at tremendous speed. And the Germans, quite understandably, did not want aircrew to be released, sent back to the UK where they could start flying again. And so they put us on what then became known as the Long March over the Oda. It was 87 miles to be covered, I think, in 18 days, with next to nothing to eat. Temperature: minus 20.

A few died on the way, but they were men who had been in prisoner of war camps for a long time and were weakened with lack of food. I had no difficulty…In fact, I wound up carrying what little baggage another man had, as well as my own, because he couldn't manage it…We got to Stalaag 3A in Luckenwalde, just south of Berlin.

There was a horrible sight: Russian prisoners of war. Russia had not signed the Geneva Convention so the Germans didn't feel they had to feed them. And they gave them next to nothing to eat. We gave them what food we could possibly spare them. And a few days later the Red Army arrived, and we were free.

Next day, I was taken to an airfield not very far away and flown home. My uncle was a doctor in the Royal Army Medical Corps. He found out I was there, sent his car for me, who drove me to my aunt in Slough.

I bless her cotton socks: she treated me absolutely normally. "Hello, Frank, nice to see you. Come on in. Would you like something to eat?"

Shigeo Matsumoto *was sent to fight in China at the very tail end of the war. It took a while for him to discover that Japan had lost the war, but eventually he was rounded up with his comrades by the Russians.*

We were told we would be returning to Japan, and they forced us to walk around the mountains. Since we were finally going back to Japan, we had to endure it.

They squeezed about 50 people into a cargo train. There was a small hole in the corner of about 30 centimetres, as wide as one's shoulders. Some people tried to escape from there. We all went to the bathroom in this hole. That was October, and winter had already arrived. Everyone had diarrhoea from the cold. Everything was sticky and dirty…

We suddenly stopped somewhere and were all ordered to get off. We then walked through old buildings and arrived at a building that was in shambles, without any lights or electricity. We were thrown into a hut that was cold with no heater. Since winter was coming, it became dark as night at 4pm. At dusk, the room became completely dark and cold.

There was one man, who shouted out loud for everyone to listen carefully. He said we were [somewhere] totally different from the port we were heading towards. Japanese were assigned to forced labour for 20 years. The Germans, who committed crimes that were even worse, were prisoners for life…

I said, "What is this? Weren't the Japanese supposed to go home? Who decided this?"

I had no idea what was going on…Looking back, I had no physical stamina, I was so weary. I had no comrades, couldn't speak Russian and couldn't escape. I had no weapons so I couldn't resist. It was cold. It was the first time I became hopeless. While people in the room next to me were rowdy, I became increasingly quiet. I still clearly remember the date: that was the night of October 22, 1945. Winter had come.

I found out at dawn the next day that seven captives had committed suicide. There was nothing else for us to do but to die…Siberia is vast, it continues on until Europe. The captives were dispersed all across Siberia all the way to Moscow—600,000 of them…

I was frequently doing work involving making brick walls. I built many cottages…This work helped me become really efficient in my present work. We lined up the bricks, plastered mortar from one end to the other and we all worked really hard. We mixed the mortar, carried it to the site, and lined the bricks.

Our group discussed how to carry out our work and we concluded there was so much that was inefficient. In groups that didn't deliver, five to six Russians would be monitoring them and make them work fast, but to us, they were very inefficient. While they were still stacking the bricks, our team would be finished. Like Toyota-method…

After the Japan-Russian war, an order was given out by Stalin. The Japanese military had carried out serious crimes, including the Siberian intervention, which is hardly taught in Japan. Russia lacked labour to advance the nation's recovery after the war…They were exhausted. There was no food. Many Russian soldiers were shot by the Germans. The government demanded Russia rebuild its economy, that's why the POWs were overworked…Under the five-year-plan, Japanese POWs played a major role, the national plan was nearly completed in three years. We were able to return because we delivered. Russia's economic reconstruction seemed to be proceeding as planned—it's an amazing thing.

About 10 percent of the POWs died and those who did were all left naked and placed in a ditch, like they were thrown away. But when Japan asked for the return of Japanese soldiers' remains, only about half of them were returned.

Shigeo's family had been told that he had died in Manchuria. He was finally able to send them a letter two years after they had received the death notice. His sister, who was very ill, did not survive to see him return home, but she died knowing that he was still alive.

SECTION THREE

Remembering the War

Chapter 19

You Want to Say "Stop Crying"

The enemy

Faced with intense propaganda, it can be hard to feel compassion for the enemy. My own motivation to see the other side of the story was challenged in Tokyo when I visited the extremely partisan Yasukuni Shrine, which showcases some interesting twists on history. Narratives that suggest Korea was eager to be annexed by Japan or that China's behaviour forced Japan to occupy Manchuria take no responsibility for Japan's aggression against its neighbours and almost seem too absurd to be officially sanctioned.

Similarly alienating are those official museums which use victimhood to score points against other nations, such as The Memorial Hall of the Victims in Nanjing Massacre by Japanese Invaders, which seems designed equally to inform and to keep fresh old wounds and enmities—something that the Holocaust museums I have visited have admirably avoided.

But at smaller, personal, memorials there can be moments where individual tragedy resonates and shared humanity overrides all else.

I experienced one such moment in the Tsushima Maru Museum which, focussing on the ship of the same name, recounts the story of the last evacuation convoy from Okinawa. One of the veterans I met, Zenichi Yoshimine, had mentioned how his own evacuation was stymied by the sinking of the ship, which put a halt to further flight from the islands. Looking at the photos of the hundreds of children who had drowned when the vessel was torpedoed, I felt quite removed from them, not least because of the language barrier throughout the museum's mostly-Japanese exhibits.

Then I saw a photo of a Japanese child that looked uncannily like my friend's Caucasian son at a similar age and I was hit by how desperate the loss of those children must have been for their parents. Later, I heard from an acquaintance the story of her friend who had put his sister on the ship, heading for the safety of mainland Japan. He had never forgotten sending her off with a bento box of rice balls for what would be her final journey.

The veterans themselves often recalled unexpected encounters in which the enemy was humanised. And while those pitted against family during the war could not help but question the conflict, even some in less ambiguous situations had, by the war's end, begun to feel sympathy for the other side. Others were surprised to be identifying with those they were expected to fight. Lou Ayala, an engineer with the Army Air Corps, made his way to India in a liberty ship carrying 250 men of the pigeon corps. He described his sense of amazement when he crossed paths with a group of Japanese POWs as they landed:

> I grew up in an area where it was kind of a farming, rural, area where Japanese used to have their little ranch farming. So I grew up with Japanese kids…When we landed in Calcutta, I'm walking with my friends and I look at these prisoners from here to there, and I think…those kids were our age, you know? *We're fighting kids our age!*

You Want to Say "Stop Crying"

Bob Burke, too, found it hard when he came across dead Japanese soldiers.

> You look at their face and they look like just a young boy, you know? Yeah, I have some sympathy for 'em. I 'helped' the individual Japanese I could see cross the fields...
>
> The natives all let themselves be known coming in on that [Burma] road because, well, all the military was on that road. But you'd see a group or something in a far distant field there, oh, I'd take a shot there to keep 'em moving. They were running south across the open field, heading for trees and forest as sanctuary. So I would shoot—not at them, but behind them. Keep 'em headed south, away from me. "Keep going! That's right, boys, keep going that way!" I just wanted to help a little bit.

I asked him: Why shoot behind them?

After a long pause, he said, "What would you do? If they're running away from me I wish 'em God speed."

I met **Lescher Dowling** *in his California home, where he had laid out a storyboard of his war along with a pristine army uniform and books about the CBI. He outlined the racial backdrop in California after Pearl Harbor, slowly and deliberately laying out the complexity of the situation.*

> You have mixed emotions because we had Japanese kids in our class, in our school—in fact, a Japanese boy was supposed to have graduated with our class, but when he was a junior he was put in a camp. And the summer of '43, my brother and a couple of our buddies went on a fishing trip, and on the way over we stopped in Tulare to leave some comic books for the kids from Carpenteria who are now in internment camp. And because we were underage we are not permitted to see them. We were not permitted to leave comic books because they thought there might be contraband in them. And that

Lescher Dowling in 2018

was a very sad situation…We were trying to reach out to them and the military wouldn't let us get anywhere near…

Living on the coast, Japanese were very common to us and we never suspected them of being spies or anything, because an awful lot of them were born in America. But then there are other people who…maybe they didn't have the close contact…

As far as the internment camps go, I think personally that it was for the protection of the people they put there. If they were left out, they would have been…mishandled…Well, even before they got into internment camps they were abused by the civilians, and some of it even transferred to Chinese because they were Asians: an Asian's an Asian…

Even for the battle-hardened soldier at the front there could be poignant moments where the enemy was humanised.

As a child, **Harry Rawlins** *had heard his father and uncles talk about the First World War and he had looked forward to becoming a soldier and creating his own war stories. During his training he agitated to be sent to battle, finally arriving in Europe after D-Day. He*

You Want to Say "Stop Crying"

was keen to see action, volunteering for patrol duties and frequently roaming in front of his platoon so that he could be in the "front of the front"—a fearless approach to combat that earned him a medal. Despite his colourful descriptions of engagements and comrades, it was the personal encounters in hostile territory which were most thought-provoking, often extraordinary in their everyday nature.

I remember, when we were in Holland…One of our tanks had been bogged in a ditch and there was some German soldiers helping to dig it out—actually, that's against the Geneva Convention, but they were helping to dig it out and a couple of our blokes were there and a young woman—must have been about 20 or so, very beautiful girl—she came out and said, "You English or American?"

I said, "We're English."

She said, "Oh, I come from Kensington."

Well, I didn't have a chance to talk to her because the enemy was still around and I was a bit worried for her, so I coaxed her back into the house, out the way—because you can't fight and talk to people…I don't know what she was doing there. Whether she's caught there on her holidays or something, during the war…

Another time there was this lone house on the side of a long road, flat both sides. And there was a shelter at the side of this house and we went into the house and there was a stove going. There was the remains of a meal on the table and the cooking pots were there. And I went out, opened the shelter door and a woman come out with two children. There's a little boy, little girl both hanging on her skirts and they were all crying—including the woman. All crying like anything. And I felt embarrassed, actually. I had to stand there with a machine gun and I could have been shot many times because there were enemy around and…I just…

A big old German, old grandfather sort of bloke, he came out and he stood in front of them as if to try and protect them. But I ushered them all back into the shelter, shut the door. I don't know. When you see 'em out there you want to say, "Stop crying. Stop…" *[choking back tears]*…And now when I think of it, it almost makes me cry, but…I

Harry Rawlins in 2019

don't know how they got on. We left, anyway. I expect they got on alright...

I had no enmity towards the Germans. I thought they were just like us: we were doing what our government wanted us to do, they were doing what their government wanted. I didn't feel anything bad about them—in fact I rather liked them. When I took some prisoners—I come across this farmhouse and I looked in there. I had an idea there's some Jerries in there, cause we've been fired at before... and I look down into the cellar, and I saw someone waving a white rag round the bottom. So I looked down, I just said, "Come!"

And up they come, about eight of them, wanted to give themselves up as prisoners. But you couldn't blame them, half of their country had been run over...And I really felt...If I didn't have the Bren gun hanging around my shoulders, I would have shook hands with them all.

Harry died in June 2024

You Want to Say "Stop Crying"

***Jeff Haward**, having served from Dunkirk through North Africa to the Normandy landings, was also making his way across Germany at the end of the war.*

I met this German, right at the end of the war. He tried to kill me, twice, but I had no wish to kill him. He was old enough to be my father…Well, our machine gun platoons were dug in in the forest and through it were these fire breaks and farther down the forest was my original platoon. So I went to see some of my old friends, have a chat with them, because it was a bit quiet. And while I was there my friend's meal came up. Name was Alf Littlewort, and he later got his hand blown off…I remember I said, "I'll leave you to eat your meal, Alf." And I started walking back this 50 yards or so up this firebreak.

And I'd taken my equipment off, to be easy, with my revolver and everything. Walking down, I saw this old German, and he was plodding along, with his rifle on his shoulder. I remember he had wire-rimmed glasses on and I could see he was old. So he's looking at the ground. So I thought, well, I can't let him walk about and shoot one of my men. I'd never forgive myself. So I waited till he got really close, a few feet.

And I jumped out and I said to him, "Halt! Kommen zie here, schnell. Mitt deine hand hoche!"

And he looked at me, give me quite a steady look, decided who I was and then he took his rifle off his shoulder, put a bullet up the breach. I thought, *This is getting a bit dangerous.* So I dodged behind these trees—and they weren't wide enough to stand behind, only sideways. So he fired a shot and missed, so I went round this tree, and he was following me around…Fired a second shot and missed. Then he decided he'd had enough, put his rifle back on his shoulder, started walking away. So I realised he was a bit bomb-happy, shell-shocked.

By then some of my men had been aroused by the shot fired and the first one to get to me was an Irish boy. And he had a Sten gun…I said, "You'll have to shoot him, Ginty…Shoot him in the leg." Because he was dangerous, this German.

Afterbursts

Ginty wouldn't shoot someone walking away…So I took Ginty's Sten gun, put it on single shot, shot this German…Made sure I shot him in the fleshy part of his leg. And of course he fell over. And he's still got hold of his rifle. So we ran up to him and the first thing I had to do is get his rifle away, which he seemed a bit reluctant to do—let go of it. So I remember I give him a slight kick in the ear with my ammunition boots. And I remember this German gave me such a dirty look. Anyway, I've got the rifle away and of course you had to search him. They had breast pockets, and I went trying to do his breast pocket. He said, "Nein nein nein nein. Nein." I thought, *He's got something in there he don't want me to see.*

So…I took my own field dressing and pulled his trousers down, bound him up…though you're not supposed to, that's for your personal use—still, rules are there to be disobeyed. And opened this breast pocket and he got a photograph in of a lady and a little girl. So I said to the German—in my 'fluent' German…"Das is diene frau und kinder?" (Your wife and child?)

He said, "Ja."

I said, "Schon"—which I think means 'very nice'—and we all had a look at it. And I put it back in his pocket for him and it made him quite happy. And the stretcher bearers came up and I had to help carry him about quarter mile back to the dressing station, where we all sat and had a cup of tea, including our German friend.

And then a Jeep arrived—a medical jeep, they used to put stretchers across the bonnet. And I helped put him on the stretcher and I remember the last thing I said to him, "At least you're going to get home after the war, albeit with a limp, which is more than we can be sure of"—and I was right, because shortly after six of my men got killed…

But, it's what I like to think about that German, that he got home and limped around with his wife and child and had a happy life…

When the Germans surrendered, my platoon had to take charge of this company of 15th Panzer grenadiers. We'd fought them in the desert, but they'd always obeyed the rules and we were friendly

You Want to Say "Stop Crying"

enemies, if you like…So they were all lined up in the field, these Germans…their uniforms were dishevelled and dirty, and they was lined up like soldiers and they got all their kit in front of them which we had to search for any possible weapons.

So…we arrived there and I got my men lined up and I said, "Now before we start I want to tell you something. You're soldiers, not thieves. I don't want any of you to take anything of personal value off these Germans…I don't want to see any of you with a German watch or anything else like that."

And of course, they were searching and some of them were a bit keen and they were taking away their knives and forks…So I said, "What you taking their knives and forks for?"

They said, "Well they could stab us with them."

I said, "Well how they going to eat their bloody rations if they haven't any cooking irons?"—as we used to call them. And of course, we had a German who could speak good English and he started laughing…I was going round these Germans giving them back their knives and forks and spoons. He thought it was hilarious.

So later on we had to take these Germans and I had this German—he was a naval officer, I think, he had a dark blue uniform on—and I said, "You ride with me as my interpreter in my front carrier." I got quite friendly with him—it took us three days to take them…On about the third day, he said, "Can I ask you something?"

So I said, "Yeah."

He said, "If one of the prisoners ran away would you shoot him?"

"Well, why would a prisoner want to run away?" I said, "You're all going to an area where you will be interrogated and the details taken. If nothing's wrong you'll be going home! We don't want to feed all you lot."

"Yeah," he said. "But if one ran away, would you shoot him?"

I said, "Why are you asking me?"

He said, "Well there's one of the prisoners…and we're going to pass near his home. And he says he wants to run to his home."

I remember, I said to this German, "Well I think he's silly, because another couple of days or so and he'll be able to return home with a discharge document."

He said, "No. He wants to see his wife and family."

So I said, "Well, tell him to get up the front…and if, when he's going to run away, you call my attention and point something out in the opposite direction, I'll look that way."

Anyway, I looked half away and all of a sudden, he says, "He's going now." I saw this German going helter skelter across these fields…And of course he disappeared, my runaway. And he [the officer] said something like, "You're a good man, sergeant."

I said, "And you're a bloody nuisance!"

Jeff was awarded a Military Medal for "acts of gallantry and devotion to duty under fire", one of just 15,000 recipients of the decoration during the entire war.

Ted Hunt *served in Norway, the UK and Europe. By D-Day in Normandy he had begun to feel some sympathy with the other side, although the sentiment was at odds with what he had learned from his father after World War One, nor was it universally shared.*

[I've] fallen out with a dear friend of mine because he was boasting, at our last Royal Engineer meeting, of meeting a German who was looking for the grave of his dead uncle who was a hero, and he said, "If he was a German, he was…." and then he followed with great insults. To be a German was bad enough and inexcusable.

I have…I have sympathy with the German who wanted to get out of bed on Monday morning, do a week's work to raise a family, and then suddenly someone says, "On Monday you're in grey, you're called up…"

I was a river man, tug man…You've got tug skippers all over the world. And that's what they all want to do: start a week's work, raise a family. And then some politician, or military man, decides: "You're going to stop. And you're going to go out and kill someone you never met." Oh, the soldiers, fair enough—but you're going to set light to his children…

You Want to Say "Stop Crying"

I mean lots of people do not share my thoughts…[But] there were other people like me on D-Day…felt the same: that we are doing what our politicians have got us into, because the Germans got a bad—really bad—dictator. *We're going to conquer the world…We are the master race.* And it had to be answered, and that's why we're doing it. But the bloke over there, who I'm trying to kill, he was called up like all my men were…

When you think of young men putting themselves in the front line because some politician thought—way back, you know—that that's where you ought to be. "Build a barricade. That's it. Have tear gas thrown at you. We're behind you all the way"—three miles back.

In war, **Nikolai Koslov** *stated dispassionately, it was "kill or be killed". But even he, pragmatic as he was, had difficult moments when compelled to carry this through.*

I will share one of the hard cases, when we were turned from the Oder towards the Baltics…The regiment headquarters got cut off from both the regiment and the division—meaning encircled by the Germans. It was a farmhouse with a large yard. There was the regiment commander with an orderly and I was there with two scouts…I set up a circle defence.

Suddenly we discovered six German soldiers. We had just a few people, no one to guard them. I locked them in the lavatory and told them not to leave otherwise they would be shot. Some time passed, and I heard shots from the lavatory. I went there. Turned out, they left the lavatory and started running and they were met with gunfire. I came to them then. Lined them up…There was no one to guard them, I had nowhere to put them. Because they started running, I shot all five [sic] of them…

Did you feel any regret?

Yes. It was hard. But I didn't have a choice. I'm not a murderer. But what could I do? In the combat context I had to kill with a heavy machine gun, pistol and automated rifle.

War is war. Either he you, or you him…The only time…When I captured nine people at Lublin, I could have shot them all…and I wouldn't have been punished for that. But I sent them all to headquarters. In situations when it was ok not to kill, I preferred not to kill.

In some areas, especially on the Eastern Front and among populations colonised by Japan, soldiers occasionally found themselves fighting compatriots who had for whatever reason ended up on the other side. **Leonid Fyodorov** *came across one of the Soviet soldiers captured by Germany and given the choice either to fight for their captors or be executed.*

Romania at the time was very green. Many orchards, fruits were ripe. When we were attacking in chain formation we were going through thick vegetation…like sunflowers…Every piece of land was cultivated…Machine gun bullets over your head…It created the impression that it wasn't the war but something staged: rear exercises with shootings.

I was going through vegetation. My trophy pistol had only three bullets—my soldiers gave it to me as a gift. [I had] nothing else, not even a grenade. Suddenly, we were out of the thickets and from the direction of the front there was constant machine gun shooting. A small hill, 15 to 20 metres away from those thickets.

I didn't stop, of course, I kept going and saw what seemed to be a German…Huge man. Folded sleeves, tanned. Machine gunner. I approached him. "Hande hoch!" He raised his arms even before my command. I came up to him: machine gun, plenty of bullets, grenades, alone. My soldiers were nowhere around. Where were the soldiers? No soldiers.

I aimed the pistol at him. I was worried that he would hit me with his fist and a pistol wouldn't help me. I thought he was a German, and all of a sudden, he asked me in Russian. "Lieutenant, I will be executed, won't I?"

I wasn't very honest with him and told him that he wouldn't be executed. And this is when he told me his story. "I lived in Odessa before the war. I was working in a port as a loader." He was obviously a huge man. As his sleeves were folded, I didn't see Vlasov's

You Want to Say "Stop Crying"

mark[42]. "You know, I was drafted…There were failures…I surrendered. Now I want to come back."

Finally, I saw couple of my soldiers with rifles. I asked them to come. "Search him and take him to headquarters." When they left, I started wondering whether they would actually take him to headquarters. I thought that if he didn't start talking to them in Russian, then maybe there was a chance that they would take him…

Why I had my doubts: everyone had their own score to settle with the Germans.

__Nina Danilkovich__ and her family undoubtedly did. As a 12-year-old she had joined the partisans, which involved participation in dangerous missions and ultimately resulted in her younger sister's death. Despite this horror, when I asked her how she felt about the Germans she said that the losses of her own people precluded any feelings of sympathy—but she remembered a couple of young Germans who had spent time in her home and her compassion for their circumstances was striking.

For us to be able to work we needed to keep our negative feelings deep inside and pretend that we have a very good attitude towards them…Those [horrors] we did not forgive—and those Germans we didn't forgive. But there were normal people there.

There were two friends, Fritz and Paul, and they would tell stories. Fritz said that he couldn't get recruited in the army when the war started and his mother was running around, everywhere, asking to have him admitted to the army, and he wasn't eligible because he had some sort of illness. And why would she do that? Because it was in their heads that the war would be over by winter and everyone who was at the Eastern Front would receive large pieces of land with free labour in Russia…

---

[42] Vlasov was a Red Army general who was captured during the siege of Leningrad and subsequently defected to Nazi Germany. He led the "Russian Liberation Army" largely made up of POWs from Russia who joined him to avoid being starved. They were broadly despised by Red Army regulars.

Afterbursts

But he was also later sent to the front...By '43, everyone would have been accepted into the army, the ill and not ill. But he regretted that he had been recruited...He came to us, told us that he was being sent to the East, and he understood that it's unlikely he would come back...

He saw where the war was heading and that was why he talked so openly. There were Germans who didn't like the war, but they were very much afraid to talk about that.

On the other side of the world, **Dick King** *served in the China Burma India theatre. Here, too, there could be unexpected interactions. The Japanese troops were notorious for their brutality, and while Dick's service with the US Air Corps did not put him directly in combat with the enemy, he had heard the horror stories.*

We had, at Hankow, a huge—and I mean *huge*—area, acres and acres and acres of land, where we had Japanese prisoners of war...We had the opportunity—one of our officers arranged for us—to play a game of baseball with the Japanese, these prisoners...The field was lined all the way around...at least four people deep...And we had to use their baseball...

But the thing that impressed me was: those Japanese fellas, who were playing baseball, were just the same as us. Cos they no longer had the higher ups telling them what they had to do—and that was the case too, as you know, they had to do it or else they were shot...

And we—well, we beat the tar out of them, my God. I forget what the score was, it was a terrible score—cos, we could do no wrong with their ball...and I enjoyed that, too! Did they enjoy it? They sure as heck did—and all the people around. They were applauding all the time.

Did it change the way you thought of them?

Absolutely. No question. No question. They were the same as us, you know? Just ordinary guys having fun—in that case. And they could run, boy those Japanese could run...

After meeting these fellas as I did...I pity them. I pity anybody who would be so subjected to higher ups to commit the kind of crimes that they did, without...I would think they'd break down. But they're just ordinary guys...I couldn't believe that. They were not at all like what you saw, or were told...I think...I think we're all just people.

Dick King returned to Pennsylvania after the war and became a manager at an animal feed company. He married and had four children. He died in December 2019.

The most arresting tale of post-war rapprochement I heard from **Rolfe Monteith**, *the Canadian naval engineering graduate and Arctic convoy veteran. Thanks to the guidance of his commanding officer when he was a young cadet, Rolfe made his career in engineering after the war. Many years later, his brief service on HMS Hardy was to provide the unusual basis for a professional bond.*

Suddenly, the ship heeled over and we turned to starboard and we were increasing speed and we reached maximum speed really quickly. So there must have been some submarine contact. What would it be? Suddenly over the loudspeaker—most unusual—the captain, "Captain here. We've just been dispatched. To seek the German ship *Scharnhorst*."

Well, the *Scharnhorst* was a German battleship renowned for its fantastic design. It was regarded as being a tremendous menace if it was ever out in the shipping lanes. Normally she lay in a Norwegian fjord and...there's a message suddenly received from London: the *Scharnhorst* is out. It would be a hell of a menace if she dashed up and attacked the convoy.

So the commodore of the convoy dispatched HMS *Hardy* to go and attempt to locate *Scharnhorst*. And we spent 24 hours dashing around at this incredible speed, trying to find *Scharnhorst*. And never did...

The war ended, I returned to Canada, 25 more years in the Navy, emigrated [to Britain] in 1970. Joined a company called Babcock, big engineering company. [After my wife died, I became head of the marine department] and I replaced this Dutch ex-submariner, who was a fantastic bloke, and he said, "Rolfe, there's one thing I'm going to do with you. I'm going to take you to Germany to see the German company. Deutsche Babcock. There's a German chap who's very important in the naval market." So over we went, flew over, had lunch—lovely lunch, lots of German beer.

Afterwards Pim Kiepe introduced me to the head of their marine department, a chap called Gunter Weise…About a month later, Gunter Weise and I had supper together. And Gunter Weise said, "Rolfe, there's a rumour in Germany that you were in the Navy during the war."

And I said, "Yes, I was."

"Well, I was in the German Navy during the war…"

Gunter Weise was aboard the *Scharnhorst* the very night that Rolfe Monteith was aboard HMS *Hardy*, searching. We didn't find each other. We met years and years and years later, became the closest of mates. And what does that say? Life is very very fascinating and rewarding and here's an enemy becomes my closest chum.

Chapter 20

I Had to Bury Him

Aftermath

Surrender meant an end to the fighting, but for many there was no neat conclusion to the war. The friends they had lost and the events they had witnessed were far harder to put behind them. The very fact of survival could be a cause of shame, guilt and lifelong trauma.

For the losers in particular their shame was compounded by the ignominy of defeat. Both the Japanese and the Russians had been ingrained with the belief that death was preferable to surrender.

Soldiers often spoke to me of the friends that had died in the fighting, the good fortune of their own survival complicating the sense of loss.

Frank Tozer *served in North Africa and the Far East with the Signal Corps, travelling from India through Burma and eventually to China. He and Bob Burke, who had also begun his service in Africa and then gone on to the CBI, had leap-frogged their way past each other up the Burma Road, but Frank was more reluctant to dredge up much of what he called "ancient history". I asked whether he had talked much about his experiences after he returned home.*

Afterbursts

Frank Tozer in 2018

No…No. I think in general most of us were so happy just to get back home…We didn't appreciate—I don't think—enough that some of the people didn't come back, too…

I had a young man that I grew up with. He was like a brother to me. He was born five days after I was and we were very close and he went in the army and was a lieutenant, or captain or something, in the infantry, and he was killed in France. Which was unfortunate. And…When I came home, his mother and father came down with my mother and father to pick me up at the depot where I was out of the army, down near LA. And I didn't realise that he'd…They'd never told me that he had been killed in France, just after the invasion… And I felt terrible afterwards, more so every day, that I didn't commiserate…with his mother and father…

Gene Clark was his name. He was an infantry officer in France and was killed when a bomb came over and caught him in the wrong place…

I felt terrible, and always do…I didn't express my empathy to them.

I Had to Bury Him

Frank had just two framed photographs on his living room bookshelves, both portraits of young soldiers. One was of him, but the more prominent he took down to show me. It was of his friend Gene[43].

Jeff Haward's *war began with the retreat to Dunkirk and ended in Germany with the surrender. I asked him what had become of his best friend Johnny Hunt, who had shot him in the shoulder in France in 1940.*

I had to bury him.

He always used to come up to me and say, "I didn't mean to shoot you, Jeff."

I said, "Don't worry about it."

And he said to me once, "You know I aimed at your head!"

I said, "It's a good job you're a bloody rotten shot Johnny, innit?"

He got killed almost at my side at Wadi Akarit, in Tunisia…He was about six feet from me, in this little trench and—course, you're

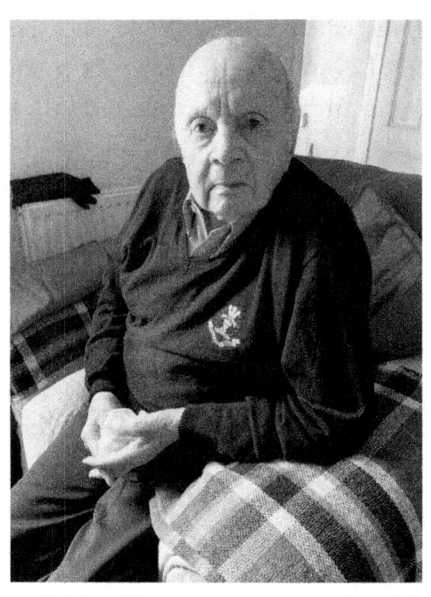

Jeff Haward in 2019

---

[43] Likely to be here: https://www.abmc.gov/decedent-search/clark%3Deugene

under heavy bombardment from the Germans and these mortar bombs and whatnot landing all around and…When it got a bit quiet, I said, "You alright, Johnny?"

There was no…no answer. And so I got out and had a look, and a mortar bomb must've burst on the edge of his trench and the full force went down. Wasn't much left…I couldn't dig him out, there was nothing to dig out. So I just covered him up with a blanket and filled the hole in.

Wasn't 'til about, oh, fifty years later…I was reading a book about it and it had all about the casualties from that Wadi Akarit. And of course, those with no known graves they put on a monument, and his name was on there…

"No known grave"…I s'pose we'd made a bit of a cross with the wood from a packing case. I suppose the winds of the desert blew it away and his grave was unmarked. Poor ole Johnny. Here's me: hundred in a month, nearly…

I do think about whether…I don't know what happens when you leave this earth. I don't believe in cherubims and seraphims and all that. But I'd like to think there's something. I often wonder—if I do go—whether some of those people I killed will be waiting to say, "Why did you kill me all those years ago? Deprive my wife of her husband, my children of their father?" I dream it—not often, but, you know, on a semi-regular basis. Haven't got an answer, have I?

Jeff died on 3 March 2022

Harry Rawlins *had relished being a soldier and received the Croix du Guerre for quick actions which disabled a German machine gun nest and protected his wounded comrades. One of his most unshakable memories, however, involved the death of his commanding officer in Germany.*

It was Operation Veritable, February [1945]…We loaded up the tanks with their ammunition because they were going to take part in the bombardment of Cleves…

We were supposed to be on what they call a piece move, which means you're moving within your own lines and you haven't got to

I Had to Bury Him

worry too much…But, I don't know what happened…They [our men] hadn't taken this part of the Reichswald Forest, and we were driving through the enemy lines and they woke up to it before we did, and they started on us…

And we had some casualties from the mortar…And the platoon commander, Michael Hewlett—fine man, he was only a year older than me I think, I was about 18, 19 at the time, and he came down the section from the top, asking everyone if they were alright. Well, I was the last one in the section…He said, "You alright?"

I said, "Yes, sir"…And I said to him, "How are the casualties?"

In fact, the section had almost disappeared with casualties from this mortaring. And I said, "How are the boys?"

I wish…I wish I'd not said anything. He said, "I'm just going back to see," and a bullet hit him in the head, killed him straight away. And that was it… Michael Hewlett was…on his back…Great gaping hole in his head and his mouth was opening and shutting as he died and…

Couldn't do anything for him, you know, it was obvious that he was dead…

I kept…I kept seeing the image of this happening again and again in front of me that day. And I…if I had nothing to do, the image would come up of him being shot…I could see it all over again. I suppose it's nerves…I kept thinking of the day and this image kept coming to me.

They buried him in the garden of a house. He was dug up afterwards, put in a cemetery. And…that was it…

I was lucky. I went to Holland last year…He'd been reinterred in Reichswald Cemetery, and I was able to go there and pay my respects. He was a fine bloke…the sort of man that everyone would want as a son…And he died like that…I'm sorry I spoke to him. I should…I should have said nothing and he would have gone.

Ken Yamada had retreated through the jungle in Burma, was wounded and eventually captured by British soldiers. He spoke of them fondly: the enemy had treated and nursed his flame thrower injury and helped him to recover.

Afterbursts

Homecoming for the defeated Japanese soldiers was difficult. Shame at both their failure and at their individual survival dogged many for what remained of their lives. Before Ken's surrender, he had made many promises to dying comrades.

I arrived in Uraga port, Tokyo Bay, two years after the end of the war. I came by the US Liberty ship…under the supervision of the British army. The captain suddenly came in and said, "Thank you for your trouble," and he sang for us…a famous Scottish song; *hotaru no hikari* (Auld Lang Syne)…I felt that we are all humans. We played rugby with the British soldiers…

I cried when I saw Mount Fuji…I went to Hakata station and everything was burned down with the air raids. I then went to my childhood village where my parents had evacuated…It wasn't easy to adjust since I saw so many horrible things during the war. My values were different compared to others. I still think about it now…It was difficult to socialise…

Ken Yamada in 2018

I Had to Bury Him

One of the soldiers cremated and brought back the remains of three dead soldiers and I brought back my comrade's remains to his house. The mother said, "These bones are not real." She said she already had his bones.

But we said, "These are his only bones," and when the mother opened the pot she had, it had stones inside.

The three mothers said the same thing: How did their sons die? So I told them that my comrade died like he was falling asleep, but that wasn't the reality. They all died in such pain. But I told all of them that they all died peacefully.

Ken was one of just two survivors out of the 380 soldiers that set sail from his hometown. On his return from the war, Ken worked in the supply department of a construction company where he met and married his wife. As our conversation concluded, he said, "I have a question for you." Rather than ask me about my work, as I anticipated, he said that he had so loved the singing of the Scottish troops who had guarded him as a POW, would I please sing for him? Once I had regained my composure I, too, sang Auld Lang Syne.

Trained as a medic with the US Navy, **Rodney Armstrong** *had first been spared death when he caught measles just before his class was deployed to Guadalcanal, where they all perished. Several more times during the war he would be the lucky survivor.*

I felt fortunate, but there was such an element of chance. For example, on one island I was seated one night watching a movie out in the open jungle. And next to me was my closest associate on that island and a Japanese sneaked up and disembowelled him while I was sitting right next to him. And it was pure coincidence that I lived and he died, with a terrible scream, next to me in the middle of the movie.

And then I had another friend…We were hurrying to go down a steel ladder down to the next deck where people needed help, and this bomb went off behind us, and he was smashed right against the side of the steel ship. And I was blown down on my face down to the next deck below, which damaged my teeth—but I was alive and once again the next fellow was dead.

Rodney Armstrong in 2017

So…the element of chance was always there.

Despite the constant proximity of death, Rodney still spent some of his time at sea looking to his future.

There I was, drafted out of high school, no high school diploma, and I sat on that aircraft carrier in the South Pacific and wondered, "What am I going to do…?" So…I sent off a simple-minded letter to the admissions office at Williams College and explained that I was in the armed forces and I'd had four years at a good boarding school and I wanted to go to Williams when the war came to an end…

So a nice letter came back, said, "Take correspondence courses from the University of California in Berkeley and have them send the results of those correspondence courses to our admissions office." So…that's exactly what I did…

So…when I got my medical discharge I went directly to Williamstown, keeping on my uniform. I weighed at that point about 100lbs, and part of my hair was white—and I deliberately left on my uniform so that they could see the purple heart and all of the rest of the stuff I had up here…And they took one look at me and said,

"We'll take you in in September"—and this was April of '45—"and if you last the first semester, you're in for good."

And looking back on it I was a terrible candidate for Williams. I couldn't get through a night without waking up the neighbourhood by screaming and yelling.

After he graduated, Rodney worked as a librarian at the Philips Exeter Academy. I asked him why he had opted for life at a secondary school.

I think I'd been through so much in the war that what I was looking for was a useful life at an interesting and happy level. And I think it has taken me a good portion of my life to get over what I went through…And I think what I was going for was…a life where I wouldn't be involved with all sorts of drama, decisions.

Even though he may have desired a low-key career, Rodney nonetheless ultimately became a recognised expert in his field. He died on 13 April 2021, not long after his 98th birthday.

Richard Dayhoff *too suffered from memories that were hard to bury. He was fortunate to miss the fighting on Iwo Jima—his ship arrived during the battle only to bob around off the coast for three days, he and his shipmates all too seasick to fight—but he was not spared close combat. After Iwo Jima he was sent to Guam where he came face to face with a Japanese soldier who crept into his tent one night—the soldier escaping as Richard struggled to grab a weapon. The experience left him unable to sleep for fear of being killed.*

There were other events that lingered: shooting a couple of Chinese who were attempting to steal US munitions after the Japanese surrender and dealing with a US officer who had raped a Chinese woman. He said that he felt the man's behaviour had demeaned him, too, as a fellow soldier. Richard's demeanour was gruff and admissions such as this were startling. The final thoughts he shared with me were the most unexpected of all.

It's really tough to kill a human being. It's you or them. You understand? I didn't like killing a human being…But…we were

Richard Dayhoff in 2018

taught: don't hesitate. If you hesitate, you're dead…I believe I was lucky…I hate to tell you: I loved to fight…

[But] I can't sleep. Unless they give me knockout pills. And you know, I don't understand that—why after all these years, I can't go to bed and go to sleep without this stuff coming back?…

I can see them little Jap babies[44] floating down the Yangtze River…It was misty and there's two Chinamen standing down here at a small tree. The one guy hollered, you know, "Hey, Joe! You look! He, he, he!" Babies floating down the river.

I got so damned mad, I come down off of that bridge, walked up to the Chinaman, I grabbed him, I said, "You crack another smile, I'm going to drive your teeth to the back of your mouth." That solved

---

[44] It is possible given the location that Richard meant Chinese babies, but he had also told me that Chinese women who had been raped by Japanese soldiers often kept the child as it entitled them to a better food ration.

it. He didn't smile anymore. But can you picture: chunky Japanese babies floating down the river? It sticks with you.

Yoshiko Shimabukuro *was one of the "Himeyuri", senior schoolgirls from two merged boarding schools who were conscripted by the Japanese Imperial Army to serve in field hospitals. Initially stationed in caves which had been specially prepared for the purpose, they were forced to retreat, taking shelter in dank limestone caverns as the Japanese lost ground.*

When I returned [home] after the war, my older brother and sister had died…My parents thought I was dead…I also lost a lot of friends, there were only a few who survived. So I worried then if it was ok for me to be alive. So many of my friends and teachers died and I felt very guilty. But after seeing both my parents, I apologised to my friends who passed away and told myself that I must keep on living…

When we went to the battlefield, we all said to each other that it's the same to either live or die, but it was difficult for me to keep living. It's only after the [Himeyuri] museum was built that I thought it was ok to live—up until then, I didn't want to see anyone. At dawn, there were some who fled their houses and hid until sunset. In the north, where one of my friends died, their parents asked me what happened to their child, but I couldn't say…

After a memorial service was held on the opening day of the museum, I feared people would shout at me for being alive while so many had died. That's all I was worried about. I apologised.

Then someone came up to me and said, "It's because you survived that this building was built!" Parents said they didn't know anything about how their daughters had died and thanked me. People finally found out about their siblings, and they thanked me.

We then gathered at lunchtime and acknowledged that it's ok for us to live.

For those who experienced the devastation of Hiroshima and Nagasaki, the suffering was compounded by ignorance. No one understood at first that they had witnessed an atomic bomb because no such thing had previously existed. The post-war American administration's efforts to suppress the information—which the Japanese government was in no position to resist—added unnecessarily to the medical fallout.

Only after the American occupation ended in 1952 did people begin to learn more, but suspicions about contagion and hereditary effects disadvantaged anyone who admitted they had been present—and this stigma continues to plague their descendants.

Survivors consequently underwent not only the initial trauma of the blasts and their aftermath but also this continuing prejudice against "hibakusha", with the obviously sick both unemployable and shunned. **Yoshio Hara** was at first too scared and ashamed to admit his hibakusha status—even in later years when the Japanese government began to offer compensation.

Near the end, the soldiers that survived were to be taken somewhere to examine what happens to A-bomb survivors. There was this rumour going around that that was the reason we were being kept there. This was actually more terrifying—that even after the war was over, we thought we would be taken away, and we thought about how much longer we would be able to live, what kind of symptoms we would develop. We knew nothing about the A-bomb, we didn't even know the word…So we were faced with a new type of fear…

The 45 days between August and September 17, that was my youth. My 45 days of youth. It's a sad youth. My next youth was returning to school. Many of my comrades had died, so I kept silent as an A-bomb survivor—as seen from my [official survivor] notebook[45], which I refused to have issued for 50 years. My comrade Sasaki, who was also a teacher—we swore we would never have an A-bomb notebook issued for ourselves, and we tried to keep this promise no matter what happened…We would never receive compensation from the government through this notebook. It was a lifetime promise…

[T]hose who died before us…all those corpses, they received nothing. How can we, who survived contentedly, receive such compensation from the government? I would never be able to forgive

---

[45] Atomic Bomb Survivor's Health Handbook, a document entitling Nagasaki and Hiroshima survivors to Japanese government support.

I Had to Bury Him

myself for that. Back then, many young soldiers felt that way. I finally received the notebook 52 years later...

[I did not directly tell my wife I was a survivor]. She had noticed that I would always sit, genuflect and pray on August 6 in front of the TV in my latter years—and in front of the radio when I was young. I would sit silently, and she would be worried about what I was doing...Then the TV era began and she could see, through the TV.

When I received my A-bomb notebook, I was honest with my wife about it, and we went to visit Hiroshima together and we brought flowers and kneeled down, the two of us together. We brought the bouquet of flowers and told the victims that although I've been in a shell, I will speak up from now on. And that there is a *hibakusha* group and I will become a member. From then on, my life completely changed—together with that of my wife. I began making presentations at the memorial...

As teacher, as an educator of junior high school students, I never talked about my experience to other teachers or students, so now I am doing this to atone for my sins. To talk about my experiences is my lifework until I die. This is my mission...I am doing this for A-bomb survivors—and having lived for this long, there are many old people who are bedridden or hospitalised. Only a few who are alive can do what I am doing now. No matter what position you are in, I must speak for those who were not able to say their last words.

Chapter 21

When I See the Graveyards

Remembrance

War cemeteries, with their rows of identical, neatly spaced markers, are profoundly sad places. Each headstone sends out tendrils of grief that reach through space and time to form an invisible web connecting the visiting mourner to distant bereaved families. The severance of betrothals that were never consummated and the voids left by children never born have an almost physical presence.

One of the inspirations behind this book came from a winter in the Ardennes during which I watched Band of Brothers, struck by how awful it must have been to have fought in that area in the depth of winter, so far from home and so lacking in comfort. There are cemeteries all around the region from both so-called "world" wars. Among the most lonely graves must surely be those of the fallen Germans, some as young as 17, who are buried far from home in land which would have had little sympathy for them.

I visited a couple of cemeteries where substance was given to some of the names carved on the tombstones. At Maastricht American War Cemetery, on a whim, I looked through the record files for a familiar

Afterbursts

name. I was taken aback to find that of William Heister Dukeman, whose death was featured in an episode of Band of Brothers. I was aware that the series was based on real people, but finding his name there made me feel I had lost someone I knew, even if just a little. It made the loss more personal and the war itself more immediate.

At the Rhone American Cemetery and Memorial in Draguignan, the superintendent offered to share with me the histories of some of the dead. As we walked among the rows of immaculate headstones, two graves were undressed of their grass, the brown earth freshly revealed. America maintains a team researching what are known as X files, in an attempt to give names to those in Unknown graves. Recently, two sets of remains had been identified with reasonable certainty and were being exhumed to be sent back to the US for DNA testing against relatives. Previously, a soldier from that cemetery had been identified via his surviving twin. In his 90s by the time his brother was returned to him, the bereaved sibling said, "Now we can finally be buried together."

Cemeteries hold great significance for war veterans, many of whom pay their respects to fallen comrades on anniversaries while the public mark the peace for which they fought. For those without specific friends to visit, such cemeteries serve as a reminder of the waste of life occasioned by war. Ernest Hilton's wife, saddened as we surveyed the graves in the cemetery at Kanchanaburi—where the dead ranged from British solders aged 18 to Dutch East Indies settlers in their 50s—suggested that before any world leader was allowed to declare war they should be made to read a roll call of the dead interred in these places.

For all the many reminders of the waste of life occasioned by war, we continue to fight. As thought-provoking as the war cemeteries I have visited was an installation I happened upon while meeting CBI vets on the West Coast. Every Sunday, volunteers from Veterans for Peace lay out red, white and blue grave markers in memory of US soldiers killed in current wars.

Row upon row of crosses stretch for hundreds of yards at this makeshift memorial they call Arlington West, red crosses deployed

When I See the Graveyards

Memorial at Bayeux cemetery

to represent ten US service personnel due to the rising death count. Beside the flag-draped coffins symbolising those who have died in combat in any given week, the patch of blue crosses also grows with the suicide of each veteran of our modern-day conflicts. If crosses for the enemy troops were included, they would cover the entire beach of nearly five kilometres.

An explanation reads: "This memorial is dedicated to the men and women of our military who have made the greatest sacrifice and to those who live on with their wounds." It continues, "We veterans believe these wars have wasted the lives of our children, family members, neighbours and the countless other inhabitants of this planet deemed 'enemies' by our government and military leaders."

The volunteers manning the information tent are often veterans themselves, or come from military families. Occasionally, they told me, they suffer abuse from passers-by who mistake their stance against war as a reproach of the troops that prosecute it—but they are not against the serving men and women themselves, just the policies that send youths to their deaths or bring them home so badly damaged mentally or physically that they can no longer function.

Afterbursts

French children celebrate veterans on D-Day 2019

Attending a commemorative event with veterans is a huge privilege, one gets a small insight into the sacrifices they made, the friends they lost and the grief with which the war left them. I was lucky enough to join a group of British veterans for the 75th anniversary of the D-Day landings, a huge gathering of war nuts coming to pay homage to the war heroes, hear their stories and watch or take part in re-enactments. The atmosphere was a mix of mournful pilgrimage and joyful carnival by turns. I felt perhaps that one of the saddest aspects was the absence of a noticeable German contingent among the masses, but even three quarters of a century on, the wounds on both sides still ache on these anniversaries.

World War Two veteran visits to overseas cemeteries often coincide with attendance at commemorative events, which are especially lively in continental Europe. As well as a chance to pay their own respects, the Allied soldiers appreciate the rapturous welcome they receive—for many of the British veterans I met, the recognition feels more marked than any afforded them at home. Perhaps this is because for those whose homelands were occupied, liberation felt more immediate. When it comes to the US and Britain, there are no battle sites around which to congregate: their soldiers mostly died "over there".

Ron Johnson went annually to mark the liberation of Holland and attend commemorations of the Battle of Arnhem.

I don't think the people in this country [Britain] ever feel it in the same way that the Dutch do. When we go to Oosterbeek, in pretty well every house there at September time all the banners come out. And you see everywhere Airborne forces banners, celebrating…

Still, after all these years they appreciate what happened. And when you go in May, they celebrate the Liberation. There's about 100,000, I think, line the routes when we go. You go in a golf trolley up the high street and they're absolutely packed solid…all clapping and cheering…

My wife didn't like to hear about it [the war] at all…And I think she had just reason. I was…On one occasion, I was unwise. We were in the cemetery at Oosterbeek—and she only went there with me once. We were on the way to see family in Germany and we went to Oosterbeek on the way, and I took her to the cemetery. And while we were there I said, "There's something I'd like to show you."

And I took her along to the graves of two young boys aged, I think…21…And I go and look at their graves each time I go there. They're twins and their numbers were next to one another and they were killed at the same time at Arnhem. And my wife didn't ever forgive me for taking her…I think she put herself in the position of being their mother, and losing twin sons in a battle like that.

There are 41 sets of brothers, including one set of stepbrothers, buried in the Netherlands American Cemetery in Maastricht.

The surrender came in 1945 and the first Armistice after that, November the 11th they flew 20 glider pilots across to Arnhem. We were very apprehensive, the 20 glider pilots. We thought, *well what reception are we going to get?* because their houses and Oosterbeek and these places were so—in the battle—were so knocked about. And in Arnhem itself. *What reception are we gonna get?* And it was wonderful. And it's been wonderful ever since.

And as you know the children each year put the flowers on the graves at the ceremony, at the service in Arnhem. Wonderful that is…I was there the first time they did that and there were 20 glider pilots, I've just mentioned, and we had the service and we didn't know the children were coming. And when they came out…tears streamed down our faces.

I asked Ron how he would feel if we had another war.

Oh, I think it would be absolutely terrible. War is…There can be a "justified" war, as there was with Nazi Europe—it was well justified. But war is never glorious, war is horrible. Really horrible.

Ted Hunt, *too, returned often to Europe after the war, welcoming the occasion to reminisce in an atmosphere of celebration. I asked him why he went to Normandy and Arnhem on anniversaries year after year.*

Well, I'm in company with veterans, which is good…And we have a similar background, and an appreciation of each other. Jeff Haward—Military Medal. Wonderful man…Now, Military Medals—what, one in 10,000? So rare! I know what that Military Medal means. Most people don't—oh, it's just another medal—but I know. My goodness! He's got to be something extra, extra special—and what a wonderful story he can tell…

Fred Glover? Paratrooper. Lied about his age. Eighteen on D-Day, arrives in a glider, he gets wounded on the way down and lands on the guns at Ranville, which they knock out. Now, the guns at Ranville were all designed to fire on Gold Beach, so when Glover arrived, badly wounded in his knees and legs, and put out the guns—and lost a lot of his mates putting out the guns at Ranville—he stopped those guns firing on me on Gold Beach.

That's what I go for. That's what I go for. [To] talk to them…And there's all that banter which goes on. And you think, *No one else can enjoy this…*

When I See the Graveyards

In Holland—because I was in the 49th division in Norway, the only division to serve in the Arctic—we had polar bear flashes. So on my blazer, I got a polar bear. Now, the city of Utrecht was liberated by polar bears. The first two vehicles…5,000 people wanted to touch—they waited for years for these bloody vehicles to come, and there they were. And when I walk through Utrecht, twelve-year-old girls come up to me saying, "Thank you for our freedom." Millionaires can't buy it.

__Fergus Anckorn__ went to visit his fallen friends in Thailand decades after the war. He was particularly touched by the way the Commonwealth War Graves Commission cared for the graves.

All of these places—so beautifully looked after. I went out to the one at Kanchanaburi looking for my great friend who I knew was dead. And there was an old dear there but the office was closed and I thought, "Well, we can't spend all day going up and down looking for his name."

And I asked her and she said, "Well ask that boy there."

There was a man who was tending the graves, cutting the grass with scissors. And I went up to him and I said, "Could you tell me where Lester Martin's grave is?"

He said, "It's the third one in on the second row."

And I said, "How do you know that?"

He said, "I know the names of everyone on the patch where I'm working. And every time I go to work there, I think of the man underneath."

And there was Lester Martin's grave.

Fergus died on March 22, 2018.

Of all the veterans, __Yoshio Nakamura__ most explicitly talked about the cost of war in terms of lost potential. I met him the day after President Trump in his first term had ordered the successful assassination of Iranian general Qasem Soleimani. As he gave his recollections of World War Two, Yoshio drew parallels between the outcome of that war and the cost of actions such as the one that Trump had just overseen.

Afterbursts

Yoshio Nakamura in 2020

We should be very careful in sending people to battle. It should be the last thing you do, not the first thing you do…Because when I see the graveyards—I saw them in Italy, and I've seen them in France and I see them in Northern California, here—each grave represents a very young person who could have been something. I just think, *I could have been one of those guys and no one would ever know who I was*…Another guy there could have been a senator, or could have been a congressperson or a professor, or an engineer, a parent and grandparent. And I just think of how lucky I am that I have been able to experience this.

When you're getting down to having war or no war, then I hope the people who are in decision-making positions consider the young people who are asked to serve…I see these crosses in these military graveyards and just to think how many thousands of these people could be doing something really great…

In fact…I've read a lot of letters from the daughters of the "rescued [Texas] battalion"… because they would [otherwise] never have been born. One of my friends in Hawaii said, "Gee. It's such a heart-warming thing that these people would write that: *we would never have known about my father…We wouldn't even be here if it hadn't been for you…rescuing them."*

Because at that time they were surrounded by the German troops, in this German forest in the mountains in northern France. And they were running out of food, they were running out of ammunition. Some of them were getting sick. And the 442nd was able to break through—but the casualties were three times the ones who were rescued…I think the governor at the time in Texas, later on, made the 442nd honorary Texans because they were so grateful…

[US Senator Daniel Inoue] was in the Hundredth Battalion. And he was injured in the last battle, breaking the Gothic Line, in Italy. But he was in many of the battles before then and he wanted to be a surgeon, a doctor, and when he lost his arm he couldn't be that…so he went on to become an attorney…He won the Medal of Honour for his heroic action…

I think about him and all the others who might have had the opportunity to be something, could have been someone who discovered a cure for some disease. That's one of the things I learned about, being in the service, is that you should be very careful in ordering people to go to war…It's not as easy as just shooting something, there's actually people who are going to be destroyed—and *our* people, it isn't just the other person, the other side.

Chapter 22

A Huge Manipulation of Knowledge

Alternative truths

History is supposedly written by the victors. During my travels, however, I did not really find this to be true: history tends to be written by the nation that wrote it—especially if you are in one of its museums. Each country peddles its own narrative, whether it be to promote national pride or justify (if not omit entirely) national misdeeds.

I came across a number of examples of this, however the most arresting related to the histories of the US submarine *Bowfin* and the Japanese *Tsushima Maru*. USS *Bowfin*—otherwise nicknamed the Pearl Harbor Avenger—is one of several vessels open for tours at Pearl Harbor. A fleet attack submarine, it was launched just days after Pearl Harbor and carried out nine tours of duty during the Second World War, receiving a Presidential Unit Citation and a Navy Unit Commendation along the way. It is a beautiful and well-preserved vessel and walking around it one can imagine how tough it must have been to serve in her cramped quarters for weeks on end.

In Okinawa, there is a museum to the *Tsushima Maru*—where I had been struck by the photo of a drowned child who looked so like the son of my friend. The vessel was an evacuation transport which met its end in August 1944 as it carried more than 800 schoolchildren and a similar number of adult evacuees from Okinawa to the Japanese mainland, hoping to spare them the looming Battle of Okinawa.

On the *Bowfin*'s sixth patrol, for which it received the Navy citation, the submarine sank several vessels in a convoy it intercepted, including the *Tsushima Maru*. She went down, taking all the evacuees and their teachers and crew with her. Just 59 of the children survived. The sinking of the *Tsushima Maru* does not feature in the *Bowfin*'s tourist introduction in Pearl Harbor—nor, to avoid denting morale, were the submarine sailors given the full details of their successful mission.

At the Tsushima Maru Museum, meanwhile, when I visited in 2018 the only English language exhibit gave the specifications for the *Bowfin*. There was no other English explanation of how Japan and America arrived at such a terrible intersection in the war where an enemy submarine might end up responsible for the deaths of so many innocents.

There are plenty of more troubling examples of one country's pride being another's outrage. In the Yasukuni Museum, as a testament to Japan's engineering prowess is displayed the locomotive that first steamed along the Burma Railway—otherwise known as the Death Railway, for its role in the loss of nearly 300,000 lives of labourers and POWs. Over in the US, the Enola Gay, which dropped the atomic bomb on Hiroshima, is displayed at the Smithsonian Institution's Air and Space Museum.

Different perspectives on history create disputes not only between nations. Some Japanese citizens, too, object to their government's revisionist interpretations of the military's more brutal actions. The re-designation of comfort women—women forced into sexual servitude for the Japanese military—as willing prostitutes and a denial of military culpability in the deaths of civilians in the Ryukyu islands have caused dismay among survivors keen for their country to acknowledge and atone for its military aggressions.

A Huge Manipulation of Knowledge

Sueichi Kido, who witnessed the Nagasaki bomb at age five, said of the Yasukuni Shrine:

> I went. But it made me feel very sick. How can human life be devalued to this extent? I really felt so sick, but I thought I had to see it at least once…In my view, the Yasukuni Shrine enshrines those who protected the Emperor—the imperial family, that's the start—so it enshrines those who dedicated themselves to the country. And the leaders who created the nation are politicians and those in the army, so these people are honoured there. But the majority of those who gave their lives are not these people—particularly those who died in war are not these people, they are not leaders. Although they are victims, they reverse this to make it seem as if they aren't, they change our mindset. That's what it means to make people into gods…all the victims. They tell them they will become a god in order to make the many victims think that they are not.

After the war, he had been a history teacher, and felt that the reason many Japanese denied the comfort women issue was due to exploitation of the passage of time.

> People do not know and have not been properly educated about the facts—however, right after the war everyone knew, even if they didn't talk about it. The reason being, soldiers that were sent to China, they were fathers, right? It's often said that in the battlefield, the soldiers were devils in Korea and China but they became the kind father back at home. So the fathers didn't speak about it, but everyone knew.
>
> But once these people die, the reality known by people who know the facts starts to fade away, and people who are close to power, including politicians, begin feeding false information

that this didn't happen…People are indoctrinated…So I am involved in an event in Gifu, where I live, to help arrange a discussion on 150 years since the Meiji era. To tell the people the truth, and to have everyone think about it together. Even if it takes time, I must do this.

After all the conversations I had, I couldn't but wonder whether a more unified approach to the evils and losses of this globally devastating conflict—one which most people would wish to avoid repeating—would not be more constructive. Keith Lowe's The Fear and the Freedom noted in 2017 that one brave museum curator in Poland was attempting to do just that. He was fired the following year as his nation's leaders swung to a more right-wing, nationalist, stance.

I began writing this book before reinterpretations of national history started to sweep the West. Prior to that, it seemed as though history was one of the few fields which had not yet begun to take a more diverse look at its approach. Business, religion and society were already being re-examined through the lens of ethnic and gender diversity. In so many realms our societies had begun to question traditional thinking—but history had remained immune. Then, over the following few years, statues of Confederate General Lee were toppled, as were those of some philanthropists credited with funding the creation of colonised nations.

The history of World War Two is often cynically deployed in service of uniting a nation. In Brexit, "Blitz spirit" was invoked. Facing economic challenges, China turns attention to the enemy without, Japan. Even modern wars are no exception: Clinton was saved excessive scrutiny from his sexual peccadilloes by the war in Iraq, and Trump successfully diverted attention from his first impeachment with an assassination in Iran. Amidst all the sabre-rattling aggression, the individual realities of conflict are buried.

Perhaps because Japan lost the war this seemed to me to have led to a great deal more introspection and soul-searching among individuals at the grass-roots level. It is perhaps harder in hindsight to accept how one could be motivated for attack than it can ever be to accept the greater virtue inherent in defence. Visiting museums and veterans I encountered a highly engaged community desperate to understand, avoid and even atone for the mistakes of their nation's past. This contrasted with the official line, which has flip flopped between denial and contrition for its wartime misdeeds. Japan's relationships with its neighbours consequently remain consistently more tense than those of European neighbours with Germany, whose authorities enshrined repentance in all its post-war institutions.

__Nobuo Okimatsu__ was among the veterans who felt that better education and institutionalised contrition for its former aggression might foster better relations.

For himself, after the war he had had no interest in studying in order to get a job, become rich and obtain a high position. Somewhat akin to Rodney's post-war yearning for a quiet life as a school librarian, Nobuo simply sought the happiness he felt lay in "ordinary day to day living".

I returned to Kure City...After I found out I could attend university I wanted to study in order to learn why Japan had lost the war. At the time, I realised how miserable it was to lose a war. I saw so many cases of people who died in the war and families that became economically strained. Losing the war meant that the nation lost its power and confidence. There were many crimes and the police couldn't do anything. Japanese people looked different to me.

To lose in war is a tragedy...If the nation chooses the wrong path, such tragedies occur, so I now feel that people must become more informed. We feel it's unfortunate there are so many Japanese who have been wrongly educated about Chinese history. Japan and China have a bad relationship now and there are many Japanese who dislike China who do not think about what Japan did in China during the war.

A more fundamental issue is that since the Japanese military believed Japan was superior, they believed they could do anything. This kind of mentality creates strong racial discrimination...

Nobuo's studies led him to believe that Japan had adopted Western learning too selectively during the Meiji period—incorporating science without rational scientific thinking and eschewing democracy based on its own spiritual and cultural superiority.

I also learned that education led Japan to lose the war, so I aspired to become a teacher...I taught at Kumagaya high school for 45 years...social studies.

When a war starts, ordinary people don't know about it. During the Sino-Japan War and the Pacific War, it was not discussed in the Diet, there was no debate on starting or not starting a war. We are suddenly told we're at war and we just followed...

In any country, governments act arbitrarily to a certain extent. In Japan, based on the Meiji Constitution, the Emperor was the supreme commander of the military and it was a system that ignored the people's opinions. While there were some people in Japan who believed we should be at war, there were many who didn't want to go to war. Back then, Japan had created an environment in which it could easily enter war...

Japanese high schools do not teach students about modern history, the reason being there isn't enough time. We study from the Jomon period and by the time students graduate, there are many schools that do not manage to make it to modern history. Modern history is seldom taught even at university. The reason is that the interpretations remain divided. So Japanese students are unfamiliar with modern history.

Modern history is mainly comprised of the Meiji era. Many teachers and textbook writers also share this perspective so it's difficult to have a proper understanding of China.

When speaking to Chinese students, they are well-educated in modern and contemporary history but they do not know much about ancient history. Japanese students only learn about ancient Chinese history, so it's difficult to communicate. It's a major problem that Japanese schools do not teach about modern Chinese history.

[Textbook censorship is a factor] too, but that's only one facet, it's not the essential issue.

At the core is that conservative politicians strongly respect the Meiji government and believe it was absolutely right. I don't think there's much fabrication [in the textbooks] since there are those who would oppose this, but there is omission and purely listing the facts so people cannot make a proper judgement...Many Japanese people do not know about the terrible things Japan did in China, and establishing friendly relations between Japan and China will not succeed unless people are educated about this history...

It's natural for Chinese people to have anti-Japanese sentiment. If anything, I think Chinese people are broad-minded. [I have been to China] about 20 times. [In 2016], I gave a lecture at Beijing Normal University. It was one room...about 30-40 students majoring in Japanese. They listened attentively. I didn't have any problems...

Japanese have many misunderstandings about China, so the only way is to work on this from the grassroots level. Talking to Chinese students it's surprising to find so many students who love Japan, so if Japanese people also support these people, I think Chinese people's anti-Japanese sentiment will change.

Choho Zukeran had been a teenager during the Battle of Okinawa, later becoming a statesman and advocate of Ryukyu identity. He too advocated for a more honest accounting of Japan's behaviour during the war. Most controversially for Okinawans, attempts were made in the 2000s to alter history books and erase references to the mass suicides of civilians encouraged by the Japanese army. Others took exception to Japan's denials about comfort women—an incredibly divisive issue that, due to the influence of Japan's conservative lobby, has to this day been only partially acknowledged.

The [Japanese] government says there was no massacre [suicides of civilians in Okinawa]—it really made me furious. The textbooks tried to change that, but I said *Look at all of these victims...*

The Japanese government denies there were comfort women, which is ridiculous. When I think about this, I think there is nothing more irresponsible...

China, South Korea, North Korea all condemn Japan. This is inevitable...Actually, Indonesia, Malaysia, and the Philippines should also be ill-disposed towards Japan. The Japanese military and the government also did such horrific things in South Asia, but the government has not repented for these acts and just makes excuses.

In the case of China, during Mao Zedong's ascendancy, the then general secretary Zhou Enlai had studied in Japan as an exchange student and the Japanese prime minister at the time, Tanaka Kakuei, advanced the normalisation of relations between Japan and China. At the time, Zhou Enlai, who was well educated on Japan, said to let bygones be bygones for all that Japan did during the war and asked for both countries to move forward.

The following year, I visited China as a representative of Okinawa. Many honourable people were so welcoming to me that when I was in Shanghai, I asked: why are the Chinese being so nice despite all the Japanese military did to China during the war? They said we are both victims, and that if we talk about war, the alcohol won't taste good so please talk about something else, and they brushed the issue aside at the restaurant. I remember being very impressed...

When Deng Xiaoping became the leader and advanced a policy to open up the Chinese economy, the people gained knowledge about the truth, so things were completely different on my second trip to China...As the general public became more knowledgeable, anti-Japanese sentiment became increasingly strong. Since Japan won't repent, China publicly opposes prime ministerial visits to the Yasukuni Shrine and the suppression of what the Japanese military did during the war...

What's most important is to advance citizen exchanges. In any country, bilateral relations prosper through trusting trade. The most important thing is trust. War doesn't happen if there is trust. If you lose trust, you lose everything, both at the state and individual level.

A Huge Manipulation of Knowledge

Keiko Ogura *was eight when the bomb was dropped on Hiroshima. Later in life she began actively to speak about her experiences, travelling as far as the US to give lectures. In her work she has experienced first-hand the power of people-to-people diplomacy, as both Chinese and Americans have reassessed their positions in response to her personal story.*

Last year [in 2017] when I went to an American college and university, I met so many people. Staying ten days, I had to give so many different lectures…And then, during that time, at lunch time around 30 or 40 students came in and asked questions and I answered.

One Chinese girl started to cry and then—a young girl—she said, "Until now I didn't like Japanese. Especially politicians—but not only politicians…Fundamentally I don't like [the Japanese]. But this is the first time I found that I like Japanese, after talking with you."

Then she started to cry and couldn't stop crying. "I cannot forgive myself, who hated the Japanese so much. Why did I hate so much? Why, now, I like you—and also, I feel like I like Japanese? Why?" She continued to cry around 30 minutes, 25 minutes…

She herself was surprised. So that she said, "Not only me, but my friends and other people…can't forgive the Japanese, what the Japanese did."

So that's the problem. Fundamentally, they don't like Japanese and they're always competing, China and Japan…

Last year I went to Syracuse university, I was giving a lecture and there were more than 200 students. After that we visited a veterans' club. There were around 200 veterans. And there I met one veteran who was 95 years old. He knew Enola Gay, the bomber and he was talking about that and I said, "Yes I know that."

He was *so* happy there is somebody who knows. He was proud of the B-29: how big, how wonderful…

I couldn't tell him, "I am one of the survivors."

Also, two years ago I went to California. The mayor asked me to tell the story to people, aged people, who know World War Two, and they said, "How I envy the young people who can visit Hiroshima directly." Then a short video and I told my story.

Afterbursts

They started to cry. Everybody started to cry. There were two tissue paper boxes going around...And I started to cry...And then they hugged me, "Keiko, we did not know anything..." It was the first time they had heard this story Because, the first time I went to America, 100% they believed that dropping the bomb was the right decision...

As a boy, **Yoshio Nakamura** *and his family had suffered from prejudice against Japanese Americans in the aftermath of Pearl Harbour. I asked him whether he felt that times today were much different—specifically when it came to misinformation of the sort that had encouraged much of the American public simply to stand by as his family was put in a camp.*

No, no, it's not different. It's different in the sense that there are many more avenues for things to get out...It is worrisome in that when an individual looks at a person who has brown skin and comes from Mexico—or the parents, or their grandparents, came from Mexico...To call them rapists, robbers and drug dealers. I think that there is a generalisation that is really pretty dangerous...

And, well, a stream of people coming from Honduras and from South America this way, and looking upon them as rapists and robbers...And there are little children and mothers who are coming up...

So it's somewhat similar, in that sense: that they want to paint this ugly brush on everyone. Most of them are legitimately leaving a very dangerous situation. So, I would say that there is a similarity between what was in 1942 and now...

But fortunately, too, there are plenty of people who are willing to stick their necks out today. During the early 1940s, the Quakers were among the very few groups that felt that what was happening was wrong.

Even the American Civil Liberties Union was not very protective of us, you know...It's amazing what a heavy dose of propaganda can do to people.

Yoshio had been concerned in particular about the jingoistic and frequently xenophobic messaging of the president of the US when we met in 2020. The end of President Trump's first term sparked some of the worst partisan violence seen in the Capitol since the civil war, and Asians of all origins were subject to abuse as a result of prejudices stirred by corona virus rhetoric.

Propaganda has always been a useful tool. In the years after the war, it was redeployed as countries which had been allies of convenience became divided by ideology.

Ed Fulwider, *who served as a marine towards the end of the war, was posted to China where he repatriated surrendered Japanese soldiers. At the time, he was "crazy about China" and recalled using his leave to visit the Great Wall, the Ming Tombs and the Summer Palace. He returned to the country in the 1990s with his wife, Loralie.*

As World War Two was ending, though, China's civil war was gaining momentum. While publicly promising not to pick sides, the US supported the Nationalist Chinese government and remained its ally: veteran pilots told me how they ferried Chiang Kai-Shek's troops between battles despite their supposed neutrality. Consequently, despite its contribution to driving out the Japanese, the US ended up pitted against the eventual winners of the war and leaders of China, the Chinese communists.

I ended up in the paymaster's office at the dispersion camp [in China]. I was just a junior clerk over there and they were having occasional fire fights between the Communists and the Nationalists… We were supposed to be on Chiang Kai-Shek's side. I wish we could have just been left out. And there was so much corruption. Billions of American dollars went over there…wasn't spent where it was supposed to be spent. They were more interested in what was in it for them—I'm just saying, we weren't high enough to know what was going on.

The Communists were ambushing us every day. Ambushing convoys, ambushing trains, attacking the arsenal, attacking ammunition dumps. They were just kidnapping Marines on the street and holding them for ransom. Every day there was some kind of an incident…

At the same time, I can understand why the Chinese people accepted Communism. Because there was just no middle class…I

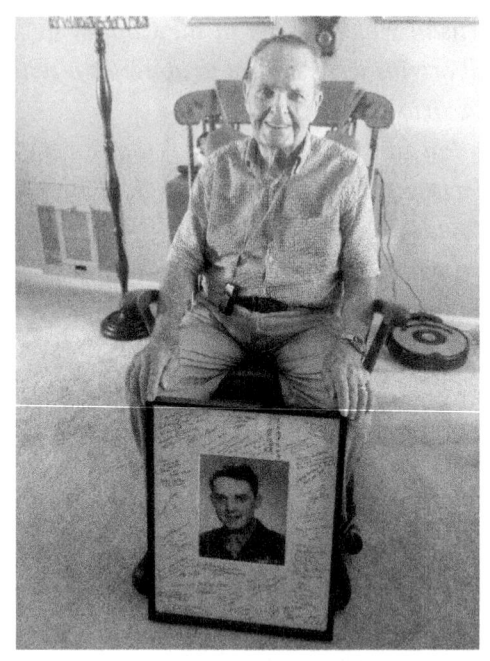

Edgar Fulwider in 2018

mean, you were either filthy rich or dying of starvation almost. And if I had been a Chinese citizen, I probably would have figured: it's got to be better than what we've got. Every morning, there'd be dead kids and old people in the street that froze during the night. No food. No shelter. Yeah. I would have said, "Well, whatever it is, it's got to be better than this."

On this trip [back to China in 1991], we picked up a city guide… This guide met us at the airport the evening we landed. We talked a bit on the way to the hotel and the next few days we got to be really buddy-buddy. He was a 27-year-old high school teacher at a girls' high school, history teacher…And on the third day we were out at some hot springs, and he says, "And this is where we captured Chiang Kai-shek."

And I said, "I didn't remember that when I was here before."

He says, "You were in China before?"

A Huge Manipulation of Knowledge

"Yeah."

"When were you in China?"

And I told him I was with the Marines.

He says, "You helped Chiang Kai-shek? You are the enemy!" And he never talked another word to me. And this…this is the slant he's teaching the Chinese people.

Lorelie Fulwider: It was such a beautiful friendship up until then. He wanted to go to Hollywood to be a singer. He was studying Chinese music, American jazz, rock and roll. And so he would sing to us on the trip. Very personable guy—but he really liked Ed.

Edgar: We met some old Chinese that remembered the Marines being there and we got along fine with them…cos they knew that the for the greater part the Marines took care of them—and kids, especially, we actually adopted some of them and clothed them.

Lorelie: One of them said, "You saved our children."

It's not what [the young] are being told.

I met a few amateur historians in China who were disappointed that the modern narrative no longer acknowledged the contributions of American soldiers, particularly the Flying Tigers. Chinese soldiers, however, could be even more cruelly affected by post-war politics. Those who had fought with the Nationalists against the Japanese were marked out for discrimination for decades after the Communists won the civil war and claimed victory against the Japanese for themselves.

Liu, *who as a child had fled the bombing of Nanjing, described his years after the Nationalists had lost the civil war. Like many others, he glossed over the specifics of what had befallen him during the Cultural Revolution, a particularly brutal time for those who had fought beside the Americans in defence of their country. I met Chinese veterans who had been incarcerated in the 1960s and '70s and one Chinese man whose father had been hounded to death for this perceived treachery.*

[After we lost the civil war] the PLA of course were very considerate towards us. They knew that we had worked in logistics and had nothing—we had handed everything over and we didn't have guns, we didn't have weapons. So they dismissed us with severance pay, gave you expenses for the road: you go home. Those of you who want to join the PLA, then join the PLA. If you didn't want to join the PLA you went home. At the time I had a wife and a small child…so I went back to Nanjing.

After we got back to Nanjing I applied to enter the Nanjing branch of the East China People's Revolutionary University. After the Communist Party came to power, because they were short of personnel, they called on a few youths who were originally from the Nationalist period to take an exam to go through training and get to work…At the time I was only twenty-something.

That university wasn't like today's universities, it only did political thought education. [My classmates] all were Nationalists…all former staff. Mainly it was about thought reform, changing our point of view. That way we could "Serve the people"…

The "improvement" process didn't even take a year. I went into the school in December of 1949. As it happened, in '50 the [Unnamed] River flooded, a historically rare, catastrophic flood, and they desperately needed men, and Chairman Mao put out a call…I gave 35 years of my career to the [Unnamed] River, and I got a commemorative medal, awarded by the CCP…

War of Resistance veterans…our hidden history really needs to be written. In the past, my experience is that veterans of the War of Resistance didn't dare talk about it. The minute you brought it up you were showing off, "What are you bragging about?" I'd avoid the topic.

I'm obviously a veteran of the War of Resistance—and we knew that overseas and in Taiwan, veterans from the War of Resistance are revered…But of course in China at the time, before the Reform and Opening up [of 1978], there was still some censorship, so we also suffered from some unfair treatment.

I'll give you two examples. The first was that I stopped receiving promotions. In the early period of liberation when I had been working for a year, I was promoted from a clerk to a member of the administrative section. But that was as far as I went, to administrative staff member. Right up until I retired…I was recognised by everybody in

A Huge Manipulation of Knowledge

the work context...[But] it didn't matter how good your work was, every year when they came to evaluate which unit was advanced and which individuals, it wasn't your turn. You didn't even make it into the evaluation. All the way up until after the Reform and Opening Up in 1978. The first year of the Reform and Opening Up, I was assessed as an "advanced worker".

In addition, my children were affected—work, schooling, everything was affected. They couldn't get into university even though they went to top high schools and their academic credentials were recognised...But, in the past, your work could be good, your schooling could be good, but when you were filling out a registration form the most important line was your family background and individual class status. To have a Nationalist reactionary like me in the family. Haha.

First there is a political trial, called political review, and then you can have [the status] removed. Of course, an individual's class status is entirely influenced by family. Now, of my three children, two are CCP members.

When it comes to people fighting their own: during the Cultural Revolution, fathers against sons—they even "struggled[46]" their sons. Brothers struggled against each other, people struggled each other...

After the Third Plenum of the 11th Party Congress at the end of 1978[47], it changed—the key for the country was this shift towards economic work. Production rose. In the past it was class struggle: I struggle you, you struggle me. The internal divisions were extreme.

But, moving on from that...Now is the spring for us War of Resistance veterans...It's come a bit late, but a late spring is especially warm...Now, in our later years, our lives are very fortunate. These days, thanks to a push from society, the country has attached

---

[46] A Cultural Revolution era activity which involved people denouncing each other. Often, those lower down in a hierarchy would attack those traditionally considered senior to them.

[47] This was the year in which Deng Xiaoping took over the CCP chairmanship and moved China into a new era of "Reform and Opening Up"

some importance to the efforts of veterans of the War of Resistance… They value us…Even though in the middle there were some periods [that weren't so great]…at the time, we could understand. The change of regime [had to do this] in order to consolidate government authority…

[When it comes to the wartime enemy], you have to distinguish between Japanese militarism and the common people. The Japanese people were also victims, weren't they? We understand this clearly. You saw that commemoration that they held yesterday, the commemoration for the 300,000 victims of the Nanjing Massacre? There was also a representative from Japan. The Japanese representation builds Sino-Japanese friendship, this affects people…Nowadays we practice peaceful diplomacy, good-neighbourly diplomacy…These days it seems China is very close to all the countries of the world, because war truly is too cruel…

Now, as witnesses to history there are some things we can figure out…But young people, especially, they can't figure things out…That is to say: whatever you tell them, that's what they believe. We are witnesses to history…We mustn't forget the past. War has no real winners or losers, everyone makes heavy sacrifices. If you want to win, what price will you have to pay? What's more, if you are unjust, you will meet greater resistance from the people…

As far as future generations are concerned, we must urge them to cherish peace, oppose war and stand firm. This point is very, very, very important. We've lived through war. It's so cruel—especially bombing. Of course, not everyone will necessarily go to the front but when it comes to bombing there's no distinction between the front and the rear…So we must truly love peace. Peace does not come easily…How many people had to be sacrificed in order to win the war? So we must teach our children, teach the next generations: cherish peace, oppose war, remember history.

In 2015, the year marking the 70th anniversary of the ending of the war, previously overlooked Nationalist comrades in China including Liu were awarded medals for their contribution to the victory against the Japanese. Despite the challenges that his background had presented over the years, Liu enthused over China's development and how its society had become more prosperous and considerate of each other.

Soldiers returning home to Japan did not have it much easier. Many were shunned for having lost the war and for returning in disgrace (glory was accorded to those who died). Particularly discredited were those "Chukiren" returnees from a post war re-education facility in China who campaigned to expose the folly of war by recounting their own experiences. Easily dismissed as "brainwashed" by authorities, they nonetheless endeavoured to bring to public attention Japan's war crimes such as sexual enslavement and biological experimentation at Unit 731 in Manchuria[48].

Shigeo Matsumoto felt that Japan should give an honest accounting of the atrocities committed in China during the war. He had told me that his commanding officer killed a local family in China that had treated the invaders kindly.

Japan must acknowledge the fact of the irretrievable damages China has suffered due to the brutality inflicted by the Japanese army.

I was shocked when I heard South Korean President Park say right after her inauguration [in 2013]… that Korea will not forget for 1,000 years the resentment towards Japan for being colonised. But when thinking about this logically, I realise this cannot be helped. If we were in the same position, we would be saying the same thing—or even more. So this is where I always return to and ponder…

The countries have not held discussions on how they view things. Japan continues to completely refrain from holding dialogue. The government has never advanced discussions among the people. They keep saying this is a thing of the past and things have already been resolved…the issue has already been settled. What are they saying?

---

[48] I visited this remote and almost unknown facility in 1991 when a student in Harbin. Its story has since become much more widely known within China but has little recognition internationally. It is possible that Dick King's testimony about the plague victims he saw ties in with the unit since it tested biological weaponry and the spread of disease using vermin.

Maybe so from a legal perspective—but the issue cannot be resolved just by legal means…

Japan wants to become a nation that is just. It should become a country that is ashamed of disgrace and places value on culture. In that regard we cannot rely on our lawmakers. We cannot just keep paying money and answering to the complaints from all over. For its responsibility in carrying out the war, Japan must apologise no matter how many times—and it may even have to make financial compensations. It must prepare itself for the worst.

While Shigeo felt victimised for his part in the war, few were as shamefully treated in Japan as those who suffered from the atomic bombs.

Yoshio Hara *witnessed the Hiroshima bomb and its aftermath. As a young soldier he was deployed to clear the city of bodies. After the war he became a teacher. I asked him whether he felt that education remained as selective in modern times as it was in his day.*

Yes. For instance, Japan's invasion of South Korea, Taiwan, and Manchuria, and the southern islands that were suppressed—even today, there are people who still say that wasn't an invasion and it was done to support and revive those countries through building many things. Even though it was done for Japan, they say it was for their development, that Japan devoted itself to these countries…

There are still civilians who feel this way…even though they never lived during those times…They have been brainwashed that it wasn't an invasion…There are people who give lectures like this and these people are inspired by them that this view is correct. They profess we freed these people…

We believe this is a huge manipulation of knowledge…I have met many people and have explained that this is a major mistake. So even though there are aspects of these people that I can respect, on this particular topic I tell them this is a major misunderstanding that must be changed.

I am no longer an educator but am among the common people. And through my experience in Hiroshima as a *hibakusha*, I have an important mission to talk about the reality of what happened in

A Huge Manipulation of Knowledge

Hiroshima. To teach children about the history that is taught incorrectly—we have a mission to connect the next generation to our experience of the atomic bombing. We must educate today's children in a way that gets through to them. We call this peace education, and we feel it is important to cover this from a broad perspective. To just talk about the devastating experience of the atomic bombing is a denial of all the other realities of the war.

I'm 91 now. Most people who fought in the war have died, so the memories of the war are rapidly weathering...If you ask what happened on August 6 or 9, 1945, there are hardly any people who can answer that question—what's more, there are hardly any left who can answer what happened on December 8[49]... Most adults don't know—this includes Pearl Harbor. December 8 was the day World War Two started, when Pearl Harbor was attacked. No one knows about this day...So, the weathering has advanced to this extent. Through handing down these stories, we must speak from a broad perspective of peace studies, and not just about the atomic bombing...

Humanity must become clever enough so history is not manipulated. In the very end, humanity is not stupid. At some point, we want to believe in humanity's wisdom, or else you cannot have any hope. There is no future if we no longer have that. I don't want to believe that. Not only must we share stories, but we must really take action to never create any more *hibakusha* survivors like us. Through this, it is our hope that humanity is not that stupid and chooses wisdom. This is all we can hope for. This is what we believe...

So, there are now 14,000 nuclear weapons—they are fewer in number, and there are also aged nuclear bombs...But more than 90 percent are possessed by the US, Russia and the UK. They do not shake hands...What is more, their [the bombs'] power has become incredible. What's often said is their performance is several thousand times larger than the bombs dropped on Hiroshima and Nagasaki... This number [of nuclear weapons] is capable of wiping out humanity

---

[49] In Japanese time, Pearl Harbor was on December 8.

three times. Yes, three times! That's what the scientists say…Nuclear weapons cannot coexist with humanity.

When you consider this, nothing will happen in the international community unless these two nations [Russia and the US] shake hands. This is the first task the UN should work on. It is a hopeless situation as long as conflict continues between these two countries. Nothing good comes from conflict. Many bad things are created. The world cannot be saved unless they understand this.

Epilogue

On a crisp November morning in 2016 I stood on a platform looking over a river more than 1000 metres below. Morning mist lay thickly in the deep V, shrouding the water and curling over the trees that spilled down the hillsides. Mountain ranges stretched eastwards as far as I could see, the winter watery colours of the foreground darkening into deep shades of blue.

In the pine trees, two birds piped at each other, their four note refrains emphasising the stillness of the forest. In this tranquil place seventy years before, the Chinese army had finally succeeded in routing the occupying Japanese forces, blowing the top off the mountain and reopening the Burma Road, a vital supply line that had been blocked for more than two years. This hard-fought victory in the summer monsoon of 1944 marked the turning point in the China Burma India theatre, heralding the end of China's eight-year war with Japan.

Stepping back off the platform, my companion and I followed a wooden walkway which wound through the trees. Completely denuded during the war, the mountainside had now been reclaimed by the forest. Fallen leaves littered the ground, the vegetation muffling the chatter of distant tour groups. Ferns pushed up from foxholes and the trenches were filled in with the layers of years.

As we corkscrewed to the summit, intermittent captions explained significant positions and earthworks, accompanied by the occasional photograph. We passed the tunnels dug by the Chinese engineers to lay explosives; the flat ground where the occupiers would exercise and flash their buttocks at the Chinese defenders on the far bank of

Pine Mountain memorial

the river; and sections of the eleven kilometres of trenches and fortifications in which the Japanese had lived and held this strategic piece of high ground for 26 months. A picture showed corpses slumped in the ditch, beside a paragraph saying that in the end the fighting had been so fierce that 62 pairs of combatants had died locked together, tearing chunks from each other with their hands and teeth.

According to the small museum near the mountain, the win was the Chinese army's first meaningful victory over a fortified position after being at war with Japan for seven years. It would not have been possible without American assistance—the most significant coming from the air, but also on the ground in planning and, as the battle was underway, medical support.

It was visiting this part of China that inspired me to speak to those who fought in the most recent world war. The tranquillity in that region overlays the horrors it witnessed, in much the way the

Epilogue

peaceful old age of the war's survivors belied the traumas of their youth.

I spent four years interviewing men and women who lived through the war, always in person, in countries from Belgium to Russia. Sitting with them in their homes, I was frequently choked up by their tears. Until I met them, the war was something I read about—politics, statistics, maps, theoretical analysis. Feeling the pain in their memories, events decades old but as fresh for them as yesterday, war was given a human face.

They all lost friends and loved ones and I was struck how many felt bewildered at the "luck" that had spared them. On more than one occasion I found myself counselling veterans who wondered why they lived on, estranged from the families they had tried and failed to build on the ruined foundations of their youth. How do you console someone so traumatised in their formative years that love became too great a challenge?

They all witnessed the worst (and sometimes the best) of human behaviour. Their youthful naiveté and patriotic enthusiasm was manipulated and twisted by indoctrination and propaganda, so that both sides were marched into war thinking they were doing the right thing.

The major combatant nations from World War Two, now mostly leaders in their spheres of influence, have dwindling first-hand experience of how devastating the outcome of conflict can be. An Okinawan caught as a child in the crossfire between American and Japanese soldiers told me, "Forgive…But never forget. That's very important—because anything you forget you do again…I think we are forgetting…And that's dangerous, isn't it?"

Some survivors have worked ceaselessly to keep us alert to the dangers. In 2024, the Nobel Peace Prize was finally awarded to Nihon Hidankyo, the Japanese nuclear survivor organisation led by Sueichi Kido, himself a *hibakusha* from Nagasaki. Representing survivors of the only nation to have experienced nuclear bombs dropped in anger, it has been agitating against nuclear arms for decades, working out of crammed and pauperish premises even at its Tokyo head office. (There is not much money in peace.)

Since I began this work, war has erupted again in Europe. After everything the region has been through, surely it is this "forgetting" about war—along with lashings of propaganda—that has made marching its people into another conflict even remotely possible. Thousands are once more being traumatised by combat and the spectre of nuclear conflict.

And when the dust has settled, what does it all achieve? Allegiances are so capricious. Jerry Yellin, author of *The Last Fighter Pilot*, told me of his war experience, how he had been based out of Iwo Jima as the US marines struggled to secure the island and of the horrors he had seen: dead marines with their genitals cut off and placed between their lips, the gold teeth ripped from their mouths.

He told me of his sense of bewilderment when the US befriended Japan so soon after he had lost many friends and comrades in the bitter conflict.

He had flown the last mission over the Japanese mainland as the emperor surrendered on August 15th 1945, losing his wingman that day even as the war was ending. He had hated the Japanese for years afterwards—until he visited in 1983, when he began to see them as "just people", and when his son went to Japan and fell in love with the daughter of a Japanese World War Two veteran, he learned to embrace his former foe as family.

In Jerry's final days, he talked to me about peace. "My journey of knowledge leads me to the belief that we are not Catholics, Jews, white, black, or yellow. We're all human beings." China and the US, now entrenched rivals divided by ideology, once united against a common enemy. It all seems such a waste, when yesterday's enemy can become today's friend—and when, as in the First World War, even today's enemy can take a break to play football over Christmas. At the individual level, too many lives are spent, ruined or changed irrevocably due to actions of an ambitious few.

Epilogue

Given there is always a potential to find mutual interest, perhaps one day we will heed the words of those who have lost their best days to conflict and learn no longer to sacrifice our youths, our future, to war. There can be no real winners when so many lives are destroyed.

Fergus Anckorn, former prisoner of war on the infamous Death Railway in Southeast Asia, was one of so many with whom I spoke who felt it important that the realities of war should be understood. How a man who loved nature and the countryside as he did could end up inured to horror.

> Some of the stuff that happened when we were in action—terrible! One of the first jobs we had to do when the fighting finished: take all the heads off the fences. Every fence post had a head on it—Chinese, mostly. We had to take them off—and that was just a job. No revulsion. In those circumstances: let's just get rid of those heads. "Chuck 'em in"
>
> So it's an entirely different world when you're in that. And the things here that would make you sick—out there, you just do it, there's nothing wrong with it. And you can't explain that to people. I mean, you might say, "How could a fellow like you kill someone?" Well, I'd knock his head off if he was gonna kill me. And having knocked his head off I'd walk away…In those circumstances it's normal procedure.

War does not leave its participants willingly, and the repercussions can be felt well into later in life.

This is true even for today's wars—which, counter to the forecasts of many, have not been fought by technology. They have still demanded the sacrifice of young men and women, battling to and fro in the trenches. If we were better informed beforehand about how this destroys even the youth that survive, perhaps we would think again.

As a modern-day soldier, a senior retired officer who saw action with the Parachute Regiment in Northern Ireland, the Balkans, West

Africa and Iraq, explained to me, "When you sign up you don't know what to expect. You've seen films, you've read books. You've heard stories and you've applied your imagination, but you can't imagine what happens when you cross the start line. Nobody ever imagines that *they* are the one that would be injured in operations, or horribly disabled. The things that you have seen, done—and not done—are not easily erased from your mind. For most of us it's stored in the back of the mind, and it will come back later. You can't know what the trigger will be."

Afterbursts

Keep the peace

I want to say: I am deeply deeply disappointed that leaders cannot see their way to the greater good, and where are we all going? What is the purpose of it all? [Canadian]

Unfortunately in the world it seems to be a blossom time for tyrants. During my lifetime there was Hitler and Mussolini and then there was Tojo...I'd say that there were some bad people who were in charge...and we let them get away with it, too. [American]

Contemporary weapons are so powerful it presents a danger for all people in the world. Not just particular states, but all people...And we need to think about that. [Soviet, Russian]

If nuclear bombs are used in a nuclear war, it will destroy humanity. Nuclear bombs do not contribute to security. They do not prevent wars: there are wars going on everywhere around the world... [Japanese]

With atomic power...perish the thought of a major conflict! While people were shooting one another with rifles was bad enough, but now, when they can let loose with all this atomic stuff...[Australian]

Did you know that any one nuclear submarine carries the destructive power of 14,000 Hiroshimas? So, we've got four. Do we really need them? But then, Russia and the Americans have thousands. So between them, they've got millions of Hiroshima equivalents. Millions. That is actually mad. [Briton]

War is originally a form of madness. It's not something that can be done under a normal state of mind. [Japanese]

When people begin to squash different opinions you have to be very much aware of what's happening and willing to take a risk to be against that. [American]

You know what war is, but...you don't really know how traumatic it is. [American]

How much grief it brought to people, that war! How many material assets were lost that had been created! [Soviet, Russia]

How outrageous that 23 million Russians died...Five of my schoolmates, gone. My nine [fellow sailors] killed three weeks after I left. Why? What was the goddamn reason? There's something strange in this world that we human beings go around shooting each other...[Canadian]

When you think of young men putting themselves in the front line because some politician thought that that's where you ought to be. "Build a barricade. That's it! Have tear gas thrown at you. We're behind you all the way"—three miles back... [Briton]

What's wrong with society, to cause these upheavals where that part of society with the greatest prospect of giving life to their society is killed at birth? Animals don't kill their young...[Briton]

We are the only creatures on the planet who kill for any other reason than for food. Look: everyone's killing everybody now. What for? [Briton]

We're all human, so we've got that in common...People become brainwashed. [Briton]

People from other nations have exactly the same right to live. You shouldn't build up images of hate because some people are "not as smart" or are "worse people in general". This propaganda has to be banned [German]

Hate the Japanese common people? I don't agree. Their husbands also died. Their fathers and mothers also died...You should hate the people who started the war...You must educate...distinguish clearly for the young who are the people who started the war, who are the victims... [Chinese]

No matter how hard I try, I can never forget. No matter how many years go by, may it be 100 years, I will never forget the atrocity of war...War is the greatest evil, so it must be stopped at all costs. [Japanese, Okinawan]

The new generations should remember that the generation that is passing sacrificed so many lives...so the current generation should work on preserving this peace for their children and grandchildren. I would wish it to everyone: both the citizens of Russia and everyone abroad. [Soviet, Russian]

This "peace", it's not easy. Cherish it...You are blessed. You have to cherish what you have now because it was hard won, it all comes from the sacrifice of your elders, they shed blood and lay down their lives in exchange for today. [Chinese]

Acknowledgements

So many people helped this book to come to fruition. My family and friends—especially my long suffering husband and mother, each of whom read myriad versions and gamely maintained their enthusiasm for the work. My father, who died before the book came to print, but who understood how much I wanted it to resonate with its readers and always had suggestions on how this could be achieved. Those who read early drafts—thank you for taking the time, even (and especially) if I didn't incorporate all of your thoughtful suggestions. The friends who chivvied me and never told me I was insane to attempt something so huge. You know who you are, from Hong Kong to Europe to the USA. It has taken more than a village.

I had input, advice and encouragement from other writers and historians far more storied than me, for which I am very grateful. Translators and go-betweens guided me in Germany, Russia and Japan—and especially in China, where I had many conversations with keepers of memory about China's very particular wartime politics. I cannot and in some cases should not name them all.

Thank you also to those who introduced me into veteran communities in the USA and the UK, all of whom, such as those in the Taxi Charity, give their time and energy to ensuring these survivors are honoured in their latter years.

Above all, I am grateful to the men and women who spent hours sharing their experiences with me—and their families, who often welcomed me into their homes. Many of the survivors have died since I met them. Even though not all of them made it into the final pages, each of their stories is lodged in my heart and in this small way, they live on. Thank you all for your service.

About the Author

Born into a family of globetrotters, Lucy Colback was made in Africa and has lived in India, Pakistan, Hong Kong, Singapore, London and New York. She has spent her life roaming the world, including hiking mountains in the Himalayas, taking ferries between islands in Greece and Asia and trains around Europe and China. She graduated from Cambridge university with a degree in Chinese and has a working understanding of Mandarin and French. She has studied in Beijing, Shanghai, Taipei and Hong Kong. After twenty years in the finance sector, she became a writer for the Financial Times. She has a keen interest in geopolitics, particularly the impact of World War Two history on modern international relations, and in people's life stories. She is married to an Australian pilot and with him continues to explore.

Afterbursts